A LIFE-CHANGING KNOCK ON THE DOOR

"What the . . . ?" Jimmy said.

Jeannie was the first to reach the door and open it. She peered outside. A large man adjusting his rimless glasses stood there; others were nearby. Not one of them was smiling. "Is your husband home?" the man with the eyeglasses asked.

"He's home."

"Ask him to come out here, please."

Jimmy pushed past Jeannie, out through the door. "What the devil's going on?"

"Are you Jimmy Taylor?"

"That's me," he said good-naturedly.

"Jimmy Taylor, you are under arrest for first degree murder on a warrant from Jackson County, Oregon."

Jimmy's half-smoked cigarette fell to the porch floor as his hands were wrenched behind his back by one of the police officers. Handcuffs were snapped onto his wrists.

Jimmy couldn't believe what was happening. "There has to be some mistake," he said. He caught one last look at a stunned Jeannie as he was assisted down the steps.

MURDER ON SHADOW MOUNTAIN

JIMMY DALE TAYLOR
AND
DONALD G. BROSS

**Expanding
Horizons**

An imprint of New Horizon Press
Far Hills, New Jersey

Expanding Horizons books are published by

New Horizon Press
P.O. Box 669
Far Hills, NJ 07931

All Kensington Titles, Imprints, and Distributed Lines are available at special quantity discounts for bulk purchases for sales
promotions, premiums, fund-raising, and educational or insti-
tutional use. Special book excerpts or customized printings can
also be created to fit specific needs. For details, write or phone
the office of the Kensington special sales manager: Kensington
Publishing Corp., 850 Third Avenue, New York, NY 10022,
attn: Special Sales Department, Phone: 1-800-221-2647.

ISBN-13: 978-1-933893-09-9
ISBN-10: 1-933893-09-5

First New Horizon Press Hardcover Printing: 1996
First Expanding Horizons Mass Market Printing: October 2008

10 9 8 7 6 5 4 3 2 1

Printed in the United States of America

CONTENTS

AUTHOR'S NOTE

Murder on Shadow Mountain is a true story told from the viewpoint of Jimmy and Jeannie Taylor. The events and dialogue have been reconstructed from court records, letters, interviews and the memories of participants.

Some names have been changed in order to protect the privacy of individuals and in some instances physical characteristics have been altered. Jimmy Dale and Jeannie Taylor, as well as the others in this chronicle, have all experienced the joys and the hell described herein.

ACKNOWLEDGMENTS

Special thanks to my attorneys, Myron Gitnes and Richard Garbutt, along with private investigator Paul Arritola, for pursuing the truth and finding it.

To all my family and friends for sticking by me during the darkest of times.

Also, thanks to Donald Bross for seeing to it that the story is told.

—J. D. T.

Special thanks to Joan Dunphy, Editor-in-Chief at New Horizon Press, for her patience and persistence. Thanks, Joan, for providing us with this opportunity

—D. G. B.

PROLOGUE

Jimmy sat at the table, steam rising from the coffee in his cup. He lifted his head and smiled at slender little Jeannie with her dark eyes and long brown hair. Time only increased the love he felt for this woman. He couldn't imagine life without her.

The years had been kind to his wife, he realized looking at her. After seventeen years, he still liked to hear the sound of her voice. She had retained her classy Boston accent. He still felt that intense attraction to her. *I hope she feels the same about me,* he mused.

Jeannie eyed her man as, lost in his thoughts, he toyed with his coffee cup. He had cared for her. He had provided for his family. They had seen the country, but they had suffered through some lean times, too. She wished he didn't look so tired, that they had more time to just be together. She didn't like the long hours Jimmy was having to work, but he was bringing home a good and steady paycheck.

And they needed every bit of it. The ever rising cost of raising three children made sure they hadn't set aside the nest egg they had always been planning to.

"Hey, Babe, cheer up," Jimmy said. "It's a good day."

Jeannie forced a smile. "Who can be cheerful at this time of the morning? I'm not so sure the day is going to be all that good, Duke. Don't ask me why, but I have a feeling something is going to happen."

"Something with the kids?" he asked, suddenly fearful.

She shook her head. "I don't know what. I just got this feeling."

"Oh, it's probably nothing," he said. "You know how sensitive you are."

"You're probably right." She smiled back at him. "Are you going to be working in town today?"

"No, I'll be out west. I'll pick up Matt in a few minutes and head out. Probably won't be back until late."

At an hour when most people were just rising, Jimmy left for work. Jeannie sat alone. She felt a cold chill pass over her, as though someone had rubbed ice on her neck. *What in the world is wrong with me?* she wondered.

In another part of town the posse was assembling. Two deputies from Jackson County, Oregon, had flown in to take control of the prisoner. They hoped to escort the fugitive back to Medford where he would stand trial.

A deputy was already cruising the alley behind the man's home and soon reported back: "Too late. His work truck is gone."

Now they would have to wait. And hunt. Patrol the neighborhood. Perhaps he was still in town. They couldn't ask his boss. If the fugitive got word of their pursuit, he might leave his family and run.

It was the middle of the morning. The children had gone to school, and Jeannie had switched to drinking hot tea when Tina's sharp bark sounded an alarm. Looking out the back door, Jeannie thought she caught a glimpse of a police car driving down the alley before it disappeared behind their long shed. *Or was it a sheriff's car?* She shivered.

Why would a police car be here? Jeannie wondered. They certainly hadn't committed a crime. Their worst brush with the law, so far as she knew, was when Jimmy had received a ticket for not having an inspection sticker on their car. They hadn't paid it yet. They don't send officers to your house for that, she told herself. Don't be paranoid, she told herself.

She looked out the back door again. Jeannie thought the view out front to be somewhat rustic. Their front yard was small but had a flowering redbud tree and narrow, rough-hewn stone steps leading down to the street. The steps were quaint-looking but treacherous, and kept intruders away. Once again, she experienced that ominous feeling she had earlier.

Something wasn't right. The police had to be searching for someone. Why would they be looking toward her house? Or was it her imagination?

It was early afternoon when Jeannie's phone rang. She plucked the handset from its cradle and spoke a low, "Hello." Her voice carried a worried inflection.

"Hey, Babe, you sound kind of down."

"I'm about to go batty, Jim."

"What's the problem?"

"I feel as though something bad is about to happen. I'm feeling that way more and more. Police cars keep driving by like they're looking for something. What do you think it is?"

"Who knows? Can't be us."

"Where are you working?"

"Piedmont. I've been all over today."

"What time will you be in?"

"I dunno. Probably about six. We get back to town, I'll drop Matt off and then I'll be home as quickly as I can."

"I'll be glad when you're here. Every time I look outdoors, there's another police car driving by. They keep driving up and down the alley, up and down. Out front, too. Maybe some criminal got loose."

"Jeannie, your imagination is getting away."

"No, Jim, I know what I see."

"Hell, we're not criminals, and the chance that some

fugitive comes around our place is remote. Hang in there, Babe. Don't let it get to you."

"I wish I could," murmured Jeannie, as she hung up the phone.

A visible noose was tightening. Every officer who would be involved with the arrest knew where the fugitive lived. Also, they knew he was driving a blue Ford pickup with identifying letters on each door. Some overzealous cop had already stopped a similar pickup and frightened an innocent citizen.

Sheriff's department and police cars watched the home. They knew he wasn't there. They did not know where he was and they did not know when he would return. Whenever, they would be ready. At the appropriate time, a dispatcher would phone just to be certain.

The hours ticked away, a minute at a time. Jeannie looked out the back door to see yet another car with a star on its door drive by. She hurried to the front but the street was empty. Just then, Andy came home from school. "Hi, Mom," he called out. He headed for the living room and plopped down on a chair.

"How was your day?" Jeannie asked.

"It was okay."

"You want something to eat?"

"No. Why's a police car in the alley?"

Jeannie shivered. "I don't know," she admitted. "I just don't know."

The girls came in and went straight to their bedroom to change into play clothes. Soon Julie went outdoors with Andy to play.

They returned to the house and Julie said, "Mamma, there's a police car out back. It looked like it wanted to turn in and then it went on. What's it doing?"

Jeannie shook her head. "I don't know."

Some time later, Jimmy shuffled tiredly through the kitchen door. "Hey, Babe, how's it going?" he asked.

She frowned. "Hon, you're going to think I'm crazy now, but there's one of those police cars parked outside in the back."

"Aw, you're worrying over nothing."

Jeannie followed Jimmy into the living room. Suddenly the phone rang. Jimmy picked it up. "Is this Jimmy Taylor?" a man's voice asked.

"That's me."

Jimmy heard a click as the line went dead. He replaced the handset. "Whoever it was, they hung up," he said, puzzled. "Sounded like it was me they wanted to talk to, but then they hung up."

Jeannie wondered, *is this another omen?*

Andy sat in a corner chair, eyeing his parents. Grownups were always getting upset over nothing. He shrugged and decided to go out back again and play. Three police cars were in the alley, pulling into their back yard. For a few moments, the boy stood and stared.

Inside, Jimmy dropped onto the couch, lit a cigarette and shared it with Jeannie. Only three remained in the pack. "I need to get some more," he said.

"You want to pick up some fast food, too?" asked Jeannie. "I've been so worried something was going to happen that I didn't take out anything for dinner."

He squeezed her hand. "It's okay, Babe. Let me rest a minute or two and then I'll go out and get some burgers or something."

Within moments there were traffic sounds out front. They looked at one another as they heard car doors slam and anxious voices.

"What the . . . ?" Jimmy said.

Jeannie was first to reach the door and open it. She peered outside. A large man adjusting his rimless glasses stood there; others were nearby. Not one of them was smiling. "Is your husband home?" the man with the eyeglasses asked.

"He's home."

"Ask him to come out here, please."

Jimmy pushed past Jeannie, out through the door. "What the devil's going on?"

"Are you Jimmy Dale Taylor?"

"That's me," he said good-naturedly.

"Jimmy Taylor, you are under arrest for first degree murder on a warrant from Jackson County, Oregon."

Jimmy's half-smoked cigarette fell to the porch floor as his hands were wrenched behind his back by one of the police officers. Handcuffs were snapped onto his wrists.

Jimmy couldn't believe what was happening. "There has to be some mistake," he said. He caught one last look at a stunned Jeannie as he was assisted down the steps.

After being turned over to two other strangers and pushed into the back seat of a car, Jimmy heard a third man who had climbed into the front say, "The law requires that you be advised you have the right to remain silent; that anything you say can be used against you in a court of law; that you have the right to the presence of an attorney; and that if you cannot afford an attorney, one will be appointed for you prior to any questioning if you so desire. Do you understand these rights?"

Jimmy could hear Jeannie protesting. Someone was screaming; it sounded like Julie. "Yeah, I understand."

"I'm Peter Jones. Are you willing to talk to me?"

"Yeah."

"Have you ever been in the State of Oregon?"

"No, never have." Jimmy twisted his head trying to see what was happening in his front yard, but couldn't.

"Were you born in Tennessee?"

"Yeah."

"Would you be willing to talk to me about a homicide that occurred in 1967 in Jackson County, Oregon?"

Jimmy shrugged. "I don't know anything to tell."

Another man got in on the driver's side and started the engine. As the car pulled away, visions of home and family were gradually pushed aside. The veil of time parted and Jimmy glimpsed a dark night on a jagged mountain peak, twenty-one years earlier. He was seeing events as though the nightmares were happening to someone else. Unfortunately for him, they weren't.

1

A NATION DIVIDED

In 1967, the country was running scared. Confusion reigned. During the past four years hope had eroded as one devastating event followed another. That dreadful day in Dallas was still etched upon the memory of those who had watched and prayed as their leader, John Fitzgerald Kennedy, was killed by an assassin's bullets. In death, JFK had captivated a nation's attention even more than he had in life.

The war in Vietnam had escalated to the point where it was the new president's, Lyndon Johnson's, obsession. He seemed convinced that he could bomb Ho Chi Minh into submission. During any pause in the action the leader of the North Vietnamese would order his people out of their holes and they would rebuild what had been destroyed, working with a demonic fervor until the next wave of bombers roared in. It became evident that LBJ was not a field general. His constituents remarked about how he'd aged.

At home, a civil war was being fought. Not between the states, but between the generations. The antagonists were parents and their teenage children, young people who were rebelling against the assassinations and the war. Once the hippie movement gained momentum, it rolled like a mighty river towards California, carrying with it rebellious children from families who were devastated by the disappearance of their offspring. Highways were lined with hitchhikers, most heading west.

One day a child would be at home, resisting parents who were out of tune with the times. The old folks were willing to continue bombing until the bastards surrendered; the younger insisted we walk away from Vietnam and mind our own business. Many youths felt as though communism might even be preferable to our corrupt capitalist government. They cried out for new leaders. They wanted Robert Kennedy and Martin Luther King.

Many of the younger generation fought tradition, corporations, and established forms of organized religion. It was important to them that they identify with one another, not with the warmongers who were running America. They liked colorful flowers, beads and bells, and psychedelic drugs. Their long hair, hard rock music and questionable morals earned them the nick-name, "Hippies."

A horde of these dropouts followed the sun until they met the placid waters of the Pacific. Thousands migrated to San Francisco. Many homes throughout the land were missing one or more of their children. Parents often wondered if the fault lay within. Stunned by this sudden shift in values and culture, most suffered in silence.

Seeing the United States after three years in Uncle Sam's Navy, Jimmy Dale Taylor was suffering from culture shock. His ship had docked at San Francisco when he had received his discharge, and he had stayed there.

Now, as he strolled towards his afternoon job in the Tenderloin area this Monday, Jimmy reflected on his current status. He worked at a bar down near the wharf. It wasn't the kind of job he really wanted but he was employed, which was more than many of San Francisco's new citizens could say.

He came from a family of eight children. His father was a disciplinarian who expected patriotism of his children. His devoted mother said of her son, "Jimmy wore his heart on his sleeve. He was a bit of a Romeo, but he would get hurt real easy and he'd always believed in showing women respect. It was the way I brought him up."

It was no wonder Jimmy felt somewhat out of place among the hordes of hippies. He was clean-shaven, even if he had long sideburns. His dark hair was no longer cropped with whitewalls, but neither was it long and unwashed. It was of a length that could be combed straight back.

He stared as a bus roared up the hill, probably headed for Haight-Ashbury or Golden Gate Park. The vehicle was packed with the young and foolish. They shouted inaudible sounds. Hands were in constant motion. These were the flower children. They came from varied backgrounds and from all over the country. The bus belched black fumes and passed out of sight.

Girls wandered the streets. Many were homesick but felt cut off from their families. Now they were reaching out for whatever affection they could find. Give them a joint or a hit of acid and they would love you all night. Or until they passed out. Few of either sex had a steady job or a reliable source of income. To the extent possible, they cared for their own. They laid claim to parts of the Haight-Ashbury section. There they would often live together in vacant houses until they were discovered and thrown out by the cops. These same cops sometimes got their kicks by waiting until rain was pouring before tossing hippies out into the muck.

As Jimmy pressed on, he wondered if the country was tilted towards San Francisco. Hippies from all over the country rode a numb thumb to the Bay Area. It seemed as though the coast was a sediment trap for the malcontents. These rebels liked to march down Market Street, protesting the Vietnam conflict. A familiar cry was, "Hey, hey, LBJ, how many kids did you kill today?"

Here there was a war, too. A constant struggle between the old law and the freethinking hippies. Jimmy was not willing to conform to what these dropouts considered to be a nonconforming society. He might puff on a joint now and then but he steered clear of hard drugs. Beer he liked. Maybe a little wine.

Jimmy wanted a change. He wanted to get out of San Francisco. He'd fastened on a place that had captured his imagination: Seattle. He'd heard there was clean air, good jobs, and more normal-looking people in Seattle. And girls who weren't stoned.

As he moved along, cars crept down the street, horns honking. At a red light, a long-haired hippie, barefoot and bearded, probably stoned out of his skull, crossed the one-way street by leaping from one car hood to the next. There were the usual curses and shouting from drivers and honking of horns. The guy jumped off on the far side, shot them all the old right-hand bone, and went merrily on his way.

Jimmy shrugged. Similar occurrences could be seen every day. Time to get out of town. *Maybe go to Yuma and visit my folks*, he thought. It had been some nine months since his last trip home. Then his thoughts turned to Seattle once again.

Glenn True Clark believed he was a man born out of season. In just twelve days he would be forty-six. There hadn't been any of this "anything goes" attitude during his youth. Now he lusted after and might even lay the meat to a hippie chick on occasion, but most of the younger generation would laugh, call him an old grandpa, and express doubts that he could still get it up.

Well, they were wrong. He had experience and staying power. When their legs were spread, they didn't complain. He was the one who should be complaining. Some dingy broad had sure enough passed her crud on to him. He'd had to make a quick trip to Salt Lake City to see a doctor acquaintance who could be discreet. There had been little if any improvement. That was just too bad. Some stupid chick had infected him so he had no compunctions about screwing it into others.

Yeah, he had two pretty daughters who were about the age of these hot little runaways. This didn't keep him from lusting. Their mother would be watching them. She'd damned sure better be.

He was running low on money, but this condition was only temporary. If a man was smart, and Glenn figured he was smarter than most, he could always drive a car without buying it and have a gun he could lay hands on in a hurry.

Glenn had spent Saturday night at a motel nearby. There he had slipped out and, taking advantage of the darkness, lifted a tag from a disabled car. It never hurt to have an extra. Time to get rid of the Utah plate and put on another.

Sunday morning, following a shower and shave, Glenn had stayed in the town long enough to have breakfast with his brother and sister-in-law. Their mobile home was only a block or two from where he had lifted the tag. After a couple of hours with his kin, Glenn had moved on. Sure, family ties were important but he was too different to feel comfortable around his relatives for extended periods of time.

Sunday afternoon he had cruised into San Francisco with the intention of getting laid and then moving on. Didn't pay to stay too long in one place. Not when you're hanging hot paper and traveling on stolen credit cards.

He had not found a willing woman. Not one young enough to suit his taste, anyway. And so he had spent Sunday night in his car, near Golden Gate Park. Alone.

Now he was cruising the streets of San Francisco, feeling more and more horny with each passing moment. The Oldsmobile purred like a mechanic's dream as it climbed the hills with little effort. And why shouldn't it? He'd had the foresight to visit the used car lot for a test drive before returning the following night to help himself. Some of these hick salesmen never seemed to learn that a smart man could have duplicate keys made.

Other than a few items left behind at his folks' home on the coast of Oregon, all he owned was in this car. His gold-plated watch swung on the turn signal handle. A hand-carved billfold containing several stolen credit cards, fashioned by his brother who was a guest in Utah's State Pen, lay in the glove compartment.

Still, there were times when a man needed cash. This might be the time to hit a store and then move on. Head up north. Where the chicks weren't guarded night and day by some hippie punk.

In the car's trunk were two .38 revolvers from a recent burglary. Wired to the underframe of the car was a rifle. A little insurance. Yeah, he had all he needed. All but a chick. Soon he would lay one and then he would be on his way.

As the car approached a deserted looking street, Glenn was surprised to see an acquaintance, Marty, standing on the corner waiting for the light to change. He pulled to the curb and called through the open window, "Hop in, buddy."

The bar was swept out and the shelves were stocked. Jimmy would fill in while Eric took a break. First he stepped outdoors to escape the sounds and odors from within.

He leaned against the building, smoking a cigarette and looking at the girls passing by when he spotted Marty, an acquaintance, coming out of a nearby liquor store. A brown paper bag was under his arm and a man Jimmy didn't know was by his side. Well, he had work to do. He flipped his cigarette into the street, waved, and had turned to go back inside when Marty called out, "Hey, buddy, wait up!"

Jimmy watched them approach. The stranger was big, not only tall, but heavy, with sharp features and thinning hair. He wondered what in the hell the old fossil was after. Probably panting after the young chicks.

Marty swaggered up to Jimmy and said, "Hey, my man, this is . . ."

"Jay," Glenn True Clark said as he lifted his hand for a shake. The less any stranger knew about him the better. "Call me Jay."

Jimmy's slender fingers gripped Glenn's thick ones. The man was strong.

Marty shot Glenn a quizzical look and said, "Okay, Jay. Since you're Jay, this is John."

Jimmy decided if they were going to play games, "John" would suit him as well as any other name.

Marty jerked his head towards the alley. "You want to go in there and have a swig of the good stuff?"

"Naw, I gotta go to work."

"Then take my buddy, old Jay here, and buy him one or two, will you? He's running a little short on cash today, and I got a hot one waiting. You know what I mean?"

Jimmy knew exactly what he meant. Marty would grab the first chick with hot pants and a cold conscience and they would hope to find a place that wasn't too public.

Jimmy wasn't happy with the prospect. Before he could decide whether or not to stake this guy to a beer, Marty left on his mission.

Turning to the man he knew only as Jay, Jimmy said, "We might just as well go in."

Glenn studied his new acquaintance and grinned. He preferred to travel alone but there were times when another good man was needed. He had big plans and young John just might fit in. And hell, the dude wasn't big enough to be a threat.

"Sure, John. Why the hell not?"

While Glenn headed for a table, Jimmy drew a beer and handed the money to Eric.

"Who's your buddy?" Eric asked.

"Damned if I know. He got dumped on me."

"You want some advice?"

"Not especially."

"He looks like trouble."

"He's just an old guy out for a good time. Give me a minute or two and I'll take over."

As Jimmy approached the table, Glenn said, "Women and money. That's all there is, ain't it? What I'm looking for is an eighteen-year-old nympho with a fat bank account."

Jimmy grimaced. "They aren't too plentiful. Drink this while I tend bar."

"I'll buy the second round. That's 'bout all I'm good for at the time, but I'll have plenty of money later."

For twenty minutes Jimmy served as the lone barkeep. As he was turning the duties back to Eric, Glenn swaggered over and bought two beers. Jimmy followed him to the table.

Glenn fingered circles in the condensation on his glass and said, "So, John. What's coming down? You been over in Vietnam?"

"Close enough. Too damned close."

Jimmy shivered. Too damned close, all right. He had been off the coast aboard a tanker, a refueling ship. A target the enemy had tried its best to destroy.

Jimmy's ship had sat in the middle of the fleet. You have to protect your fuel. Everywhere Jimmy looked he could see a ship. Until then he had never seen ships' guns firing at sea. It had scared him.

"I was in the last one," Glenn said. "Not just close, but in the son of a bitch. Came out of it disabled. There's some work I still can't do. What I can do though is find ways to make a living. Old Gl-, Jay, might be a little short on cash, but that's temporary. I'll have money soon. Money and a chick. How about you? Got a lady to call your own or do you play the field?"

"Neither." Jimmy shook his head.

"That's one way to do it. But you need to have one you can fall back on at any time. As for me, I don't want to be saddled day and night with no whining woman. I'll just take 'em as I need 'em. Ain't no trouble for old Jay to get laid."

Jimmy listened without comment as Jay raved on and

on about his conquests over women and his ability to make money without working. He was wishing Marty would come and take this old guy off his hands when he heard the word that captured his undivided attention: Seattle!

"What did you say about Seattle?" Jimmy asked.

"I'm thinking about heading up there. You want to go?"

"Seattle sounds good to me," Jimmy said. Did it ever!

"Let's get out of this town then," Glenn said. "How you fixed on cash?"

"I got a little."

"We'll hit the road after dark. You ready to leave this place? Got something I want you to see."

"Suits me." Jimmy hurried to the bar and said to Eric, "Need any more help?"

"Naw, I can handle it."

"I'm cuttin' out then."

"Better watch that guy."

"You're not my parents, man. Give me two six-packs to go."

They stepped out into the afternoon sunlight. Glenn stopped to get his bearings, then said, "This way." He led Jimmy to a white two-door Oldsmobile. "How you like this?" he asked.

Without really considering, Jimmy said, "It's okay."

"Okay, hell! It's a beauty, man. I can get me a car anytime. We get tired of this one, I'll get another."

To Jimmy, this sounded like just plain bull from a man without money, but he didn't comment.

Glenn keyed the door, climbed in on the driver's side and unlocked the passenger door. "You still wantin' to go to Seattle?"

"Yeah, I want to go! I just need to pick up a few things."

The journey to Jimmy's place took them through "Haight," the name young immigrants had given Haight-Ashbury. It was a neighborhood filled with large Victorian houses once inhabited by the well-to-do and now by youths in torn jeans and miniskirts. Many of the guys had beards and ponytails. Their password was, "Freedom." Some stayed; others moved on.

The community had certainly been transformed. Rock bands were plentiful. The Grateful Dead had bought a mansion here as had the Jefferson Airplane group.

As they drew near to Golden Gate Park, the atmosphere was charged. You could feel the excitement, sense the tension. Police cars cruised the area, hoping to keep the animals corralled. Young girls wore flowers in their hair and sold bouquets. Glenn visually undressed them all.

They decided to stop. Glenn parked, locked the car, and they strolled in. Jimmy carried both six-packs in a paper bag. As the fog closed in, they heard a ship's horn out in the bay. Gulls cried as if trying to be heard over the raucous sounds from below. The birds were fighting a losing battle.

The two men entered the park and were bombarded by a cacophony of sounds. Individuals who thought they alone had found the profound meaning of the decade were shouting their messages. Some guitars played a soft melody; others blasted out hard rock. Jugglers vied for attention. A young girl with long brown hair sat beneath a tree, playing a sad tune on a flute. Many looked in need of a bath and a meal. Acid and grass were more available than was food.

Above the waist either sex might wear anything or nothing at all. Some girls, proud of their boobs, went topless. Some with tiny boobs went topless, too. Maybe the sunshine would help them grow.

As they wandered deeper into the park, they saw many couples embraced in the clutches of love, only partially concealed by bushes. It was as though the area had been set aside as a reservation and, so long as the inmates didn't stray, they were left alone to satisfy what they considered to be basic needs.

Jimmy thought the park resembled a circus. Everywhere he looked, something was happening. There were jugglers and clowns, and music coming at them from all directions.

Glenn thought of it as a huge meat market. He was anxious to make a selection. Maybe a little rump roast, or breast of chick.

"Enjoy the view," Jimmy said. "You don't want any of these girls. There's all kinds of disease down here. I don't know much, but I know that."

Glenn wasn't ready to confide to Jimmy that he could spread a little infection around, too. After finishing one six-pack and starting on the other, they returned to the car. Glenn, who had done most of the drinking, was bug-eyed.

He opened the trunk and removed a brown bag. Inside the car, he glanced around to see if they were being observed. Satisfied, he pulled two revolvers out of the bag. Both were snub-nosed. One was blue steel; the other a shiny chrome with a cracked handle grip.

Glenn pushed the shiny gun towards Jimmy. "This one's got your name on it," he said.

"What in the hell would I want with a gun?"

"Protection, man. Everywhere you look, there's weird people. Never hurts to be prepared."

"Where did you get it?"

"What difference does it make? Take it."

Hesitantly, Jimmy took the gun in his hand. "Is it loaded?"

"I'll load it for you. Ain't no way you can protect yourself with an unloaded gun."

Jimmy felt a certain amount of pride. This was the first pistol he'd ever owned.

Glenn took ammunition from a box and loaded the cylinder. Beside the glove compartment, under the dash, was a metal ledge with a curved lip. "Keep it up there," he suggested. "Long as it don't bounce out, nobody will ever know."

Glenn plucked a leather pouch off the floor, placed his gun inside, and lay it between his feet. "Let's see your gun. See if the safety is on."

"Man, I know all about guns." Jimmy didn't want him to think he was a novice.

"Oh hell, yes! I'll bet you're some kind of an expert,"

he said, looking at Jimmy and laughing. "Well, here's how you hold it, sharpshooter." He looked at Jimmy fumbling with the gun. "Now, where's your pad?"

"Up ahead."

Glenn parked outside a large house that had been divided into small apartments.

Jimmy gathered up the few items he needed, threw them into a duffel bag, and headed out.

"Where to now?" Glenn asked.

"Let's stop off at the bar. I need to get some more money."

As they were leaving the car, Glenn slipped his revolver out of its pouch and into a hip pocket.

"What in the world do you need that for?" Jimmy asked.

"Just for self-protection."

They went into the bar together. Jimmy used the pay phone to call his boss. He told Troy he was going to be out of town for a few days and asked for some of the money owed him. Troy told him a couple of hundred would be sent within the hour.

Eric waited until Glenn had wandered off, then asked, "Who in the hell is that guy?"

"Like I said, I dunno. Jay somebody."

"He looks like trouble to me."

"You're repeating yourself. Don't sweat it, man."

"Listen to me, Jimmy. I bet you two-to-one that if you go off with the old fart you're gonna have more trouble than you've ever seen. I know the type."

"Let it go, man. Give me a beer."

A half hour later Jimmy's money arrived and he was ready to head for Seattle. He found Glenn trying to make time with a blonde who seemed to be having some difficulty choosing between this new guy who was bigger and talked one heck of a line or staying with her escort who was a shrimp with a fat wallet. Before she could decide, Jimmy told Glenn they had to go right away.

"Dammit, John, you picked one hell of a time to hit the road. I was ready to get me some of that."

"We'll never get to Seattle if you go after that kind." Jimmy swallowed hard and then said, "That guy can't do you any good."

"What guy, you asshole? I was after the blonde."

"That's the guy I'm talking about."

Glenn stopped and gave Jimmy a hard look. "You're putting me on."

"You don't believe me, go back and see for yourself."

"You mean I was trying to put the make on a man? He's one hell of an impersonator, I'll give him his due."

"Yeah, he is." Jimmy had no idea of the person's sex but he suspected she was as female as any woman in San Francisco. From the looks of her, probably more than most. What mattered was he'd convinced Jay.

As they approached the car, Glenn said, "Hey man, how about sharing some of that money? I got things to buy before I get to Seattle."

Jimmy wasn't in any mood to take a bus or hitchhike. He peeled off three twenties and handed them to the old man. It looked as though this was going to be an expensive trip.

They both got into the car. Jimmy slumped down into the seat and fished a cigarette from the pack. He lit it thinking he didn't care much for Jay, but the man was going to Seattle. The timing was just right. Jimmy was ready to put thoughts of the war behind him. He was ready for a new life.

2

QUAIL ON THE FLY

In Portland, Oregon, Terrie Trina Tidwell, pretty, eighteen, and naive, had endured a troubled summer. She had lived with her mother and then, following a disagreement that had severed ties at least temporarily, shared quarters with two girlfriends. Still, she was not content. And so she had phoned her father, a successful financial consultant, to see if she could come to Los Angeles to live with him and her stepmother.

She could. Not only that but Brian Tidwell sent his daughter sufficient money to buy an airplane ticket. That Terrie did not use the money for this purpose but for the girl stuff, would, in a very short time, come back to haunt her.

About the time that "Jay" was goggling at the sights in Golden Gate Park and "John" was anxious to head for Seattle, Terrie was waiting for Gregory Winslow to arrive and go off to meet some friends in Eugene.

She had first met Greg at a party around the first of August. He was some six feet tall with dark hair and bedroom eyes. He was also lots of fun and they liked being together. Since that time they'd been together, but this jaunt would be their last fun trip. When she reached Los Angeles, she would be required to play a different role.

Terrie rode in the blue jeep to Eugene, Oregon, and arrived at the apartment of Phil and Tracey, friends of Greg's. Here they would spend the night. Maybe party a little. She would miss Greg.

Where is that fool? Jimmy wondered. Sitting on a tall stool at the short end of the L-shaped bar, he had not seen Jay for some ten or fifteen minutes. Jay had remained with Jimmy only long enough to drink part of a beer. Then he'd said he was going to the rest room. Now here it was 11:25 at night, the wall clock said, and Jimmy was beginning to wonder if he'd been left behind. Perhaps the Olds was long gone. The way things were going, they would be lucky to reach Seattle by Thanksgiving.

Suddenly Jimmy heard noises, curses, and shouting coming from around the far end of the bar. Even though the commotion was out of sight, Jimmy slapped a hand to the side of his head and cursed the wicked gods who had brought him and Jay together.

As the man came running over, advising him to get his friend out, Jimmy had a good idea of what was going on. Why oh why had he ever left San Francisco?

Jimmy hurried down to the other end of the bar to investigate.

Sure enough, Jay was standing near a booth and arguing with two men who were half his age. Seated beside one of them was a plain-looking girl with green eyes and long yellow hair who did not look old enough to visit taverns.

A young man with a red beard and even redder eyes said in a gruff voice, "Listen, you old son of a bitch, you don't say things like that to my girl."

Glenn advanced a step, causing each man to stand while the girl tried to hide, her big eyes opening even more as she wondered if these three men were actually going to do battle over her.

Jimmy doubted that anyone had ever fought for her, much less over her. But she had shapely legs and was breathing and so, to this weird guy he was driving to Seattle with, she was surely a work of pure beauty.

"All I said was she's the prettiest little piece in here," Glenn said. "Any asshole offended by those words ain't got his head on straight. What say we let her decide? You want to leave with me, pretty little piece, or do you want to stay here with two assholes?"

The girl didn't say a word. Her hands trembled and her lower lip quivered. Red Beard said, "You wanna keep your teeth in your head, you old fart, then get out. Now!"

Jimmy slid between them. He didn't mind a fight but Jay was an idiot. "Hold it," he said to the two men. "Come on, Jay. We're getting out of here."

"Oh hell, not you again. I suppose you're going to tell me this one's not a woman either, like you done that last time."

"I'm just saying we're leaving. You guys back off."

"If he's your friend, you'd better teach him manners or keep him out of here," Red Beard said. "You don't, we'll kick his ass up between his shoulders."

Though Jimmy was small, he was strong. He grabbed Jay by the arm, hoping the man wouldn't resist. For some reason, maybe because he'd had too much to drink, Glenn surrendered. He winked at the girl and said, "You get tired of these guys, look me up. You sleep with a real man and you'll spit on these assholes."

Jimmy pushed him towards the door. "Come on, man, let's get out of here."

When they reached the car, Jimmy waited until Glenn climbed in before he went around to the passenger side and did the same.

"You're gonna have to quit interfering with me," Glenn said. "Next time I get my hands on a girl, I'm gonna screw her and you're gonna have to stay out of my way. I like you, John, but people who cross me tend to get hurt. You've been warned. Don't forget."

"Yeah, okay. Let's get on the road. I'd like to live long enough to see Seattle."

"We'll sleep here," Glenn said. "I'm gonna pull the car over under the light and we'll drink beer, piss, and sleep until we're ready to move on."

Sunlight poured through the side glass and burned Jimmy's eyelids. Jay was folded into the front seat in some obscure way, not visible, but there was no doubt he was there. His snores vibrated throughout the car.

Seattle seemed light years away.

A few minutes later Jay's snoring caught in his throat and rumbled to a stop. He thrashed around for a moment and then sat up. "Got a damned crick in my neck."

Glenn rubbed his stubble of beard. He liked to start his day with a razor. Slap on a little aftershave to please the girls. Oh well, they would have to stop for gas in Sacramento and he could always clean up in the rest room.

Jimmy stared at him, wondering what the older man was thinking. His lips fit together too tightly, and Jimmy thought he knew why. The man wore false teeth. He must have taken them out to sleep. Glenn ducked his head out of sight and soon reappeared with teeth intact.

"Somewhere in California," Glenn said. "Ain't important just exactly where we're at. Don't worry one little bit. We're on our way to Seattle. Told you I'd take you and I will. Old Jay says he'll do something, he'll do it."

Somewhere down the highway they stopped at a McDonald's. Jimmy went inside and ate a hamburger and French fries while Glenn decided to stay in the car and drink. Soon after they hit the road again, the driver stopped and bought more beer.

After that they drove silently for a few hours. "We need gas," Glenn announced, breaking the quiet. He left I-5 at a Sacramento exit and drove until he found an Atlantic

Richfield station. He might as well use the credit card until the balance got so high they cut him off. While the attendant filled the tank, Glenn checked the oil. Take care of your car was his motto. Treat it better than you would a woman. Cars are hard to come by. Women are plentiful. At least they used to be. They would be again, of this he was certain.

John had hurried to the rest room. After signing the credit card slip, Glenn pulled his shaving kit from the trunk and followed. Damn John and his Seattle. Glenn knew he would not, could not, wait that long to have a woman. Somewhere along the road he'd find one and have his way. If she didn't like what he had in mind that was too damn bad. There were ways to handle them kind of women. He got back on the highway continuing the drive.

Hitchhikers of both sexes, many traveling alone, lined the road. Most were thumbing their way in the direction of San Francisco. A multitude of shapely young ladies were already being mentally raped by Glenn True Clark. He was sorely tempted to stop. But for one reason or another he passed them by.

Meanwhile, Greg had dropped Terrie Tidwell off on the highway. It was 3:00 P.M., the hottest time of the day. She put up her thumb in the customary manner. It wouldn't take long to get a ride.

Watching Glenn, Jimmy decided that, when the early settlers moved across this country, they must have made better time than he was making with Jay. Them old covered wagons would have passed them by already, left them in the dust. The sun was standing at midafternoon and they had yet to reach Redding. The mountains were in sight but still far away. And now here was Jay taking another exit. *What is it with this man?* Jimmy wondered.

"Where we going this time?" Jimmy asked as the older man paused at a stop sign and then turned right.

"Keep cool, little buddy. I got a little chore to do. Have you back on the road in no time."

After driving a couple of miles, Jay shot a left and turned down a side road. He soon stopped, pulled a pair of pliers and screwdriver out of the glove box, and got out. Jimmy followed.

Jay opened the trunk. Inside was a license tag with a name, letters and numbers that read California IVX-380. "Time for a little insurance," he said. "We're gonna make a change."

"Why?"

"Because this is a hot car, that's why."

"I should have figured that," Jimmy said, wondering what had ever possessed him to hook up with this damn nut. As soon as they got to Seattle he was going to make some excuse and cut out.

"Picked it up off a car lot in Salt Lake City. After they closed at night, that is. I like this little beauty. We keep swapping tags and we can drive her forever."

"Where'd you get that tag?"

"Off a junk car a block or so from my brother's house in Tracy. Nobody ever misses a tag off a junk car."

Within five minutes the chore was done. Glenn tossed the old tag back into the trunk and the tools back inside the glove box. He said, "I gotta drain my radiator before we go on." As he started to urinate, he grimaced. "Some bitch caused me to have a leaky dick," he said. "I'm doctoring it though, so it's just temporary."

What else? Jimmy thought, but kept quiet.

When Jimmy didn't respond, Glenn said, "Let's pull up under a tree and take a nap. I don't feel like I've slept in a week."

Within five minutes, Terrie had her first ride of the afternoon. It was with a man. He was alone in a pickup truck. He looked innocent enough. She hoisted her suitcases into the back and climbed into the cab. They eyed one another briefly. He lit a cigarette, then offered her one.

She declined in favor of one from her own pack. There was no air-conditioning, but at least she was off the hot highway.

"Going far?" he asked.

"To San Francisco," she said.

"I'm only going twenty-five or thirty miles. You can ride that far and stop off at my place for a while if you care to."

Was that a proposition? Terrie glanced at his left hand and saw that he was not wearing a wedding band. There was nothing conclusive about this. Lots of married men didn't. Perhaps he had a wife and six kids and was just being friendly. Either way, she didn't want to stop this early on her trip.

"No thanks," she said. "I have a long ways to go."

"That's fine," he said. "I just wanted you to know you were welcome."

During their brief time together he fished for information as to who she was and why she was hitchhiking. She told him little. He spoke of being a rancher and a horse-shoer. A nice enough man, but she wasn't going to his place and he wasn't about to drive her to California. Within the hour she was standing alongside the highway again, suitcases at her side.

Finally, Redding was behind them. At least the scenery was changing. And the air was cleaner. They were now driving in the mountains. Off to the right was a snow-covered peak.

Jimmy supposed it could have been worse. They did have another six-pack of beer. And Jay did seem ready to get down to business and head north for a while. Perhaps they would drive through the night. If offered, he would take his turn behind the wheel.

"That's Mount Shasta with the snow on it," Jay said.

Although Jimmy had never been this far north in California, he didn't feel the need for a tour guide. He didn't give a damn about the name of any mountain.

Jay popped the top on a beer can and looked over at his companion. "What I want to do is take a bank. You ever wanted to rob a bank?"

"Hell no!" Jimmy said. "I ain't no criminal. I don't want nothing to do with robbing no bank. The FBI gets after you then. You get caught, you're sent up until you're too old to think about chasing after women or anything else."

"We won't get caught. Long as you're with me you don't have to worry about that. Think it over, John. How many people are there these days who have the guts to rob a bank?"

Son of a bitch thinks he's Jesse James, Jimmy thought. And damn! Jesse died young. From a bullet. A bullet to the back.

The highway was lined with youths thumbing their way to California.

Late model cars whizzed by. One with a cool air-conditioner would be nice. A woman in a blue Buick slowed, seemed to change her mind, and sped away.

An old green Ford slowed, sputtered and coughed. It came to a stop just beyond Terrie. There wasn't a chance that it would have an air-conditioner. When you hitchhike, you can't always be choosy.

She wrestled her bags into the back seat and climbed in beside the driver. He was an old man with stained teeth and bad odor whom she judged to be crowding seventy.

The Ford polluted the air with a cloud of black smoke as he tromped the accelerator and pulled back onto the highway. His cracked voice said, "Going my way?"

Terrie, hands clasped together on her lap, nodded.

They rode in silence for some five minutes. Then he said, "Cat got your tongue? People who ride together oughta talk together."

Terrie stared out the window at the low mountains. "What do you want to talk about?"

"About you. You're a right pretty woman. Anybody ever tell you that?"

"Once or twice."

Another moment of silence and then he said, "Thing is, I believe that people oughta do for each other. I'm hauling you in the direction you want to go. That being so, you oughta do something for me."

"Like what?"

"I think you already know what. My wife, she won't do for me so you know what I need. I could drive us off on some side road or we could stop and get us a motel for an hour or two. Won't cost you nothing either way. Side road or motel, you take your pick."

"No!" Terrie cried out.

Her emphatic reply startled him. He jerked his head towards her. "You don't have to treat me that way," he said. "I know you people ain't got no morals and that you crawl into bed with one another all the time. How come you're so different when it comes to me?"

Terrie hadn't meant to hurt his feelings but she was not going to bed with him. Some girls would probably put out for any ride they could catch but she would never go that far.

"It's my time of the month," she said.

He eyed her for a moment, trying to determine whether or not she was telling the truth. Well, at least it gave him an opportunity to save face. "All you had to do was say so," he said. "I live at Myrtle Creek. You can ride that far if you want. I ain't goin' no farther."

He didn't go no farther. Not with Terrie, anyway.

She stood alongside I-5 near Myrtle Creek. Would the next ride take her into San Francisco or at least as far as Sacramento? It was uncertain. The afternoon sun was well along on its journey when the black Mustang stopped. Two nice looking young guys were inside. Instead of nasty old men. Two of her peers were offering a helping hand.

"Thanks," she said, as she joined her suitcases in the back seat. "How far you going?"

The driver turned and flashed a smile. He had dark curly hair and a kind face. "Eventually to Redding," he said.

Terrie smiled. "Eventually?"

The young man in the passenger seat turned sideways and said, "We know some people in Medford. We're gonna stop there and have a swim and then go on tomorrow. Why not join us?"

Terrie hesitated. "I need to go on," she said.

"Where are we at?" Jimmy asked.

Jay had stopped at a filling station to check the oil and put in a can of STP. He climbed back inside the car where Jimmy was eating a Butterfinger candy bar he'd purchased from a vending machine. "Yreka," Jay said. "We'll wait a while to gas up. How we doing on beer?"

Jimmy wondered where in the hell Yreka was. "Four left," he said.

"That'll last a while. Let's hit the road."

The boys had been reluctant to leave her on the highway alone. They seemed to actually care about Terrie's welfare. They'd had their stop planned at Medford, and she had insisted that she would be all right. And so they had taken her through the town, as far as the Talent Exchange, and wished her a safe journey.

It would soon be dark, not a good time for a woman to be stranded there. Whatever ride was next offered, Terrie Tidwell would have to take. Terrie's head was turned toward the southbound traffic. She didn't see the light-colored Oldsmobile heading north, nor did she realize that the driver had spotted her and was already dreaming of what she'd look like naked. Had she known what terror the night would hold she would have left her suitcases alongside the road and run for her life.

3

DEAD INDIAN MOUNTAIN

The day was drawing to an end. Glenn True Clark was hot, tired and horny. He was regretting all the possible lays he had passed along the highway. And then he saw her, a slender chick standing on the west side of 1-5, two suitcases beside her and leaning towards California. There was no doubt in his mind his luck had changed. Even though her purple sack dress concealed the exact formation of what lay beneath, he was certain she would be shaped just right.

What he had to do now was turn around, head back, and entice her into his car before some other stud beat him to the prize.

This one wouldn't last long. Young and supple and willing, he would bet. The sign at the exit read: Talent. Perhaps this was an omen. Glenn pressed hard on the gas pedal.

"Hey, man, what's going on?" Jimmy's head raised up from the backrest and he rubbed sleep from his tired eyes.

Seconds later, Glenn hit the brakes, throwing his passenger into the dash and causing his head to bump the windshield and his revolver to fall from its hiding place.

"Damn!" Jimmy shouted as he reached for the gun and placed it back on the ledge. "Watch what you're doing. What the devil are we pulling off for? We aren't ever gonna get to Seattle."

Glenn didn't come close to stopping at the sign that ordered him to do so. After a cursory glance to satisfy himself that the road was clear of oncoming traffic, he shot a quick left.

As Glenn gunned the engine, he said, "I spotted something across the highway thumbing her way south that looks better than anything you'll see in Seattle. Maybe she'll have a sister for you."

"She can't be that good."

"We'll soon find out. At least she's here and not a thousand miles away."

"Man, it ain't no thousand miles to Seattle. We keep driving and we'll be there by morning. You want me to take the wheel, I'll do it. I'll drive us all the way up there without even stopping except to buy gas and more beer."

"Nobody drives my car but me."

Glenn cranked the wheel again and headed down the entrance ramp to I-5 south. When he saw the chick still standing there beside her two suitcases, as appealing as a magazine model, he pounded on the steering wheel and shouted, "Hot damn! Don't go nowhere till I get there, baby."

This was going to be so easy it was almost criminal. The fact that Glenn had daughters nearly as old as the girl he was determined to pick up and use as a means of relieving tension didn't deter him for one moment.

So far as he was concerned, women who stood alongside the road were asking for it. Probably wanting it bad. She wouldn't have to wait much longer. Glenn was willing to give her a ride in his car but then he damned sure intended to ride her. A fair enough trade, he thought.

Terrie was shivering. The sun was sinking low. Hitchhiking had seemed to be a wise decision during earlier daylight hours but it now threatened to become a nightmare. The competition for rides was stiff. In the short distance she'd traveled this afternoon, there had been scores of hitchhikers, most going in her direction.

When the speeding car slowed and pulled off the road near her, Terrie looked relieved. Two men were in the front seat. No problem. It was the one-man rides that gave trouble.

The passenger side door opened and a young man stepped out. He didn't say a word but folded the seat forward and placed her suitcases inside. As she crawled in after them, the driver said, "Where you heading?"

Terrie wasn't sure where. "Sacramento," she said. "I have a job waiting for me there. In a bank, you know."

"This is your lucky day," Glenn said. "We're on our way to Sacramento." *Tell 'em anything*, he thought. Had she said Phoenix, that's where he'd say he was going.

Jimmy slumped down in his seat. The girl was right behind him. This, they didn't need. He had no idea where they were, but there was no doubt that Sacramento was many miles away. They had stopped there some time in the morning and now here it was almost sundown.

"I'm Jay and my little buddy here is John," Glenn said. "What's your name?"

"Terrie."

Terrie settled into the white leatherette seat. But then she glanced up to see Jay eyeing her in the rearview mirror. She shivered.

Jay partially turned his attention to driving and she turned to John who had a melancholy look on his face as he sat up straight and stared out the side window. John acted as though something was really bothering him.

What in the hell is going on? Jimmy wondered as dreams of Seattle and its beautiful girls began to evaporate. Why was Jay heading back the wrong way?

Here they were, twenty-four hours after leaving San Francisco, and they still hadn't left California.

At this rate they would be lucky to reach Seattle before

winter. Although he had no idea of how far they were from Sacramento, he was certain they would probably lose another day making the round trip. Maybe two, depending on what his new acquaintance had in mind. All because old Jay was horny enough to stop for any hitchhiker wearing a dress.

He looked over at the girl. She looked tired, real tired. He looked at his driving companion. He knew what was in the old guy's head. Jimmy sighed.

As Terrie closed her eyes, looking relaxed, it was obvious she didn't realize Jay was watching her and planning just what it would take to get her panties off. First he would have to get her filled to the gills with beer and wine so she would see things his way. At least soused enough so that she would offer very little resistance. And then . . . What came next depended on her. He was damned sure going to get him some of that within the next few hours. If she resisted—well, there were ways to handle those kind of women.

The car slowed. Terrie opened her eyes. There was a sign proclaiming the Ashland exit. Jay, watching her in the rearview mirror, said, "I'm thirsty. Why don't we stop at a store and get some beer. You like beer?"

"Yeah, sure."

Jimmy didn't pay any attention to the name of the town. He knew only that they had traveled south for a few miles and now they were exiting. Maybe this meant they would soon turn north again. With Jay, you never knew. They had been on the road a day and a night and it didn't seem as though they had gone anywhere. Maybe they'd only been going around in circles. Could be Jay needed a compass and map to get him out of California.

Glenn turned left and soon pulled into the parking lot of the South Side Market. "I'll get us something," he said.

Although Terrie couldn't see what he did next, Jimmy did. "What the hell is he doing now?" Jimmy muttered to himself. Glenn deftly slipped the pistol out of its leather pouch and shoved it into his right back pocket. He left his round gold-plated watch on the turn signal handle, pulled his wallet out of the glove box, left the car, and swaggered through the front door.

Left alone with Terrie, Jimmy offered her a cigarette. Again she declined in favor of one from her own pack. "How long you been on the road?" he asked.

"Since two or three o'clock. That's long, you know. It seems as though nobody is going any distance today. It's taken me three rides to get this far. Now you and your friend are taking me all the way to Sacramento."

Jimmy didn't answer. Sacramento, hell! If Jay took her all the way back they might as well forget Seattle. He felt sorry for this young chick, stuck out here by herself, but she wasn't alone. Everywhere you looked, girls were hitchhiking. Especially those who were trying to reach San Francisco.

Terrie wasn't that much different from a host of others he'd seen. She did have big blue eyes and a nice body. Anyway, what he had seen of her legs looked nice.

Glenn returned, climbed into the car, chucked his wallet back into the glove compartment, threw a box of Kleenex onto the front seat, slipped the gun back into its pouch, and pulled a six-pack of Olympia beer out of a brown paper bag.

Before he could hand one to Terrie, she said, "Let me out. I want to go inside for a moment."

"You'll be back, won't you?" Glenn asked.

"Now where else would I go? Of course I'll be back. I want to buy a few things."

Jimmy opened his door, got out and raised the back of his seat.

"I'll just be a minute," she said.

After she had entered the store, Jimmy said, "Man, what are we doing here? I thought we were going straight to Seattle."

"We're on our way. Let me finish with Terrie. Then we'll let her out and we should be in Seattle sometime tomorrow. You can wait that long, can't you?"

Jimmy knew he didn't have any choice. Not unless he got out and started walking. Or hitchhiking.

He popped the top on a can of beer and took a sip. Damn, but that was good.

"Look at her," Glenn said, as Terrie stepped out of the store, balancing a soda and ice cream bar in one hand and clutching a small bag containing grapes and a peach in the other. "Man, she's built just the way I like 'em."

Jimmy suspected by now that the way Glenn liked them was female and breathing. If they met those qualifications, more than likely they passed the old man's test.

Glenn told Terrie to watch her soda and backed the car out of the parking lot. Instead of heading west to where they could get back on I-5, he turned east. "Now where in the devil are we going?" Jimmy asked.

"Oh, just driving around a little." Glenn wondered if there was any easy way to get rid of his buddy until he was through. Two bulls sniffing around after one little heifer in heat wouldn't work. Get a combination like that and somebody was going to get hurt. If somebody did, that person would be John.

What was important was that he keep Terrie on his side. "You ain't in no hurry, are you?" he asked. "We got some friends living near here that we oughta stop and see before we head south. Sooner or later we'll get you to where you're going though. Don't you worry about that. Probably be sooner than you think."

"What friends?" she asked.

"Slim and Virginia. They own a ranch up in the mountains. Thought that since we're this close we might stop for a few minutes."

"Well, I don't know."

"There's a new singing group staying at the ranch. I can't remember what they call themselves but they are damn good."

"Sure. All right."

Jimmy wondered what was going on. This was the first he'd heard of Slim and Virginia and any singing group. He suspected that the old guy was blowing smoke for Terrie's sake. Whatever Jay had in mind, Jimmy owed it to the girl to see that she wasn't mistreated. The old man had better not use force. He had too much respect for women to ever allow that to happen.

A sign pointing to the left read: DEAD INDIAN ROAD. Glenn turned onto it. Ahead lay a winding asphalt track, snaking its way up a mountain that was bare on the sides and covered with trees on top. It had the appearance of a man with a round head and a poor haircut. Robbed of sunlight this late in the day, it looked gloomy.

"Slim and Virginia live over on the other side of Dead Indian Mountain," Glenn said.

Sure they do, thought Jimmy. *And I'm the president of Cuba and Fidel Castro is King of England and old Lyndon Baines Johnson is loved by all in North Vietnam.* He might be naive, but he wasn't stupid.

On their left was a small airport; on their right was the Airport Market. "We can't go up there with only one six-pack of beer," Glenn said. "Let's pull in here and get another."

Jimmy was not one to argue against the need for more beer.

Glenn parked in front of the store. After going through his ritual again, he went inside. Terrie wiped her hands on a Kleenex and said, "Your friend is kind of strange. Have you noticed?"

"Yeah, I've noticed."

She rolled her eyes at Jimmy. "How about you, John? Are you strange?"

Jimmy shook his head. He turned in the seat until they were facing one another. "I got it together," he said. "Being in the service did that. Your big blue eyes sure are pretty."

"Thank you." Terrie took a bite of peach.

"You really going to Sacramento?"

"I really am. Maybe farther."

"You could get hurt hitchhiking."

"I can take care of myself."

"Maybe. I don't know what Jay's got in mind, but I want you to know I respect women. Nothing's going to happen to you if I can help it."

"There's no need for you to worry about me. Jay isn't going to do anything to me even if he wants to because I won't let him. I am experienced at taking care of myself, you know."

"You might need help. Look." Jimmy plucked the revolver from its ledge under the car's dash. "I got this from Jay."

Terrie pulled back. It was a small gun that John held in his hand. It was shiny, a chrome-plated revolver with light colored grips, but it could be deadly. Guns were something to be feared. "Does it shoot?" she asked.

"It better. What good is a gun if it won't shoot?"

"But why do you want it?"

"For protection. Don't have no license, or nothing."

As he spotted Glenn coming out of the store, Jimmy hid his gun back under the dash. "Don't tell him I showed it to you," he said. "No need in making him mad."

"It's our secret," Terrie said. It wasn't clear what they were doing with a gun. From what did they need protection?

"He keeps one on the floor between his feet," Jimmy said in a conspiratorial tone.

When it isn't in his pocket, he thought.

Two guns! Terrie shivered.

Glenn climbed in, passed two six-packs of beer to Jimmy and broke the seal on a bottle of wine. He offered it to Terrie who drank first and then passed it back. As Glenn attacked the wine, she accepted a can of beer from Jimmy.

Glenn pointed the nose of the car up Dead Indian Road. They had traveled less than a half mile from the Airport Market when they saw a highway patrolman coming towards them. "Put it down," Jimmy begged Glenn. "Please, put the beer down."

He and Terrie were both looking guilty as they tucked their beer cans out of sight. Glenn just laughed and raised his in a salute as the patrolman approached. The two cars passed, and Jimmy tried to hide in his seat.

A mile or so more and Jimmy was squirming. He felt as though his bladder would burst. "Man, I gotta go," he said. "I gotta go bad. Find a place and let's stop."

Glenn whooped it up. "There's a tree," he said. "That oughta make a good bathroom. You can go behind that tree."

"Man, it's not a good enough tree. It's too little. Find us a place. I bet Terrie has to go, too."

When they pulled into the Hooper Springs Wayside Park, Jimmy jumped out and made an awkward dash to the rest room, hoping he wouldn't spot his britches. He barely made it inside without doing so. As he was going out, Glenn was coming in.

"Can't you hold your water?" Glenn asked.

"I can hold it as well as most. It's been a long time between rest stops. Besides, you went when we last stopped and I didn't. Man, what's this crap about Slim and Virginia and a ranch and a singing group? First time I've heard anything about that."

"Just because you haven't heard don't mean they're not there," Glenn said as he went inside.

Terrie returned to the car soon after Jimmy and he let her in the back seat. "Are you afraid of me?" she asked.

"No. Why?"

"I don't know. You just seem to wish I wasn't here. Is that what you wish?"

"It's nothing personal. I'm just wanting to go to Seattle."

"What's in Seattle? A girlfriend?"

Jimmy was saved having to answer when Glenn returned. His reasons for wanting to go to Seattle were becoming more and more difficult for him to define.

When they were all three back in the car, Glenn reached under the seat and pulled out a deck of cards. "Do you play poker?" he asked Terrie.

"Of course." She plucked a cigarette from her pack and Jimmy flicked his lighter. She blew smoke and added, "I know how to play."

"Count us out some matches, John. We don't want to take Terrie's money. We got us a couple of hundred apiece so we don't need to do that. Of course it would be a lot more exciting to play strip poker."

"We'll play for matches," she said.

"Yeah, okay. Dealer's choice. Five card stud is my game. I'm giving you fair warning now though. There's been many the time when I've made my living playing poker. Got my training in Las Vegas. I can beat those guys any day, no problem."

Jimmy felt certain that Jay's ramblings were only for Terrie's benefit. Nobody beat Las Vegas consistently. If they could they wouldn't have to drive stolen cars.

He counted out ten matches for each of them. As Jay was shuffling, Jimmy opened another can of beer. Damn, but he was getting hungry. It had been a long time since the candy bar and even longer since breakfast. And Jay hadn't eaten a thing all day. Just drank beer and wine.

Why were they here instead of on the road heading north? he wondered. They would never get to Seattle and the reason was obvious. Because Jay was willing to chase anything female.

Glenn saw John as a challenge for Terrie's attention. He was dealing and talking. "You like my car?" he asked Terrie. When she didn't respond, he plowed ahead. Time to take his new friend down a notch or two.

"Old John here, me and him had us a new Riviera but he wrecked the damned thing. Said it was the other man's fault. It's always the other man's fault, ain't it? You ever hear of anybody having a wreck when they would admit it was their fault?"

Jimmy studied a pair of queens. He'd never owned a Riviera in his life. Didn't even know what they looked like. Wasn't even sure who made them.

"After John wrecked our Riviera, we had to have some wheels, didn't we? You know, we didn't have a dime's worth of insurance. So it was left up to old Jay here to find us transportation. That's easy. I ain't never had to worry about something to drive. Sometimes I buy 'em, sometimes I don't. This one I helped myself to. You know what I mean?"

"Well, you know, I suppose you mean this is a stolen car." She looked bothered by the news, but said nothing further. Soon she would be in Sacramento and then these two men could go wherever they wanted to go.

Glenn laughed. "You're a quick learner. Ain't she a quick learner, John? Old John here stole it."

"Like hell I did," Jimmy replied.

"How about that, aces and kings," Glenn said. "You gotta give me a match apiece. My luck holds, we'll be playing for more than matches."

Glenn kept the deal. As he shuffled the cards, he said, "I like to give presents to my girls. Now I'll have you know I ain't no tightwad. All I ask is if we split up they give the present back. That ain't asking too much, is it?"

"Probably not." Terrie frowned.

"I was in Sacramento not long ago. Now I'm going back. For you I will. I'll take you anywhere you want to go. You sure that's what you want?"

Jay was getting drunk. The more he drank the more he talked, and the more he talked the less sense he made.

"That's where I'm going," she said.

"We oughta go down there to the airport, park the car, borrow us a plane, and fly down. Old John here is one hell of a pilot."

Jimmy knew then that the man had lost what little sense he'd ever had. Given a choice, he would walk almost anywhere before he would fly. The only time he could remember being really scared was when he'd been in an airplane.

"Let's all have a cigarette and another beer," Glenn said. "I had me a girl in San Francisco and I gave her a pair of white go-go boots. You know the kind I mean. Pretty as a painting. The boots, not the girl. And expensive, too. The girl and the boots. Both were high dollar. We split and she wouldn't give them back. Now I ask you, is that fair?"

When Terrie didn't respond, Glenn said, "Reason old John's so quiet is, his heart's in Seattle. He's got him a girl-friend there. Poor old John. He didn't much more than get out of the Navy when this girl, the one he was so crazy about, was in a car wreck. About the time John was wreck-ing our Riviera in California, his girl was gettin' herself killed up in Seattle. If that ain't a coincidence I don't know what is.

"That all happened a few weeks back," Glenn went on. "Now you know the reason old John's so sad. He's kind of ignoring you because his heart is still with her."

Terrie must have felt sorry for John. As she looked at her pair of jacks, she asked, "Were you in Vietnam?"

"Close by," Jimmy said. "It was on a boat. We were right offshore."

What was Jay talking about? He really was nuts.

Terrie won the hand with her pair of jacks. Beer cans and an empty wine bottle were tossed out of the car. The doors were open and the dome light was on. While Jay was shuffling, she studied both men. Although Jay had explained why John had not made a pass at her, the older man was doing just that. Well, Jimmy thought, she could take care of herself.

"Are you part Indian?" she asked Jimmy.

"I'm a full blood Cherokee," he said. Now why had he told her that? He wasn't full blood. Less than half.

Jay was old. Not as old as the pervert who'd proposi-tioned Terrie earlier in the day, but he had to be past forty. His brown hair was thin and receding; he combed it straight back. His small nose had a pronounced hook and he wore false teeth.

Glenn said, "Yeah, old John's still in mourning but I ain't. Just look at me. I ain't in bad shape for already being thirty-one, am I?"

Instead of answering, Terrie asked Jimmy, "How old are you?"

"How old do you think I am?"

"Oh, I'd say nineteen."

Jimmy nodded. He figured that was close enough. He didn't tell her he was twenty-one. What was the point?

"He ain't even dry behind the ears," Glenn said. "Me, I got experience. That's what women like, a man who knows how to satisfy 'em. Ain't that what women like?"

Terrie didn't answer. "Let me out," she said to Jimmy. "I need to go to the bathroom again."

By now it was well past sundown. It was near enough to the darkness Glenn had been waiting for. "We'll all go," he said. "Then we'll drive down to the store for more refreshments before we head up to Slim and Virginia's. You can sit up front here with us any time you want," he said to Terrie.

While Glenn was in the store, Terrie took him up on the invitation. She slipped her shoes off, stuffed them into a suitcase, then climbed over into the front seat. "Hi," she said to Jimmy.

"Hi."

"I was getting lonesome back there."

"Okay, now you're up here. No more need to feel lonesome."

Glenn came out of the store with another bottle of wine and two more six-packs. When he saw that Terrie had moved up front, he grinned. The girl was ripe for picking. Ready to satisfy old Jay.

They headed up Dead Indian Mountain, all three riding in the front seat and drinking beer and wine. The night was black. Glenn followed his headlights around sharp curves, driving too fast, causing them to lean hard first one way and then the other.

"Man, slow this mother down," Jimmy said. "You're scaring Terrie."

Glenn laughed and pressed the accelerator. They looked for the wayside park but somehow missed it. Once more he pushed the car too fast on sharp turns.

"Man, you're gonna wreck this mother," Jimmy said.

"Piss on you," Glenn growled.

"Man, don't talk like that around Terrie."

"Piss on you, I said, and I'll say it again. You or nobody else will ever tell me how to drive. Tell you what, I put one dent on this car, I'll bang my head against a rock. Hand me a beer. Don't try keepin' it all to yourself."

They popped the top on three more cans. Terrie looked frightened by Jay's antics. "When are we going to get to the ranch?"

Glenn took several side roads, but always came back to Dead Indian Road. Terrie looked so tired she couldn't keep her eyes open. She lay her head on Jimmy's shoulder and went to sleep. She looked content. Safe. Secure. When she awoke, her personal hell would begin.

4

GUNFIGHT

Even in late August, the nights can get bone-chilling cold in the mountains of Oregon. So cold that before morning your teeth chatter and you shiver and dream of ways to find warmth. Enough wine and beer consumed could make you feel comfortable, deceptive though the feeling might be.

A crackling fire can offer comfort although you might have to turn yourself like a rotisserie, cooking one side at a time, feeling overdone in some spots and somewhat raw in others. Even so, a fire on a mountain clearing can certainly offer one the illusion of warmth.

The driver favored the comfort promised by liquor over that of a fire. That and the heat from a young woman would be enough to satisfy his needs. The night was young enough so it was only chilly, not cold. That would come later.

Yes, Glenn True Clark had his own idea concerning the best way to stay warm. As he turned off Dead Indian Highway onto Shell Peak Road, she was sitting right next to him. Breathing the deep even breaths of one who feels secure in a peaceful sleep.

Sure her head was on John's shoulder, not his, but what the hell? When you're asleep, your head might go any which way. And that damned John wasn't paying the least bit of attention to her. He acted as though Terrie was inferior to the girls in Seattle. Like maybe them broads up there were really something special.

So far as Glenn was concerned all women were the same. This one was put together plenty good enough for him. And one thing for damn sure, she was here, and they were still hundreds of miles from Seattle and John's fantasies where he and his driving buddy might find something they could bed and they might not.

Take what you can get when you can get it was Glenn's motto. And there was no doubt in his mind that, if he could get it, one way or another he damned sure would.

Now, he'd started to think that when he stopped for Terrie he should have kicked John out. Let the son of a bitch hitchhike to Seattle if that's what he wanted. Yeah, John for Terrie would have been a good trade. Except he might need a man's help before long. Terrie probably wouldn't be worth a damn at robbing banks.

Speaking low so as not to disturb Terrie, Jimmy said, "Where are we going now?"

Glenn knew where he was and where he was going. He had lived at Central Point, near the Dead Indian Mountain, long enough to be familiar with the countryside. He'd even brought a girl or two up this same road or one similar. Not one had complained. Neither would Terrie. Once he got her warmed up, she would beg for more.

"You gotta take a leak again, don't you?" Glenn asked, looking at Jimmy.

"Hell yes. I'm about to bust."

"Well, dammit, hold your water a little longer. I'm taking us to a place where you can piss a stream from here to the ocean."

Terrie stirred. Glenn felt her pressed up near him. He couldn't hold off much longer.

As the Olds bounced over the rough road, Terrie lifted

her head. Glenn peeked in her direction. In the soft glow of the car's interior light she looked even prettier than she had before. Better than anything he'd been close to in a long time. Way she was built, he didn't much care what she looked like. Still, a pretty face made it all that much better.

"Where are we?" Terrie asked. Trees surrounded them. She didn't see any lights that identified a ranch. "Are we lost?"

Glenn laughed, hoping to reassure her. What he didn't need was a panicky chick. All he had to do was get inside her and she would like it. He would make sure she did. This might be her last time ever. If so, he owed her the best she'd ever had.

"We're a long ways from lost," he said. "Virginia and Slim's place is right on up Shell Peak Road. My little buddy here has to relieve himself. We all can."

"I don't need to yet."

"Suit yourself."

They had turned off on a dirt logging road and were now some hundred yards or so west of Shell Peak Road. A clearing loomed ahead.

"Man, stop this thing," Jimmy begged. "I'm about to bust."

Glenn pulled into the clearing and killed the motor. He turned out the lights and they were enveloped in a darkness that was near absolute and frightening.

"Give me some light," Jimmy said as he jumped out the car door and ran towards the bushes.

He assured himself that he wasn't afraid of the dark but he didn't want to trip over a rock or slam his face into a tree. Glenn pulled the switch and white light slashed through the darkness.

"My little buddy is afraid of the dark," he said to Terrie. "You wait here and I'll be back before you hardly know I'm gone.

For the first time since climbing into the car, Terrie looked like she was having second thoughts about accepting this ride. Jimmy wondered if like him she was even beginning to doubt there was a ranch or a Slim and Virginia who had a singing group staying with them. The clearing in front was lighted until it reached the trees, near where John had vanished.

As Jimmy stood there passing water, relief spread over him. He was zipping up when Jay joined him.

"Man," Jimmy said, "I think we oughta take the chick back to the highway and let her out. We aren't ever gonna get to Seattle if we keep stopping all the time."

Glenn relieved himself and they stepped out into the open. "Seattle can wait," he said. "We'll get there. But first I'm gonna get me some of that."

"Some of what?"

"Little Terrie, you asshole, that's what."

"What if she doesn't want to give it?"

"I didn't say I was going to ask her for it, did I? You remember me saying that? What I said was, I'm gonna get me some of that. If she don't want to give it, then I'll take it. For damned sure though I'm gonna flick her in the next five minutes."

"Are you crazy? We don't need that kind of trouble. You force yourself on her and she'll go running to the cops before we're out of sight. Besides, you told me yourself you were infected."

"Don't let it worry you, little buddy. Cops won't bother us. Some chick like her is the reason I got a leaky dick. Look around. There's plenty of room to bury her up here where she'll never be found. She raises too much fuss, that's exactly what I'll do."

Jimmy felt a chill start at the back of his neck and spread over his entire being. What kind of a man had he teamed up with? First the old bastard wanted to screw anything he could find and then said something about a bank job. Now he was talking of rape and, worse yet, maybe murder. If Jay was willing to kill Terrie, wouldn't he go even further and decide to leave no witnesses?

Jimmy's jaw set in the characteristic way he'd had since

a small boy. Why was he even thinking this? The man wasn't going to kill anybody. Not if Jimmy Dale Taylor had anything to say about it.

"You just stay away from the car," Glenn warned. "Don't come around until I say I'm through. This is one time you ain't gonna interfere. I'm telling you for sure there's plenty of room to bury two people up here. If you get in my way, that's exactly what'll happen."

Jimmy couldn't believe what he was hearing. He was tempted to run down the mountain, even though the night was dark. No, he would have to ride it out. Even had his own life not been threatened, it wasn't his nature to stand by and let something happen to a woman.

Besides, where would he go?

But there was no way he could stop this big son of a bitch from doing what he wanted to do. Not unless he had an equalizer. He had to have that gun. Just in case. For protection, that's what Jay had said.

"Wait till I get something out of the car," Jimmy said. "I don't want to sit here waiting without something to drink."

"Get what you need now. No matter what, don't come back to the car until I say you can. When I climb on top, I don't want no interruptions. Or no audience either. You gotta pay if you want to watch and you ain't got that kind of money."

Room to bury her where she'll never be found. These words rolled over and over through Jimmy's head as he hurried towards the car, angling to his left where he could make his approach from the passenger's side. *Room enough for two if you interfere.*

Terrie's window was rolled down. She was shivering. Jimmy bet it wasn't from the cold.

"Why are we still here?" she asked. "Jay said we were only going to stop for a minute or two. What have you and him been talking about?"

"I'm going to get something to drink. Hand me the wine bottle, will you?"

"Where are you going?"

"I won't be far away."

"What is he going to do?"

"I'd better let him tell you what he's got in mind." Jimmy opened the car door and sat on the edge of the seat. He felt under the dash until his hand touched the pistol. "I got the gun," he said. "Don't tell Jay I'm taking it."

She stared at him. "John, don't go." She grasped his arm, but he pulled away. "Don't go and leave me alone with him. I'm afraid. Why did we stop here?"

Voice trembling, Jimmy said, "Ask Jay. He's driving. I don't know where we're at or why we're here. But if you get in trouble, yell out. I got this gun. I ain't afraid to use it if I have to."

Terrie looked startled, like a fawn. She was sobering fast, and she didn't look like she wanted his partner, not to Jimmy anyway, but maybe he was wrong.

Glenn was moving towards the driver's door. Terrie grasped Jimmy's arm again. "Please don't go."

"Time for you to get away from here and entertain yourself," Glenn said to Jimmy. "Gimme a swig of wine first though. And just remember what I said," Glenn warned as he climbed in on the driver's side, pulled a couple of swallows from the wine bottle, and passed it back. For a moment the two men stared at one another. Then, taking a beer, Jimmy headed for a tree stump at the edge of the car's lights, some forty feet away.

The gun in his hip pocket felt uncomfortable. He didn't like touching it. Would he use the pistol if Terrie needed help? He didn't want to have to find out.

Terrie wasn't any virgin. He would be willing to bet on that, he told himself. She was mature enough to know what she wanted and if that was the old man it was all right with him. After they were through, they could get back on the road or they could let her off, whatever she wanted. Still, he didn't feel good about it.

Jay was becoming weirder all the time. He drove a stolen

car, and the man wanted to rob a bank. Was he capable of cold-blooded killing?

He looked around. There was no doubt there was plenty of room up here to conceal two bodies. They were really hidden from the world. Jimmy listened but couldn't hear the sound of a car on the road or a dog barking. They must not be anywhere near an inhabited area.

All he knew was they had parked in an isolated clearing. Tall trees grew up all around and far overhead there was a sky filled with stars.

He wondered where, exactly, they were. Somewhere far up in northern California, he supposed. The last he remembered they had left Yreka and headed north. Yeah, they must be close to Oregon.

Or somewhere on the back side of the moon, for all Jimmy knew. Exactly where wasn't important. Survival was taking center stage in his troubled mind. As he took a swig of wine, he wondered if Terrie and the old man were getting it on while he froze out there alone.

Hell, they would never get to Seattle. By now he would have been willing to bet on that.

The chilly night air was filled with the scent of pines. Jimmy heard the call of an owl and not far from where he sat some large animal ran through the brush, spooking him.

Out of habit, Glenn had taken the keys when he'd left. Now he poked them back into the ignition slot.

"What are you doing?" she asked.

"Nothing that you should worry about."

"You're not going to drive off, are you? You wouldn't put me out and leave me alone up here, would you?"

"You know I wouldn't," he said. "You're much too important to me."

"What do you mean? I thought we were going to see Slim and Virginia."

"They can wait. We're not in a hurry. You be a good friend to old Jay and I'll take you to see Virginia and Slim and the singing group, too. But first we gotta have us a little fun."

Not that far from them, Jimmy was sitting on the stump

lifting the wine bottle to his lips. Though he could make them out, he felt far away.

Glenn scooted across the seat. Nothing could stop him now. He had waited too long. He'd picked the bitch up, spent money on her, and let her drink as much as she wanted to get herself ready for the celebration. Now it was payback time.

Whether or not he would have to bury her up here was hardly significant at the moment. What was important was that he have his way with her while she was still breathing. It was more fun if the girl cooperated but he was determined to plunge into her no matter what.

"Stay away from me," Terrie warned. Her voice was rising fast. Jimmy caught only its echo. "What are you doing? Don't come any closer."

Glenn didn't answer. One hand gripped her shoulder as the other slipped under her dress, determined to pull her panties down. His cool hand against her bare belly caused her to gasp.

She pushed him with all her strength, and he fell back.

"Bitch!" he growled. "You might as well like it. Makes it better for both of us."

Glenn fell on her, his mouth a whisper from her lips while one hand stroked her neck and the other shot back up under her dress.

Terrie screamed.

"Shut up, bitch! You're asking for trouble."

He grasped a handful of hair and pulled her mouth to his.

Jimmy had just taken another swallow of wine when he heard Terrie scream. He hesitated momentarily, wondering. Was it a scream or a squeal? He knew that sometimes girls squealed out when they were aroused. Maybe old Jay was having that kind of an effect on her. Might be she was only crying out for more.

There was banging and thumping coming from the car. He set the bottle on the ground and got to his feet. The car seemed far away. Dammit, he shouldn't mix beer and wine. He was feeling a little tipsy.

"Help!" Terrie shouted. Her scream rose until it became one of desperation. "Help me!"

There could have been some doubt as to whether the original sound had been a scream or a squeal but there was no doubt as to her call for help.

He vacillated for a moment, wanting to get away from the scene, tempted to head down the mountain on foot. Take a chance on what might be out there. Bigfoot, or whatever. Since Terrie was resisting, Jay sure as hell would kill her. And the old man wasn't about to leave a witness. He would kill them both!

But Jimmy couldn't run. Neither could he stand idly by and listen to Terrie's cries for help.

He stumbled towards the car, pulling the small gun out of his pocket. *Why*, he wondered, was he so protective towards women? There was a girl in trouble and he was rushing to the rescue. Stupid! He was no Clint Eastwood.

The car lights were still on. Inside, the dash lights provided a dim illumination. His only hope now was to try and get the upper hand. Standing outside the door, Jimmy eventually found his voice that wasn't all that firm and was able to say, "Get off of her."

Glenn lifted his head and Jimmy saw a look of pure hatred on the man's face.

Jimmy lifted the gun and pointed it at Clark. "Just leave her alone," he said, his voice trembling.

"What the fuck do you think you're doing?" With an astonished look on his face, Glenn glared at him as if he couldn't believe this little man could be threatening him. Not if he expected to live. "Put that damned gun down and get away!" Glenn shouted. "Don't you remember what I told you? You or nobody else is stopping me this time. You'd better run while you still can."

"Get off her. Leave her alone. Get out of the car!"

As Glenn raised up uncertainly, Jimmy grabbed the passenger side door. Terrie was crying and trembling uncontrollably. She climbed out. "You get out the other door," Jimmy said to Glenn.

"You ignorant son of a bitch, let me tell you something," Glenn growled. "There's room enough to bury the two of you up here. Hell, I already told you that. You'll lay there and rot in the ground. Don't think I won't do it. Put that gun away or you're a dead man!"

"Get around to where I can see you in the headlights," Jimmy said. In spite of his fury, Glenn wasn't ready to argue with a loaded gun. With his shirttail hanging, he backed out the driver's door. Jimmy could see the leather pouch on the floor, the pouch that had housed Glenn's pistol.

Terrie, crying, didn't seem to understand what either man was saying. She had run around to the driver's side and was too busy dragging her two suitcases out from the back seat.

Jimmy was quite certain Glenn had the gun somewhere on him, but where? Most likely in a hip pocket. First he would have to find it and then he would—he didn't know what he would do next. Jay was big. To Jimmy he seemed so large that without his own gun he would not stand a chance against the man. Unless he could get the other gun off Jay what came next was immaterial. There would be two new graves on the mountain. If the man even bothered to bury them. More than likely he would leave them for the wild animals to feast upon.

"Get your shirt off," Jimmy said. The gun had to be on Glenn somewhere. Had to be!

"Damn you! You stupid bastard! You've really had it now. Your ass is dead! Don't think it ain't. You hear me, asshole?"

For Terrie, there was only one frightening reality. She was a long way from where she was supposed to be, alone on a mountaintop with two lunatics and one of them had a gun. What had John said? Was it, "I'll protect you" or "I'll kill him?"

She dragged her suitcases away from the car. It was too late now.

"Dammit, get your shirt off!" Jimmy shouted. "I'll kill you if you don't."

"I'll take my shirt off, you son of a bitch. It's you who's gonna get killed though. You ain't man enough to kill old Jay. I was shootin' guns before you was born."

Jimmy knew what he must do. If he could find the other gun, he would first take it away. Then he would force Jay to crawl inside the car's trunk. Close the lid and lock him in. He and Terrie could drive to the nearest town and leave the car. Then they could hitchhike out, her one way and him the other. Or maybe they could just leave Jay there without his shoes and take the car. Jay wouldn't have too many miles to walk for help. Whatever they did it was important that Terrie stay.

Now that he'd stuck his neck out for her, he didn't want her wandering off down the mountain. He'd take her where she wanted to go. Sacramento or wherever. As for Seattle, there was no longer any hope of going there now.

Jay's shirt was off. There was no gun to be seen. Where was Terrie? Where was the gun? When Jimmy could hear anything other than Jay ranting and raving, he heard Terrie crying and screaming. Jimmy's sense of direction was confused. "Where are you, Terrie?" he called.

"Don't go. Please don't go. I'll shoot him if I have to. Don't think I won't kill him."

Jimmy didn't know how long he would be able to hold the gun on Jay. His hand was trembling. Would it even shoot? If he had to pull the trigger, would anything happen?

Although the gun was heavy, it seemed awfully small. Was it powerful enough to stop a wild man like Jay? Hopefully, he would never have to find out.

Terrie was screaming as she moved away from the car. She was making such a lot of noise that Jimmy wondered if she had been shot or cut or something. What had Jay done?

Jimmy turned away for only an instant, searching for a sign of the girl and at the same time trying to keep one eye on the old man.

When he turned his full attention back to Jay, his worst nightmare was taking shape. Jay's right hand was whipping around from behind his back. Jimmy caught sight of the gun as it was coming up.

Oh, God! There was no time to consider his next move, no opportunity to make a rational decision. Jimmy quickly raised his gun and silently prayed it would fire. As he squeezed the trigger, Glenn snapped off a shot.

Terrie was moving across the clearing, dragging her suitcases down the logging trail, trying to reach the road they'd come in on. She heard what she thought was one shot. She let out a loud cry and walked even faster. Her screams intensified.

Jimmy felt a sharp pain as Glenn's bullet tore flesh from his right forearm. The small gun threatened to slip from his hand. His bullet had hit Jay high on the chest. Jay's mouth flew open and his left hand clutched his breast as he bumped the car, stepped to his right and dropped to one knee. Terrie glanced back only long enough to see the old man kneeling down. Tears filled Jimmy's eyes. Supporting his right hand with his left, he brought his gun to bear on his nemesis.

Jay's gun lay within reach. Jimmy started moving to his right so the old man wouldn't have a clear shot. Don't do it, Jimmy silently pleaded. "It's over, man, it's over," he said aloud. "Get your hand back. I'll get you to a doctor. You'll be all right."

"You rotten son of a bitch, you've shot me. Damn you to hell, you've shot me. I'll kill you! Kill you!"

Nothing short of death could prevent Glenn from trying. No little guy was going to get the best of him. The gun was within reach. From one knee he twisted around. His hand touched the cold steel.

Terrie cried out when she heard a second shot.

5

FALLING DOWN THE MOUNTAIN

Silence. A total absence of all sound. Had someone whispered, Jimmy felt as though he could have heard every word.

Only moments before, the noise had been maddening. There had been yelling! Screaming! Cursing! Terrie was crying. Sounds had seemed to attack his senses from every direction. And then came the most shattering explosion of all: the roar of gunfire. The little pistols had made more noise than he would have thought possible. Louder than the big guns had been when he was aboard ship off the shores of Vietnam. These were little guns that hurt bad.

Those sounds had evaporated. Now it was as though all the nocturnal animals were frozen in place and holding their collective breath. There was only silence. Stark silence. Deafening silence. Jimmy was certain that this silence was louder than all the noise had been earlier. He felt as though he was in danger of going mad and losing all sense of reasoning.

He closed his eyes but the silence increased in intensity until Jimmy feared his head would burst. And then it was interrupted by a repetitive sound that grew louder and louder, a sound that closed in and threatened to beat him to the ground. Any noise would have startled him but this one was devastating beyond all measure. Some moments passed before he recognized the sound of his heartbeat as his breathing grew shallow and rapid.

Gradually he realized that if he didn't gain control there was the danger he might collapse. As helpless as Jay seemed to be, this he could not allow. If he quit now, he would never get down off this mountain.

He willed himself to take deep breaths. His forearm burned as though someone was pressing against it with a hot coal. There was a real danger that he might pass out. This he could not, would not, allow to happen.

Was Jay still alive? He didn't know. All Jimmy knew for certain was that a few moments earlier he had been in a situation where he had to shoot or be shot. Kill or be killed. His life or Jay's. All because Terrie had screamed and yelled for help.

Where was Terrie? He hadn't a clue to what direction she had taken. Why had she run? She had no reason to fear him. What he'd done, he'd done for her as much as for himself. He couldn't stand by and watch any woman be abused. And once he interfered, Jay would have certainly killed him if given the chance. Jimmy was convinced that the old man had intended to kill them both, no matter what.

Jay wasn't moving. He lay face down, as still as death. Not a muscle twitched. His gun was nearby. Damn those guns! Jimmy couldn't leave them.

Where was Terrie? He spoke her name softly. The sound of his voice shattering that stark silence frightened him. He called out again, this time somewhat louder. She did not reply. Why would she be afraid of him? There was no reason to be. He'd done what had to be done to protect her. To save her life even. Did she know Jay had threatened to kill her? To bury her on this godforsaken mountain where she would never be found?

There was no way she could know. Jimmy hadn't wanted

to say anything that would frighten her even more than she had already been frightened. Jay damned sure wouldn't have told her. How do you find somebody at night on a strange dark mountain unless they want to be found? he thought, staring first in one direction then another.

Terrie grabbed her suitcases and turned left on Shell Peak Road, each step taking her farther and farther away from the Dead Indian Highway and the way they'd come. Moving downhill it was easier to walk. Deeper and deeper into the night forest she went.

Jimmy had to act. He couldn't stand still forever while time passed and God alone knew who might come along. They hadn't seen a sign of civilization but that didn't mean they were completely alone. In spite of how solitary he'd felt only moments earlier, poachers could be roaming about. Lovers could be looking for a perfect place to park. Jay had seemed familiar with this spot. Others might be also.

Jimmy took a tentative step towards Jay, willing himself not to look at the man. He picked up the black gun, dropped it into his coat pocket and then, satisfied that he was in no imminent danger from Jay, dropped his gun in the other. He tied his handkerchief around his wounded arm and wiggled into his jacket. He rolled Jay over, hooked his hands under his shoulders, and dragged him over the rough terrain. He left Jay face up and hurried to the car.

The lights had been on a long time. This thought crossed his mind as he wondered if there was enough juice left in the battery to start the engine. He pushed the light switch and was as startled by the darkness as he had been earlier by the lack of any sound. Thankfully, Jay had left the key in the ignition. Jimmy didn't want to spend the time it would take to hot-wire the vehicle.

The motor turned and caught. He switched the lights back on and pulled the shift lever into reverse. He managed to back up without plunging down the mountain and then headed towards Shell Peak Road. Where in the hell was Terrie?

Terrie grasped the handles of her two suitcases and groped her way down the mountain, away from Dead Indian Road, away from any possible chance of finding help that night and, although she did not know it at the time, away from a dead man she knew only as Jay.

Accompanied by a fear that was worse, much worse, than the fear of flying, Jimmy turned right on Dead Indian Road and tried to get the feel of the Oldsmobile as it climbed towards the peak. But there were too many horrible memories crowding into his mind to concentrate on driving or anything else. He was operating on instinct.

Scarcely more than twenty-four hours after leaving San Francisco with a man he hardly knew, Jimmy's world had come crashing down. It had fallen on him like a concrete wall. Unless he found a way to turn back the clock and relive these last hours, his life would never be the same.

As he reached the mountain peak and started down, he kept telling himself it had been shoot or be shot. Kill or be killed. Even so, the nightmare remained. Would he awaken and find it had all been a bad dream? That none of this had happened?

But no, the events of the night were real. Jay was real. And Jimmy was afraid that the old man was really dead. Where was Terrie? After driving two or three miles around the twisting road, he considered going back and trying to find her. He even slowed the car looking for a turnabout, but then accelerated again. There were all sorts of side roads that turned off this one. There was no way short of a miracle he would ever be able to find the one Jay had turned on. Jimmy was beyond the point of believing in miracles. It was too late. One dead man and one frightened girl too late. He wondered if Terrie had returned to the clearing and found Jay, or if she was running down the mountain, even more terrified than he was.

Deep shadows. Tall trees on either side and only a hint of starlight in between. Terrie's feet were suffering from blood-covered stone bruises. She sat on one suitcase and opened the other. Tears streaked her face as she pulled out a pair of brown shoes made of soft leather.

Although Terrie had no way of knowing it at the time, Jay's stolen car was not on its way to Seattle. Nor was it on its way to San Francisco, where Jimmy had decided to go. At the moment, the Oldsmobile, of which Jay had been so proud, was not on its way to anywhere.

Having realized the hopelessness of finding Terrie, Jimmy headed down Dead Indian Road in search of 1-5. He drove too fast, skidding around curves, wanting to put as much distance as possible between himself and Jay. Luck played a large part in the fact that he did not crash. He wasn't certain the big man was dead, not one hundred percent certain. Even so, there seemed to be little doubt.

And then, before Dead Indian Road flattened out, the engine sputtered and died, as dead as he feared Jay to be. One look at the gas gauge and he knew why. That damn fool, who'd been willing to rape and kill, had been so preoccupied with Terrie that he had failed to fill the tank.

Jimmy coasted to the side of the road and stopped. He sat there for a moment, his head buried in his hands. His right arm throbbed where Jay's bullet had torn through. It was the middle of the night. Would any help come along? Did he even want it to? Or would it be better to abandon the car?

No! He had to have the car to return to San Francisco. If he drove through, he could reach the city quicker. Besides, with a bleeding arm, he didn't want to depend on catching rides. Several miles to the southwest, he could see the lights of a town. Perhaps he could buy gasoline there.

Jimmy climbed out of the car. The guns weighed heavy in his pockets. He was considering what to do with them when the highway patrol car pulled up behind the Oldsmobile and stopped. Like a cornered animal, Jimmy was trapped in the headlights.

Terrie kept on walking. It must have seemed as though she had been on the move for hours, but it wasn't that long. Her feet hurt. Her arms ached from carrying and dragging the suitcases.

There had not even been one house since she'd started down the mountain. Once or twice there was the sound of cars on a road nearby. It wasn't a very busy highway. And by now she didn't have any idea which direction to go to look.

And then she stopped. Ahead of her loomed a dark structure. It surely wasn't a ranch. She eased forward with caution. Whatever it was, it wasn't moving. It seemed to be a vehicle of some sort. It was a truck. She breathed easier. Did she dare stop?

She stopped for a moment, and then moved on. She needed a hiding place, not a vehicle parked alongside the road.

"Got problems, son?"

Jimmy stood near the back of the Oldsmobile, outlined in the lights of the patrol car as the state trooper, looking even larger than Jay, moved cautiously towards him. Jimmy's shot arm ached and he silently prayed that the blood stain hadn't soaked through his jacket. He felt wet blood between his fingers so he was careful to keep his right hand out of sight. The guns weighed heavy in his pockets. Why oh why hadn't he left them on top of the mountain or thrown them away on the drive down? He damn sure could not, would not, shoot any patrolman.

Perhaps, just perhaps, there was a reason for him running out of gas and this patrolman showing up just then. Jimmy felt a powerful need to tell all, to let loose all the frustration that had been building and building, filling him to the bursting point. He had to have relief.

Perhaps this man would understand. Jimmy could tell him that up on that mountain was a shot man, a man who was possibly dead, and somewhere on that same mountain was a scared young girl who was undoubtedly running for her life.

It was self-defense, officer. He was going to kill me. Not only me but the young girl as well. Terrie was about to get herself raped and then shot and buried. Me right beside her. We'd rot in the ground together.

Hell, nobody would believe him.

Nobody.

"Ran out of gas," Jimmy said, hoping his voice didn't betray him.

"What are you doing out this time of night?"

"On my way home."

"You going to Ashland?"

Where in the hell was Ashland? "Yeah."

"All right, come on and get in. Not up front. Crawl into the back. We'll see if we can find a station open. I'll take you down but you'll have to find your own way back. Maybe you can hitch a ride."

"Yeah, I'll do that."

Adrenaline can carry a person only so far. When this is exhausted, fear can sometimes kick in and carry him a little farther. For Jimmy, it would need to carry him a lot farther. He didn't know how far he was from San Francisco, but he knew it was many miles. He felt that if he could only get back home he would be safe.

True to his word, the trooper had dropped him off at an all-night station and left to continue his patrol.

Even though he would have liked to have had a ride

back to the car, Jimmy was relieved to see the patrolman drive away. He made a five-dollar deposit on a two-gallon can and filled it with gas. On the four-mile journey back he hitched a ride part of the way and had to walk the remainder.

All the while, Jimmy felt the weight of the guns in his coat pockets. Had they been found on him, they could have tied him to the shooting, but he couldn't risk their being found if someone happened on the car while he was gone. Now, he didn't want to keep them on him another second. One at a time, he took them from his pockets and tossed them over the cliff, throwing them as far as he could. He poured the last of the gasoline out of the can and into the tank, then threw the can onto the floor between the seats. Then he got into the car, and headed down the mountain.

He made only one stop and that was at the same gas station to which the patrolman had taken him. There he filled the car with gas. After that he headed for I-5 and turned south.

Terrie had still not found a ride. The night was getting colder and colder. Finally she parked the suitcases on the road and got inside the old, cold truck. It smelled of sweat, oil, old leather, and brake fluid.

She left both doors open for a short while. But then she closed them. A bear might drag her out. She rolled the windows down. Within minutes, she rolled them up again. Perhaps bears could reach in through an open window.

A sob jumped from her throat as she lay curled on the seat. There would be no sleep for her this night.

As the distance between them increased, neither Terrie nor Jimmy had any idea that they would ever see each other again, and both would have been happier had that day never come.

6

WILD WOMAN

As the first light of morning penetrated the shadowy foliage on Dead Indian Mountain, a logging vehicle commonly referred to as a "crummy" bounced along on a road as rough as a cow pasture. Inside sat four men. Each was occupied with his own thoughts. At such an early hour the men usually had little to say. This Wednesday in late August was no exception.

Hank and Seth, older and experienced loggers, claimed the front seat while the neophytes, Mike and Larry, slumped on the back seat catching what sleep they could. There was no reason to believe this day harvesting timber would be any different from countless others, until the two men up front spotted the pair of suitcases sitting near the center of the road.

"What in the devil's going on here?" Hank asked as he stepped hard on the brake. "Where'd them suitcases come from?"

Seth shook his head. "Damned if I know," he said.

The squeal of brakes brought Mike awake. He bolted upright and said, "Are we there already?"

The two men up front didn't answer. They had little tolerance for cubs who couldn't stay awake at six in the morning. If these young men were going to do logging work, they'd danged sure better get used to the early hours.

"That watchman must be asleep in the truck," Seth said.

"Why would a watchman have suitcases sitting in the middle of the road?" Hank wanted to know. "That don't make sense."

Seth had to admit that Hank was right. He opened his door and said, "I'll danged sure find out in a hurry. If it's him, I'll see that the boss hears about it. Ain't no excuse for sleepin' on the job."

Seth hurried to the truck door and yanked it open. Mike raised up for a better look. Larry was rubbing sleep from his eyes when a loud noise from within the water truck's cab shattered the morning stillness.

The commotion was caused by someone screaming and lunging at Seth. He slammed the door shut and jumped back to avoid being attacked by whatever had taken refuge in the truck. By now everybody was wide awake. Whatever or whoever was behind that truck door was obviously scared to death.

During those brief moments, Terrie wasn't the only one who was on the edge of panic. First Terrie screamed at the suddenness of the door opening. But then she screamed even louder because the man who had first looked in and then slammed the door shut looked like Jay.

Before the four men could make their escape from this wild woman, the truck door flew open again. Terrie rushed out and cried in desperation, "Wait! Don't go! Please, please don't leave me. I thought . . . I thought you were someone else. Please don't leave me here alone. If you do, they'll kill me."

In her panic she grabbed Seth by the arm. He pulled away as though she were crazy.

She turned to Hank and clutched his arm, determined

that he would not leave without her. The two young men in the back seat were watching wide-eyed. Terrie had their undivided attention.

"Why don't you stay here and wait on the boss to come along," Hank suggested to her. She was jabbering away and he had no idea of what she was jabbering about. "He'll get it all straightened out and I expect he'll take you wherever you want to go."

"No!" Terrie cried. "I'm not about to stay here alone. Please don't go!"

"We can't just leave her here," Seth said. "Can't you see she's scared to death?"

"Go ahead and put her in the crummy then," Hank said, not at all happy with this unhappy beginning of their work day. He glared at the young men. "Now you young bucks keep your hands to yourself. Throw her suitcases in the back. She can wait on Frank up at the job."

Mike and Larry watched all this silently from the back seat. From the smiles on their faces one could surmise that neither was sorely disappointed when Terrie was told to climb in back. The arrangement suited them just fine.

Heading south around sharp turns and through mountain passes, the Olds performed like a thoroughbred. Like a horse going to its home barn. Jimmy didn't pamper the car as Jay had. No more checking the oil every hour or two. No more STP. Try to make it with what gas he had in the tank. All that was in his mind was getting away.

Sunup now. He was steadily increasing the distance between himself and his nightmare. Jay was surely dead, but Jimmy didn't want to think about the man. Even so, he found it difficult to forget.

Visions cramped his muddled mind. Visions of Jay lying face down beside the car. How he had looked rolling him over and pulling him away. He'd pulled like a dead man. If so, whose fault was it? Wasn't it Jay who had reached for his gun and come up firing?

Damn fool!

Where was Terrie now? Over and over in Jimmy's mind he played out his actions. His lack of choice. He'd done it to save the girl from being raped by some old son of a bitch who had gonorrhea. Worse yet, they both might have been killed and buried on that damned mountain!

Did she have any idea about the fate that might have awaited her? Had Jay been serious about killing little Terrie? About killing them both? Jimmy felt as though the man would surely have been capable of killing. And now he was surely dead.

He tried to get hold of himself. *Easy, man. Don't panic. Pull over and rest before you pass out. See a doctor; treat the arm. No! I'm not stopping for anything.*

Okay, don't pull over. Watch your speed. You don't want to get stopped by a patrolman or some small town cop. Man, you don't even have a driver's license. Police pull you over and tie you to what happened back on whatever mountain that was and you will never again see the light of day.

Just keep pushing it, man. And hope you don't bleed to death.

Terrie was half crying and half rambling as if she couldn't stop talking. The crummy lurched forward. It was rattling and shaking so much that the two men riding up front couldn't make out much of what was being said. This didn't bother them one little bit. They got paid for harvesting timber, not for pampering some crazy woman.

Not so with Terrie's two young companions. As she rattled on and on, they hung on every word.

"Oh God, oh God, what I've been through this one night. Nobody should ever have to go through something like that," she cried. Her voice was high and rising. She was trembling all over and couldn't quiet herself.

"What?" Mike said. "What?"

"I was kidnapped."

"You were?"

"Yes."

"How'd that happen?"

"Well, I was traveling from Portland to Los Angeles. My daddy sent me the money to come down. He thought I was going to fly home, but I decided to save the money and hitchhike. These two men picked me up and then they kidnapped me."

"Did they hurt you?" Mike asked.

"They tried to. One of them tried to. He tried to rape me."

Mike winced. "Oh no." To him Terrie looked so innocent. Tears trickled down her cheeks. "Where did they pick you up?"

"At the Talent turnoff. They said they were going to Sacramento but instead they turned off at the Ashland exit and then they stopped at stores and bought beer and wine, and I think they were both wanting to rape me. Then they got some more beer and wine and they drove me up into the mountains and one of them got out of the car and took some beer and wine with him, and John said if Jay tried anything he'd kill him, and Jay tried to get my clothes off and then I screamed and John came running over and ordered Jay out of the car, told him to get around in front of the car, in the lights, and told him to get his shirt off and get down on his knees. Jay was begging and pleading for John not to shoot him and then I heard two gunshots and I grabbed my suitcases and I ran for my life. Had I stayed, I would now be dead, too. I know I would."

Terrie was still talking when the crummy stopped and the two men in front got out. They walked away fast, as though wanting to distance themselves from this problem that was no business of theirs. Whatever had happened to the girl, more than likely she had brought it on herself.

Seth climbed upon his shovel, started the motor and went to work. When the boss showed up, he damned sure didn't want to be standing around doing nothing. Hank felt the same way. He fired up his Cat and went to skiddin'.

The work had to be done. Whatever the girl's problems, they wasn't none of their doings or business.

When their boss arrived, the three of them told Frank the story, all trying to talk at the same time. He heard them out, then used his citizen band to contact ROXY Radio who promised to pass the information on to the sheriff's office.

"Now," Frank told Mike, "take the crummy and the girl and head over to Dead Indian Road and Howard Prairie where somebody from the sheriff's office should be meeting you before long."

At 6:45 A.M., August 30, 1967, the sheriff's office at Medford, Oregon, Jackson County, received a call from ROXY Radio, relaying the message from the Frank Moat Logging Company that they had located a girl on Shell Peak Road, near the Dead Indian Highway. According to them, the girl said she had been kidnapped. Her name was Terrie Tidwell, age eighteen.

Detective Carl V. Seuter of the county sheriff's office was the first officer receiving the call; he left his home within minutes and at about seven-fifty that morning arrived at the junction of Dead Indian Road and Howard Prairie Lake Access. There he met up with Mike and a still shaken Terrie.

Seuter first asked Mike what had happened.

"Two of the old loggers were driving us to work," Mike said, "down on Shell Peak Road. When they spotted two suitcases sittin' in the middle of the road they stopped so short it woke me up. The suitcases were right there by a watering truck, about, oh, about a mile or a mile and a quarter north of Dead Indian Road. That's where we found that lady, Terrie. She was sleeping in the cab of the truck. Scared to death, she was. Later, she told me she had been kidnapped by two men. While they were fighting, she escaped."

Seuter next turned his attention to Terrie and asked her what had happened.

Terrie hesitated and bit her lower lip. Although hitchhiking was the mode of travel for young people all over America at this time, Terrie's dad probably wouldn't approve.

She started slowly. "I was in . . . in Medford, you know, at a coffee shop. These two men, they came up and started talking to me. They saw my suitcases sitting there and asked where I was going. I didn't want to tell them, but they were persistent. After considering it, I decided they could be trusted. So I told them I was on my way to the airport and then I was going to fly to San Francisco. They offered to take me as far as Sacramento."

Mike wondered if he had misunderstood what Terrie had said about being picked up while hitchhiking. And hadn't she said that she had been on her way to Los Angeles?

"What can you tell me about these two men?" Seuter asked.

"They said their names were John and Jay."

"What were their last names?"

"They never did tell me. They just used first names."

"All right. Describe John, please."

"Well, he said he was nineteen years old and a fullblooded Indian. He did have Indian features, but was not very dark. He was about five feet seven inches tall."

"Slender or heavy?"

"He was more slender than heavy. He had dark hair, not too long, combed straight back."

"What about Jay?"

"Jay said he was thirty-one years old. I think he was older, but that's what he said. His brown hair was going back away from his forehead, you know. I guess you would say that it was receding. It was very greasy, too. He had a small nose with a pronounced hook."

"All right, you were in a coffee shop and these two men

started a conversation and asked if you wanted a ride. Is Medford your home?"

"No, Los Angeles is my home. I've been visiting friends in the Portland area for some time. I was going to stop at San Francisco and then go on home from there. My friends drove me to Medford and let me out at a coffee shop. That's where the two men found me."

Seuter looked suspicious of her story. "What was the name of the coffee shop?" he asked.

"I—I don't remember."

"Why did they drop you off at a coffee shop if you were going to catch a plane?"

"Well, I was going to get some food and then take a taxi to the airport."

"All right. These two men asked where you were going. What did you say?"

"San Francisco. They promised to take me to Sacramento. I really had intended to fly down, but they seemed like such nice men and so I thought I would ride that far with them. We went out and got into their car. Instead of going to Sacramento they stopped and got some beer and wine and said they wanted to visit some friends in the vicinity of Dead Indian Road."

"Did you agree to this?"

"After much thought and consideration, I decided this would be all right. Since they were only planning on a short visit, I thought it would be okay."

"Who were these friends? Did either of these two men ever tell you their names?"

"Jay said their names were Slim and Virginia and they were living on a ranch and a singing group was staying with them."

"Go ahead."

"I really did think it would be all right since they were only going to stop for a few minutes, you know. But they didn't drive to their friends' ranch."

"Who did the car belong to?"

"Jay. He did all the driving. But he later told me it was stolen."

"Did you feel as though you had been kidnapped, since they didn't drive on to Sacramento as they had told you they would do?"

"Yes, I most certainly did. There was no doubt in my mind. By then I definitely knew that I had been kidnapped. I didn't want to be with them but I didn't feel as though they would let me leave. What chance would I have trying to resist two men?

"They pulled off on a road and the two of them started arguing and John threatened to kill Jay. Told me he would definitely kill Jay and I was afraid that if he did then he would kill me, too."

"What were they arguing about?"

"First they were arguing about who had stolen the car. Then Jay, no John, got some wine out of the car and went off by himself. Jay got into the car and started talking and then he made a grab for me. I screamed. John ran up to the car with his gun in his hand. When he opened the door, I jumped out. And then he ordered Jay out of the car."

"What did you do then?"

"When this happened I grabbed my suitcases and ran."

"Did John shoot Jay?"

"Yes, I think so. There was shooting."

"Was Jay killed?"

"Yes. I don't know. I think so."

"Can you tell me where this happened?"

Terrie pointed up the mountain. "It was dark. I don't have any idea how to find the place now."

"What else can you tell me?"

"While I was running, I heard two shots fired. I got lost and sometime during the night came to the truck where I stayed until they found me this morning. Then I asked them to call the police."

"After you left the two men, did you stay on the one road until you found the water truck?"

"I—I think so."

Carl asked Mike, "Are there many logging roads between the Dead Indian Road and the truck where you found Miss Tidwell?"

"Several."

"You want to help look?"

"You bet."

Past Redland the terrain changed. Mountains loomed on the right and behind him, but now the road ahead was straight and flat. Jimmy wasn't admiring the scenery.

Jimmy hadn't mapped out a route and was not giving any thought to where he was at any given moment. He felt that, if he could just keep driving, eventually he would reach a safe haven in San Francisco. The more miles he could put between himself and that cursed mountain, the better.

At about the same time Seuter and Mike, with Terrie in the car, started checking every logging trail off Shell Peak Road. They were looking for any sign of recent traffic. Maybe they would find some empty beer cans or wine bottles.

It was just before nine-thirty that morning when they reached a dirt road running west, some three-tenths of a mile north of the Dead Indian Road. Terrie shivered, as though some inner sense was warning her that this was where tragedy had occurred.

Then they saw tire tracks in and out. Also, they saw bare footprints, the toes pointing towards them.

"Yours?" Seuter asked Terrie.

With quivering voice, Terrie said, "Yes." She looked as if she didn't want to go any farther. But neither did she want to be left alone.

Mike took the lead. It was important to him that he make the discovery.

Terrie stayed between the young man and Seuter. She was shaking uncontrollably.

It couldn't be much farther now. The clear space around them was widening out. As Mike hurried forward, Terrie slowed her pace. Seuter was close behind.

"Here he is!" Mike shouted.

When she saw the body, Terrie screamed as though she couldn't stop.

7

TERRIFIED WITNESS

Seuter looked over at Terrie and decided she wasn't going to pass out, in spite of her terror. He hurried ahead to join Mike. The boy had suddenly stopped walking. Catching up to him, Seuter saw why. A few yards away, a man was lying face up. The moment Seuter saw the still form, he had no doubt that he was seeing death.

Dead Indian Mountain had claimed another victim. Legend had it that around 1854 white settlers found two Rouge River Indians dead in deserted wigwams in this area, having been killed by Kiamath Indians. They had been left where they died, as had this white man. Thus the name, Dead Indian Mountain.

"Don't go any nearer," Seuter said to Mike.

Mike had gone as near as he cared to go to the corpse. He turned his attention to Terrie.

Seuter studied the man on the ground. He was large, head bare, as was his chest. Middle-aged, for sure. Lying face up, it looked as though he had been dragged to his present location. One shoe had come off.

From where Seuter was standing the only visible

wound was in the upper right chest. On the left forearm was an obvious mark, indicating the man's wristwatch had been removed. In all probability the wallet along with all identification would also be missing.

This only confirmed Miss Tidwell's story. She claimed to have heard two shots. Could he believe her? He certainly had his doubts about part of the story, that she had been in a restaurant while on her way to the airport. About the rest he wasn't sure.

Seuter turned back towards his car. Mike helped Terrie. "Are you okay?" Seuter asked his witness.

She nodded. "Is he . . . ? Is he . . . ?"

"Yes, there's nothing we can do. Let's get you back in the car while I advise the office of the situation up here."

Jimmy's arm throbbed. The handkerchief he'd pressed against the wound was blood-soaked. The jacket was getting warm. Without breaking speed, he wormed out of it and threw it onto the back seat. He lifted the padding on his arm and noticed the blood had clotted. Good. He thought at least he wouldn't bleed to death.

In the distance he could see Sacramento. The gas gauge needle was sitting below the halfway mark. Jimmy was tempted to stop. If nothing else, he could wash off, maybe even get something to eat. But when the exits came up, he passed them by. Scenes from the night before were churning through his mind. It was fear that would not allow him to stop. He had to reach San Francisco.

Having met Corporal Thyson at the Dead Indian gravel pit, Sergeant Jay Armand, a man who was on the rise in the county sheriff's department, left his car, and the two men rode together. By now, having relayed a radio call to his office, he had been brought up to date on a body being found and had been told that they would definitely be working on a homicide.

Although he didn't yet have many details, he understood they had a witness. This should help. With any luck they would have a killer in custody within twenty-four hours. Forty-eight at most. With any luck. After that the trail would soon be as cold as an Oregon winter.

They parked near the access road, blocking it from any other traffic. Seuter was waiting. Armand also noted the tire tracks that went down to a clearing and back out, and the small, bare footprints which were visible.

They were all careful not to step on any of the footprints as they moved towards the victim and stopped, studying the crime scene.

It was decided that Seuter should head over to Howard Prairie Resort and phone Undersheriff Pauling. He was to take Terrie and Mike.

It wasn't until after the undersheriff had been called and they were on their way back to the crime scene that Terrie asked Seuter, "What's going to happen now?"

Although he thought he understood where she was coming from, Carl asked, "What do you mean?"

"When can I go home?"

"It's possible you could be held as a material witness. When we capture the suspect, we'll need you to identify him."

"You can't hold me. I need to go home."

Seuter pulled to the side of the road and glanced at Mike who had remained silent during this exchange. "I want you to witness what I'm going to do," he said to the logger. Using a Rights Advisal Card, Seuter read Terrie her rights.

"Do you understand what I've just done?" he asked.

"Why are you doing this?"

"Miss Tidwell, a man has been killed. We consider murder to be a very serious offense. We intend to catch the killer and we also intend to have your cooperation. Now, I'll ask you once more. Do you understand your rights?"

"Yes, I understand my rights." Her voice trembled as she replied.

"Good. Now, let's go see what the others are doing."

The others were doing what they could do without disturbing evidence, meaning they were mostly looking. Armand and Thyson had continued studying the crime scene. They now wrote down their impressions: the victim was lying face up about ten feet north of the shoulder of the road. His upper body was bare and his blue sport shirt was on a small log some three feet north of the shoulder. It wasn't torn and, from where they stood, there was no evidence of a bullet hole. This could mean that the shirt had been removed willingly before the shooting.

A trail of blood spots led from the vicinity where the right front fender had been to where the victim lay. In the soft dirt were boot marks with heel cleats, horseshoe shaped, and these didn't match the shoe the victim was wearing.

Seuter's report listed the suspect as: "John," Indian male adult, nineteen years of age, five feet seven, one hundred forty pounds, black straight hair, brown eyes, dark complexion, wearing nondescript sport clothing and blue striped ski jacket, also either cowboy or Italian mod style boots with full horseshoe cleats on heels.

He had pieced together the description from Terrie's account.

Some forty feet from where the car had been parked, Armand spied a wine bottle and a beer can. He wondered what significance these had. When Seuter returned, Armand decided he wanted to talk to Terrie Tidwell.

He climbed into Seuter's car, introduced himself, and said, "If you don't mind, I'd like to ask a few questions."

"I've already told the other man everything I know," Terrie said. "When will I be free to go?"

"I'm afraid I'll have to insist that you stay with us a while. And even though you've told your story to Detective Seuter, I'd like to go through it again. Now please tell me everything, beginning at the time you met the two men. What names did they use?"

"Jay and John."

"Who is the victim?"

"Jay."

"Then John is who we're looking for?"

"Yes."

"All right then. Tell me how you met them and then tell me how you happened to be with them last night. Tell me everything from the time you did meet them until you met Detective Seuter this morning."

Terrie started talking. She repeated the story she'd told Seuter, how she had been at a coffee shop in Medford and from there she had planned to take a taxi to the airport when she had been approached by Jay and John and offered a ride to California. She had intended to catch a flight to Los Angeles.

"I didn't want to go with them," she said. "It was against my better judgment."

"I'm sure it was."

Terrie told Armand that instead of continuing down Interstate Five towards California, the men had exited at Ashland and started drinking. They wanted to take her to a ranch, even though she didn't want to go. She felt as though they weren't going to let her out of the car and so she felt as though she had been kidnapped. Since they had promised to drive her to Sacramento and hadn't done so, wasn't this kidnapping?

Armand didn't respond.

Terrie continued with her story, telling Armand about the drive into the mountain clearing. John had come for his beer and wine and left her alone in the car with Jay. John also had taken his gun.

"Why do you think he took the gun?" Armand asked.

"I don't know. I wonder if he didn't intend to kill Jay all the while. From what I've heard, he stripped him of all he had and I know John drove away in the car."

"All right. You were in the car with Jay. What happened next?"

"Jay started making advances towards me. I—I don't know what he had in mind but I must have cried out. John came running over and ordered Jay out of the car. John had his gun, so Jay got out. He ordered Jay around to the front of the car, in the headlights, made him take off his shirt and kneel down, and then he shot him."

"What were you doing while this was happening?"

"I was carrying my suitcases out to the road, afraid that John would kill Jay and then me."

"Why would he kill you?"

"Because," Terrie said, "I was the only witness to his crime."

Although she could possibly be right, something wasn't adding up. "Do you think John came over and ordered Jay from the car because you had cried out, Miss Tidwell?"

Terrie bit her lower lip and shook her head. "I don't know why he would. I certainly didn't ask him to come and kill Jay. There just wasn't any reason for him to kill him. He made him kneel in front of the car and then shot him."

Armand had seen what looked like a knee print near the car, so he didn't dispute this. "All right. What did you do next?"

Terrie told how she had stumbled down the dark road until she eventually found a truck. How she had stayed there until the loggers found her early this morning and how she had gone with them and eventually with Mike and Seuter until they had located Jay's body.

They sat in silence for a few moments. Armand considered her words. Finally he said, "Let's go back to the coffee shop where you first met these two men. How did you happen to be in the coffee shop?"

"Some friends from Portland drove me down."

"And let you out at the coffee shop?"

"Yes."

"Why didn't they take you to the airport?"

"I wanted to get something to eat and drink first."

"And then you were going to take a cab to the airport?"

"Yes."

"What flight were you going to catch?"

"I—I don't remember."

"Had you called ahead to see when the next flight would be leaving for Los Angeles?"

Terrie shook her head. "No."

"What was the name of the coffee shop?"

"I don't remember." She stumbled on the words.

Armand looked up sharply. "Miss Tidwell, where did you really meet these two men? This time I want the truth."

Terrie studied her hands as she twisted them together. "I—I didn't want you to know I had been hitchhiking. You see, I wouldn't want my father to know I was trying to catch a ride with strangers."

"All right. Let's start over. Where did your journey begin yesterday?"

Was it only yesterday? "At Eugene."

"Not Portland?"

"No, not Portland. I spent the night at Eugene, with friends, and then I started catching rides."

"And where did Jay and John pick you up?"

"At the Talent Exchange, on I-Five."

"How many rides did you catch before you were picked up at the Talent Exchange?"

"Three."

"Is there any reason why I should believe the remainder of your story?"

"Mr. Armand, everything else I've told you is true."

Armand thought perhaps it was. Right now he didn't have any choice other than to believe her.

By the time Dr. Ron Southerland, Undersheriff Pauling and Detective Porter arrived at the scene, at approximately eleven-fifteen that morning, Corporal Thyson had taken a number of Polaroid shots of the victim and then he switched to a four-by-five Photographic camera. He took two photographs of the heel imprint with the horseshoe cleat. They all felt as though this might be a very important clue.

Dr. Southerland waited until Thyson finished before going to work. After examining the body, he concluded that a bullet, possibly a .38 caliber, had entered the victim's chest approximately two inches below the collar bone and four inches to the right of the center line.

Southerland then rolled the body over and discovered an entrance wound to the back of the head, approximately three inches above the hairline and about one inch to the right of center. Seuter thought perhaps some of Terrie's story was plausible. She claimed to have heard two shots fired and there was evidence to support this.

Southerland straightened up and surveyed the scene. He strolled over near to the place the killing had occurred. "I would say the man was down on one knee. Isn't that what the witness said?"

The officers agreed that it was.

"All right. Your killer was standing about this far in front of him. Just a few feet. First shot was to the chest. The right chest. The victim grasped at his injury with his left hand and his head bent forward, exposing the back of his head. That's where the second shot struck him."

"No wallet?" Pauling asked.

Southerland shook his head. "No watch, no wallet, nothing to identify the man. Anybody here recognize him?"

No one did.

Seuter's subsequent report listed the property stolen from the victim as being, "One each man's wristwatch" and "one each wallet, no further description, containing undetermined amount of cash and identification of the victim" and "one each vehicle, described as a late model Pontiac Bonneville."

The gas gauge was dipping below the quarter mark and Jimmy, fighting fatigue, wondered if he should stop at a station. He couldn't remember when he had eaten. The last food he'd seen was what Terrie had brought into the car. She hadn't offered to share. Perhaps there were some grapes left.

Not likely. She'd had plenty of time to eat every last

one, as well as the peach. He wondered what had happened to her. Why in the devil had she run off? Had she stayed, he could have explained everything. Taken her anywhere she'd wanted to go. Had they been together and telling the same story, he could have gone to the police. At least he would have told the patrolman who'd stopped to help when he'd run out of gas.

These last dozen hours or so had been nothing short of a nightmare. Jimmy wanted to be able to shut Jay out of his mind completely. But he couldn't. Terrie was somewhere out there. He wondered what she was saying.

In the back seat of the police car Terrie shivered as they pulled into Hooper Springs Wayside Park. Pauling was driving and Armand sat up front with him. She'd changed her story talking to Armand. Her dad wouldn't be pleased at the hitchhiking part.

"This the place?" Pauling asked.

"Yes. We came up here, parked, and everybody used the rest room."

"Did everybody do some drinking here?" Armand asked.

"Yes. They were drinking. I did a little."

Armand inclined his head. "Did you do anything else?"

Terrie hesitated, then in a low voice said, "Yes. We played poker. For matches. Not for money or anything else, just for matches. One of them counted out ten or twenty matches for each of us, I don't remember for sure how many, and we played for matches. Jay said he was a professional and he had, at one time, played a lot in Las Vegas."

The two men got out and bagged what they hoped would be evidence. Near where the car had been parked the evening before they found an empty four-fifths quart wine bottle, two empty beer cans, a brown paper sack containing an empty beer carton, another brown paper sack containing a book of matches and an empty cigarette package.

While the trio visited the two stores where purchases had been made, a hearse from Conger Morris Mortuary pulled into the clearing. Harold Moss and Brad Kaley loaded the body onto a gurney and slid it into the vehicle. Moments later, Glenn True Clark started his last ride down the mountain. He'd been willing to take a life, or even two, to satisfy his lust for a woman. Instead, he had lost his own.

The remaining lawmen followed the hearse out to Dead Indian Road and on towards Medford. Some fifteen miles later they passed the spot where Jimmy had run out of gas and been assisted by a patrolman. Without knowing it, they passed within a hundred feet or so of two pistols, both .38 caliber. Both had been fired. One had killed; the other had wounded.

The logging road off Shell Peak Road had received more traffic this day than it ever had in the past. It had been visited, trampled upon, photographed and sketched. Now it resumed its tranquil state. All that remained to remind anyone who happened by of the recent violence were tire tracks, bare footprints, and boot marks that were hardly recognizable since a plaster moulage had been taken of the heel prints.

The blood spots were turning brown. Soon nature would erase them completely.

8

JIMMY'S RUN

For Jimmy, as morning dissolved into afternoon, reality was becoming increasingly difficult to fathom. Perhaps he would awaken and discover that those events whose memories haunted him, even now during daylight hours, were nothing more than a weird dream. If only he could know with certainty that there had never been anyone by the name of Jay or Terrie in his life. That they were both only parts of his vivid imagination.

If only.

Sleep first, though, for he was tired, so very tired. The wounded arm needed treatment. He didn't remember a time when he had been so exhausted. Sleep for a week if need be. Then when he did awaken he could phone his boss and see where he was needed. Back to business as usual. If only he could forget all the pictures crowding his mind.

He looked down at his hands gripping the steering wheel. The damned car wouldn't let him forget. As he drove the Oldsmobile through the streets of San Francisco, the gas gauge sitting on empty, he knew it was not a dream. What had happened would be with him not only this day but for countless days to come. Perhaps for the rest of his miserable life.

A cruel reality slowly replaced a shattered vision. Jimmy shuddered as he realized only two days and nights had passed since he had left San Francisco, intent on getting to Seattle. Now he was back in the Bay Area, having never even seen his dream city.

At the moment, even in his dazed condition, he realized this was of little significance. Whatever was in Seattle could stay there. A more important decision facing him now was what to do with this car. There was no way he could continue to drive it as though it was his own. Being stolen, the cops could be looking for it even now. In all likelihood, they were hot on his heels. Also, he had a throbbing, bleeding arm to consider. As well as the gun he wished he'd never seen, even though it would probably be unfound and soon rusting on the top of a mountain.

He tried to convince himself he was the same careless youth who had left the city a few days before. Deep inside, though, he knew he would never again be the same. Nothing would ever be the same again.

He'd been in trouble before when he and his brother had responded to dares thrown their way. His mom had treated those incidents as important. And there'd been that other time. Sure had seemed momentous. Now he knew different. This was big.

As sure as he was sitting on the white leatherette seat of a stolen car, the man was dead. Jay, or whatever his name was, had gone wherever dead criminals go to spend eternity. If they ever charged him with murder, then that would be the end. Life in prison or the gas chamber. Either way he was a big-time loser.

Jimmy headed for the Tenderloin area. Although this placed him only a mile or two from where he'd met Jay, he had decided there was no way he could return to his place of employment. Cops could be waiting. He stopped in a seedy section of the city, a place where before he hadn't cared to be alone, certainly never after dark. It was dangerous enough in daylight.

He parked the Oldsmobile in front of a bar and crawled out, leaving the key in the ignition. Standing was harder now than it had been while on a ship in the midst of a war. Scowling faces studied him. Don't show fear, man, or you've had it. Without looking back, he walked down the sidewalk, moving ever farther from part of his nightmare.

What remained of Glenn True Clark's possessions stayed with the car. In all probability the gold watch still hung on the turn signal handle. A hand tooled wallet, made for Glenn by his brother at the Utah State Prison, was inside the glove compartment. A rifle was wired to the underframe of the car. An empty two-gallon gas can rested on the rear floor. To a would-be thief, add it all together and it was a touch of paradise.

Jimmy felt certain that within five minutes the car would have a new owner. They were welcome to it. His only concerns now were getting out of this neighborhood alive and deciding where to go if he did. Perhaps it would be best to hop a bus and get the hell out of the city. First, though, he had to take a leak, eat, drink, and rest.

About the time that Jimmy abandoned the Oldsmobile in San Francisco, some three hundred and seventy miles away in Medford, Oregon, the body of Glenn Clark was arriving in town. Although Clark had been primarily a loner most of his life, he was soon to command a great deal of attention and be studied more closely in death than he ever had while living.

The hearse, accompanied by Detective Porter, arrived at the Conger Morris Mortuary only to be sent to the Providence Hospital where Dr. Southerland had requested it be taken for x-rays. There, Dr. Morgan took over.

X-rays revealed that the bullet to the back of the head had broken into two pieces. The larger piece was lodged just under the skin over the left ear. Corporal Seuter arrived and began taking colored photographs of the body. One of these showed an entrance hole in the back of the head. Morgan then took a penis smear which was placed in a jar. Clark's upper and lower dentures were taken and tagged, as was all of his clothing.

And then it was back to the mortuary.

Around four in the afternoon it looked as though the Jackson County Sheriff's Office was about to get its first break in the case. Sergeant Armand told Detective Porter he needed to take a run up to Grants Pass where they had a suspect under surveillance who fit their all points bulletin.

Porter took off for the thirty-mile trip, wondering if he would be coming back with a murderer. It would indeed be something if they could put a lid on the killing in the first twenty-four hours.

Within the hour Porter was at Grants Pass, feeling more optimistic with each passing moment. Their suspect, Burt Henry, had stayed in a local motel the night before. He was eighteen years of age, five feet seven, one hundred forty-three pounds, brown hair and brown eyes, and part Indian. He had been driving a 1966 Pontiac, light blue, with California license but number unknown. It fit. It all fit!

The bubble soon burst.

When Porter arrived, suspect and vehicle were both long gone. Surveillance had lost him. Porter soon decided car and driver could go wherever they wanted without any interference from the county sheriff's office. The Pontiac had bucket seats. Terrie was certain Clark's car did not. She was positive on this point.

Also, more than one motel employee swore that Burt Henry had been at the motel the night before and couldn't possibly have been running up and down I-5 or Dead Indian Road kidnapping and killing people along the way. So much for their first suspect.

* * *

Shortly after five that same afternoon, the body of Glenn True Clark was analyzed further. Doctor Morgan, assisted by Doctor Southerland, started an autopsy. They first determined that he was five feet ten inches tall and weighed one hundred seventy-nine pounds. Not a small man, but hardly the giant he'd seemed to Jimmy. Hair was brown and eyes were greenish brown. He was in his late forties or early fifties. After splitting the man from stem to stern and analyzing everything that had at one time made him tick, they decided that, except for gonorrhea and a couple of gunshot wounds, especially the one to the head determined to be the cause of death, the old boy had been in pretty good health. For his age.

Armand and Pauling were kept busy for the next six hours or so questioning people, recording statements, trying to get some kind of a handle on who was killed and who had done the killing. As for Terrie, the police hardly knew what to make of her. She had told first one story and then another. They suspected this was probably because she'd been so nervous and afraid her family would discover she had been hitchhiking instead of flying a commercial airline home as expected.

Or maybe she was in with the killer. Whatever, other than for the workmen, she was all they had at this time. Not that they hoped to gain much from questioning the loggers, but they had to cover every possibility.

"I'll go first," Mike said.
The four men who had discovered Terrie were gathered at the sheriff's office. Armand had explained that they would be required to come in with him, one at a time, for an interview. It was 5:30 in the afternoon when Armand first turned the recorder on and began the questioning. Having been in on the search for the dead man, Mike quite naturally felt anxious to help in any way he could.

After Mike had been advised that the interview would be tape recorded, Armand asked questions and Mike opened up willingly. When asked what happened, Mike said, "Well, we were driving to work, and I was sitting in the back seat asleep and the crummy stopped so I woke up, and Seth, one of the guys I work with, got out of the crummy and started picking up some bags in the road. He thought they were just lost so he was going to set them in the truck. When he opened the door, this girl just almost jumped out of the truck, you know. And Seth just slammed the door and stepped back, because he didn't know what it was."

When asked to describe the girl, Mike reported, "About five foot two, with blond hair and wearing a dress with a pair of pants under it. Long pants," he added.

"Would you go ahead then and tell us what happened?" asked Armand.

"Well, Terrie jumped out and she was all scared and panicked and none of us knew what was going on because we didn't expect it. Well, she wouldn't let us go and, you know, leave her there so we let her in the back seat with me and Larry and she started telling us this story about being kidnapped and hauled up there and one man getting shot and so on."

"Could you describe in detail the story she told you in regard to this incident?"

"Well, I heard it four times so I think I can. She was picked up by the Talent turnoff on the freeway, I guess, and they drove her through Ashland and they picked up some beer in Ashland, I heard, and then went on up to Dead Indian and picked up some more beer and wine from the store on the Dead Indian and then drove on up past Howard Prairie and then turned off and went to Shell Peak Road and pulled into this turnoff on the road and I. . . I don't know what they did in between that, but she said after a while they were talking and drinking more beer and wine and then one of the guys came to the car and got some beer and wine and took off and left her alone and, before he left, he told her that she'd be all right, if the other guy hurt her any, that he'd kill her, kill him, so he left them alone and then this other guy got into the car and grabbed her and she made him let go and then he reached in his pocket and grabbed the car keys and put them in the dash and so she said she was leaving and then he grabbed her by the hand and pulled her back and she yelled for the other guy, I guess, and he came over and made him get out of the car and walk up in front of the car and get on his knees and made him take off his shirt. In the meantime, what's her name?"

Armand thought perhaps the young man had set a world record for talking without once coming up for air. And he surely knew the girl's name as well as he knew his own. Staring at him, he wondered how long Mike could keep it up.

"Terrie grabbed her bags and stuff and started to leave and this John, I guess, hollered at her and told her to come back, not to leave, that he was going to kill him and get rid of him and it would be all right. Well, she just kept going because she was afraid and when she got down the road a ways she could still see the car and she heard two shots and she seen this John holding the gun in front of the head-lights and so she just ran that much faster and hid in some bushes. Well, about five minutes later the car started up and came down the road and I guess he looked for her for a while and then she seen the taillights leave so she got out and started walking up the road and found the water truck and hopped in it and was soon sleeping. That's about all."

Armand asked for Terrie's description of the vehicle. Mike said, "It was somewhere between a Sixty-two and Sixty-six Bonneville Pontiac, about a light metallic blue or green, I think it's green and a two-door, and that's about all."

When Armand asked for a description of the two men, Mike replied, "Well, this John was about nineteen, she said, and about my height, about five-two or five-three, and I can't hardly remember what color of hair she said. I think it was dark black, oh yeah, it was black, real dark, and looked sort of like an Indian. That was all she said about John. And Jay, she said, was about thirty-one years old and about six-feet high, had a receding hairline and light brown hair with sort of a hook nose."

He repeated Terrie's description of John's gun. "It was a small, looks about like a, sounded about like a thirty-eight snub-nosed pistol and it was chrome with a white handle."

"What else did she say?" Armand asked.

"She said they argued one time about the car being stolen, that one of them stole the car and that they both had a lot of money on them, and they were beered up, I guess."

"Did she say how much money they had?"

"About two hundred each."

"Did she indicate to you that either of these subjects got intimate with her?"

"She claimed neither one had."

After continuing with this line of questioning for a time, Armand leaned toward the younger man scrutinizing him. "Is there anything else you'd care to add to this statement?"

"Well, just that I like the girl quite a bit after all she's been through and that I hate to see her get the bad end of it."

"You believe then that she is sincere and in your opinion was telling the truth about the incident?"

"Oh yeah. A hundred percent."

Larry was the next to take his turn in the room with Sergeant Armand. His answers weren't as thorough as Mike's, but he did recall some different details.

When asked to relate Terrie's story as to why she was on the freeway, he nodded. "Yeah. She said that she was on her way from Portland to San Francisco and her parents sent her money to go down and she was going to save her money and hitchhike so she tried it and two men picked her up and . . ."

"Did Terrie describe the vehicle they were in?" Armand said matter-of-factly.

"Nope," Larry answered, shaking his head.

"And the two men?"

"No, she didn't," Larry replied.

As he continued, Larry remembered Terrie said that she had been asleep when the car stopped. "She said one man had some beer and wine and he was going out in the brush to drink it and told the girl if that other man went and tried anything to yell at him and he'd come back and kill him."

Larry ran his hand through his dark brown hair. "He told him to get out of the car and take his shirt off and get on his knees and he did, and she apparently started running off, a little ways down the road, and she heard two gun shots and just kept running, and the man told her to come back, that the other guy wouldn't hurt her anymore and she started going up different roads and found the water wagon. That's all I know now."

When asked exactly where all this took place, Larry spoke shyly. "I don't know the name of the roads. I've only been working there a week."

It was time to interview the older men. Seth came first. His story varied little from the others until he tried to recall what Terrie had said while seated in the back of the crummy.

"She jabbered all the way up there," he said, "but I never paid no attention, you know what I mean."

"Could you describe the girl?"

Seth was hesitant. When pushed, he said, "She looked like a blonde or redhead. She was real skinny, I thought. Had on a pair of slacks and a dress over it and a coat over that, I think."

"Did she seem frightened or alarmed?"

Seth nodded. "Yeah, about scared half to death, I think."

Yeah, she'd done a lot of talking, but he hadn't paid attention to what was being said. When they reached the landing, he got out his shovel and went to work.

* * *

Hank, the driver of the crummy, was the last of the loggers to be interviewed. Large and florid faced, he sat uncomfortably on the hard folding chair. When asked to describe what happened when they approached the water truck, Hank said, "There was a suitcase and might have been a smaller suitcase in the car lights. There was an object that might have been another little suitcase which had to be moved before we could go through, so Seth went out to move it and we thought it was a night watchman in there, and he opened that door and this girl flew at him like a wildcat."

Armand wondered how he'd describe the girl and asked that next. Hank said, "Well, I guessed her age at about fifteen."

Armand changed the subject. "While on the way to the landing, did she relate a story as to the reason she was frightened?"

"She said these guys, these guys, the way I understand it, was trying to rape her and this one guy held a gun on the other one that had her down and she got away. She said she heard two shots while she was running off."

"Anything else you remember?"

Hank shrugged. "I don't know what it would be. I was only there with . . . where she was for about ten minutes and I was driving the crummy to the logging woods and it rattled and banged and I just didn't . . . I couldn't hear all she was saying, but I did hear that much. We had to be at the landing at six. I jumped out and told Mike to get ahold of Frank. That's when I started my Cat and went to skiddin'."

So much for the loggers. The lawmen wondered what they would have when they merged their stories. Probably not much.

Jimmy stumbled into the Coffee Time, a small diner in the Tenderloin area. Seated at the counter eating potato chips and drinking coffee was an acquaintance, Nick, with whom Jimmy had drunk beer and reminisced in times past. Nick was tall and lean with long, dark, shiny hair. Feeling as though he was near the point of passing out, Jimmy dropped onto a vacant stool beside his friend.

"Jimmy, you son of a bitch! What happened? I've seen dead guys who looked better than you."

"I've known dead guys who must have felt better than I feel."

"Well, where you been?"

"Around."

"What happened to your arm?"

"You don't want to know."

Jimmy ordered a ham sandwich and a cup of coffee. To Nick he said, "You got a place where I can stay for a day or two?"

"Hell yes, man. My old lady's staying but there's always room for one more. Hurry up and eat. Let's go see how drunk we can get. Then I want to talk to you about a job I've been hoping to pull." In a whisper, Nick added, "You got the guts to rob a store?"

"Yeah, I got the guts. But I also got better sense than to pull such a damned fool stunt."

Tanked up on beer, his arm packed with toilet tissue, Jimmy stumbled through a door on the second floor of a seedy hotel, where rooms could be rented by the hour, day, week, or month. Nicky led the way.

Inside was a single bed. Lying on top, wearing only a loose slip and a pair of panties, was a girl with her back to the door. Long, brown hair fanned out above her head.

"Hey, Jimmy, meet Ramona." Nick giggled like the drunk he was. "If she wasn't so stoned, she'd be able to say, 'Hi, Jimmy.'"

Jimmy waved. "Hi, Ramona."

"You hiding out from somebody?" Nick asked.

"Maybe. I don't know."

"Come on and sit down. Eddie was here but left before

I did, after a bottle of something. Christ knows what. He'll be back in his own sweet time. We only got one bed, but if you're needing a place to land, you can sack out on the floor."

"Thanks, Nicky."

"That's what friends are for. Maybe you can do something for me some day. Remember that job I mentioned?"

"What job?"

By now it was getting dark outside. Even though Jimmy had eaten earlier, hunger still gnawed at him. But more than that he felt ready to collapse. He fell into a soft chair, not really giving a damn whether or not Eddie showed.

That same evening, at 6:40 P.M. Seuter and Thyson were at the mortuary to fingerprint Clark. Once that chore was completed, they returned to the office and called Robert Anderson who was the department's fingerprint classification expert. He agreed to come in and classify the prints. After this, Anderson and Seuter began making telephone calls to other law enforcement agencies. Because of what had happened on Dead Indian Mountain less than twenty-four hours earlier, it would be a long night for them all. Of the three people who had been up on the mountain, the only one they had identified was Terrie.

Terrie was making a long distance call to her father, Brian Tidwell, in Los Angeles, explaining why she had been alone on a mountaintop with two strange men when a gunfight erupted instead of safe on an airplane winging her way home. After the dust settled, Mr. Tidwell advised her to cooperate and arranged for a local attorney to represent his daughter just in case the locals had any intentions of pulling a fast one. As a result, it was nearly ten that night before the interview started. Pauling and Armand would ask the questions.

After going through the preliminaries, Terrie commented, "Can I say that I'm not really positive of all my answers and if I say something like I think it happened this way, I'm not saying that it definitely did. Because I was pretty upset during certain periods and I'm just not positive, but I have an idea, but, or I . . ."

"Sure, Terrie, we understand."

They started by confirming that she was hitchhiking on I-5 near Talent, Oregon, when John and Jay stopped and offered her a ride. No more of this crap about stopping at a coffee shop while on her way to the airport. She described the car as a dark bluish green Pontiac. Said they'd told her it was a Bonneville. She knew it had white leatherette upholstery. Her description of Jay was as being older than the thirty-one years he claimed to be, much older, brown hair with a receding hairline, not much hair, what there was was thin, not bald, and, according to her, he was kind of fat.

As for John, she saw him as five-seven or five-eight, and not very tall or very big. He had black hair and black eyebrows. He was kind of thin, not skinny, but thin. He had dark skin, but not dark out of the ordinary. It was obvious that he hadn't been in the sun, really.

Terrie told them about the trips to the stores to buy beer and wine, the poker game, being shown John's gun, and then awaking as the car was pulling onto a logging road. She told about how Jay had said they were on their way to see his friends Slim and Virginia as well as a singing group that was staying at the ranch.

Next, Terrie was asked, "Were you alarmed by their behavior or concerned for your safety?"

"No."

"When they turned off from their southbound route, did this alarm you?"

"No, it didn't. I believed them. I don't know why, I just did."

As for being asleep when they pulled into the clearing, Terrie said, "I can remember waking up and I was very tired. I didn't get much sleep the night before."

She told about the two men getting out of the car and having a conversation she couldn't hear. How John had come to the car and taken his gun and told her, "Don't worry. If anything happens you just call out and I'll protect you. I promise, I'll shoot him if I have to."

Terrie was asked, "And you yelled for help?"

"Yes."

"What next occurred?"

"Then John came running to the car. And, with the gun, and pointed it and I jumped. When Jay saw the gun, I don't know, John said something to Jay. You know, he said 'Leave her alone,' or something to that effect. When, when, he said 'I have a gun' and when Jay saw the gun he let go of me and I jumped out of the car."

After considering for a moment, Terrie said, "Now that I think about it, John pointed the gun and told him to get out of the car."

"He ordered him out of the car?"

"Yes, yes, he was being, ordering him an awful lot. John was ordering Jay, was giving him all kinds of orders."

After admitting to dragging her suitcases out of the car and moving away, Terrie was asked, "To the best of your ability, could you continue to hear the conversation between John and Jay?"

"Well, not to the best of my ability because I was very upset at the time. I was shaking and my legs were shaking and I was crying."

"What can you recall of the conversation?"

"I can definitely recall John telling Jay to kneel down, to get on his knees, and then I remember him saying, 'Take off your shirt.'"

"Where did this happen?"

"In front of the right headlight of the cat"

"Did Jay comply with the orders from John?"

"Yes, he did. I remember him saying, 'Don't shoot, don't shoot' the whole time. 'Please don't shoot.'"

Armand leaned toward her. "Did Jay make any effort to physically resist John? Did he try to disarm him?"

"I don't know if he really tried to disarm him. I know there was some kind of physical thing going on between them, and I don't know what it was."

"You saw Jay on his knees in front of the headlight?"

"Yes, I did."

"How far from Jay would you say the gun was?"

"I don't know. It was close. I couldn't . . . That's the most hazy part, and I don't want to confirm anything because I'm not sure."

After telling how Jay had pleaded with John and how John had asked her to please stay, Armand asked, "Then what happened?"

"Then two shots went off."

She admitted to having been some fifty or a hundred feet from the two men when she heard the shots. She was then asked, "Did you look back when you heard the shots?"

"Yes, I was looking towards them. I can remember seeing the gun and I can remember seeing Jay's skin in the headlights. That's all I remember. I don't know what position they were in or anything really, I just—it was very hazy."

"Did you see Jay fall over?"

"No, I didn't."

"Did you look back momentarily or continue to watch?"

"I just walked. I turned around and I didn't run. I just walked real fast. I was screaming and crying while I was walking."

Terrie went on to tell how she had hidden when the car left, how, frightened, she had walked until she came to the truck and how she had been found by the loggers. After she'd told how she had assisted in finding the road and how they had eventually located Jay's body, the interrogators backed up and asked, "At the time John was threatening Jay with the gun and indicating that he intended to shoot him, did you say anything to John in the way of stopping him from this act?"

"No, I didn't."

"Did it occur to you at the time?"

"That he was going to shoot Jay?" She inclined her head, looking pensive. "I don't really know if it really occurred to me or not. I was just, I was so shocked from Jay grabbing me and I just kept crying and I don't know what I thought."

"How do you explain John's behavior? The fact that he came to your aid, the fact that he shot Jay in an apparent attempt to protect you, what would motivate him in your estimation?"

"I don't have any idea because I did not give him any reason to motivate him at all and I mean he was very nice to me. He kept telling me that I was pretty and that I had, he liked my blue eyes, my big blue eyes, and you know, that he respected women, things like that, but I don't know what motivated him. Now that I think about it, look back on it, I think his intentions were to kill Jay anyway."

"When he showed you the gun, was it in any way a threat to Jay? Had he indicated a threat to Jay at that first occasion?"

"No, he did not. As a matter of fact, he said they had two guns though."

"Did he tell you what the other gun was?"

"No, he just showed me one. He said they had two guns though."

"At any time did you see the other one?"

"No, I did not."

As the interview wound down, Terrie was asked if she had anything further to add. She said, "No, I don't, about the shooting and I don't want to confirm anything about it. I was just so upset at the time and I don't really know what I saw. I know I was looking in that direction. And that's all I know, really."

"All right."

"And I know that John was holding the gun and I saw Jay's skin."

Although Pauling and Armand didn't know it then, by the time they concluded the interview at 11:20 and had made arrangements for Terrie to spend the night with a Deputy,

Glenn True Clark had been identified. At 11:00 that night, a Mr. Davids of the California State Bureau called saying he had checked the classification and tentatively identified the victim as a man who had been arrested on April 5 that year by Siskiyou County Sheriff's Office, Yreka, California, on charges of unpaid traffic warrants and carrying a concealed weapon.

When Seuter saw the name, he recognized Clark as a man who was currently under investigation by the Medford and Central Point Police Departments for passing fraudulent checks.

For many of the tired sheriff's officers, the night was far from over. Had they known their alleged killer was asleep in a San Francisco hotel, they would have been ready to hang him from the nearest lamp post.

9

INTO THE FIRE

Although there were times when he was vaguely aware of his environment, enough to realize that he was in a strange room, Jimmy had no desire to open his eyes and face reality. During those moments of questionable lucidity he practiced denial. Erase all those memories from your mind and they never happened.

There was never a Jay or a Terrie who intervened in his life. No Oldsmobile that he had driven those many long miles back and ditched somewhere in a seedy section of the city. Despite his exercises in futility, he knew there was a hot car out there and he hadn't even bothered to wipe away his prints. Now that it was too late, he remembered.

It was daylight. Eddie had been in and out. More often than not, Ramona was living in a world of her own. When Jimmy wasn't sleeping, he was drinking beer or whiskey. Although this had failed to erase memories, at least they were being diluted. Once when they had been left alone, Ramona invited him into her bed. Jimmy declined. Nick was a friend and, besides, he didn't want anything to do with any woman who was on hard drugs. He rolled in a blanket on the floor and went back to sleep.

While Jimmy was attempting to forget, many of the lawmen back in Medford, Oregon, were going about their business with the assistance of large quantities of caffeine. After the interview with Terrie was complete and she had been put up at a deputy's house for the night, Pauling and Seuter stayed in the office until four o'clock in the morning in a futile attempt to locate Glenn True Clark's ex-wife, Gayle, as well as Ted Ryder, who was thought to be Clark's friend.

Late the next morning, while Armand and Seuter accompanied Terrie to a Pontiac dealer in an attempt to identify the car, Pauling, who had located Ted Ryder in a Central Point trailer park north of Medford, went there to see what he could learn. Ted admitted knowing Glenn True Clark and agreed to accompany Pauling to the Conger Morris Funeral Home. Upon their arrival, a positive identification was made.

At the Pontiac Garage, Terrie wasn't certain which was the right car. She looked at numerous used cars but was unable to identify any specific model as being identical to the one she'd been in with the two strange men. She thought perhaps the tail lights on the Sixty-two Pontiac were similar. Maybe that was it. But her memory said the speedometer in Jay's car was round rather than rectangular, the automatic shift lever was longer, and, as she recalled, there had been a shelf under the glove compartment. The lawmen concluded this space had been designed to accommodate an air-conditioning unit that had never been installed. There must have been a shelf, Terrie insisted. That is where John had kept his gun. Under there, somewhere.

Disappointed that she had been unable to make a positive identification of the car model, the two deputies escorted Terrie back to their office.

Although it was past noon, none of them stopped for

lunch. They wanted to get on with their search as quickly as possible. The more time that passed the colder the trail became, this they knew. A man was dead, murdered, shot in the head. Stripped clean. Right here in their own back-yard. It had to be murder in the first degree. They had the resources to catch the killer. With a lot of hard work and a little luck, they could do it.

Next, Seuter took Terrie to their medical illustrator who began to draw a composite picture of the suspect from the description supplied by Terrie. It took two tries before they were satisfied.

By now Ted, who had identified Clark, agreed to come to the sheriff's office for questioning. Armand and Pauling wanted to learn all they could about the dead man.

Asked when was the last time he had seen Clark, Ted said, "Early August. Last heard from him, must have been about the fifth or sixth. He'd been in town the week before and from what I know had been passing hot checks. Told him he was going to get himself into more trouble than he could get out of. He was a hard man to tell anything though. Had a mind of his own."

"Yes, sir. When did you last hear from him?" Armand asked.

"It was August fifth, I know now, because it was a Saturday. I was expecting him to come by that day and so I had arranged with the police to have him arrested. It's clear now that he'd a been a lot better off if he'd been stopped before he got in any deeper. He was a sly one though. Must have sensed something was up. Instead of coming by, he called me from somewhere, long distance. Wouldn't tell me where he was though."

"Have you any idea where he called from?" Pauling asked.

"Not for sure. Glenn told me he knew he was wanted for bad checks around here and so he decided to go where he'd be safe. Probably Idaho. He's told me more than once that he never would do nothing out of the way around Caldwell, Idaho. He saved that place where he could hole up and they wouldn't be looking for him. Said he'd see me when he came back this way."

"What kind of car was he driving when you last saw him?" Armand wanted to know.

"He was driving a station wagon. A Pontiac."

"Was there anyone else with him?"

"No. He usually traveled alone. Might pick up somebody and spend a day or two with them but he was a loner most of the time."

"Do you know if Clark had been working recently?" Pauling asked.

"I know he hadn't worked for the past couple of months."

"Did he do much drinking the last time he was here?"

"All the time. Didn't see him sober much."

"Are you acquainted with Mrs. Clark?"

"Gayle? Sure, I know her. The two of them separated first and then they got a divorce. Since then she's been hiding from him. She's afraid that he's going to kill her. While he was here, he tried to find her, but wasn't able to."

"Other than passing bad checks, do you know of any other criminal activities that he might have engaged in?" Pauling asked.

Ted said, "Well, he's dead now so what I say won't hurt him none. I know he's done some burglaries. Stole some guns for one thing. From what he said, he sold most of 'em. Always carried a gun on him and I know that was against the law. I think he used that gun in some robberies, but I ain't sure."

"What kind of gun?" Armand wanted to know.

"He was carrying a thirty-eight-caliber blue steel with a short barrel. He'd filed the serial numbers off the butt."

Numbers on the butt sounded like a Colt to the lawmen.

"Said him and another guy had gone into a hardware store after it closed and stole the guns. He'd kept this one and one other and sold the rest. That's what he said."

"Any other criminal activities that you know of?" Pauling asked.

"No, not really. He was always talking about robbing a

bank but I don't think he ever did. I know I tried my best to talk him out of it. He thought he could just walk in, pull his gun, take the money, and walk out. They'd a had him before he got to the corner."

Ted paused for a moment and then went on. "I tried to talk him into getting rid of the gun he had. Knew that if he got caught with a gun where the numbers had been removed it would spell big trouble. He got caught in Weed, over in California, one time not long ago for carrying a concealed weapon. He was telling me how they'd found a twenty-two he had but overlooked this thirty-eight revolver he had hid underneath the back seat."

"On his visits to you, was he ever accompanied by another man?" Pauling wanted to know.

"Several months back he had a hophead with him. Skinny little guy, kinda wild looking. Don't know his name. Glenn said that the two of them had been down in Mexico. When they come back, the hophead was arrested for something in New Mexico. Later on, Glenn was arrested in Salt Lake City and he thought it was the hophead's fault. Don't know how, but he thought it was."

"Anything else?" Armand asked.

"Glenn spent a lot of time in Salt Lake City. Said he knew a man there where he could get a rebuilt stolen car any time he needed one. Don't know the guy's name, but that's what he said."

Before he left, Ted provided the officers with names and locations of Clark's relatives and said, "Glenn Clark was not a good person. He liked to beat on women, I know that. He wasn't a good person at all."

It was five that afternoon when Pauling phoned Marion Parker, who was Glenn Clark's sister. She, along with his parents, lived in Oregon. Marion told Pauling that their parents were up in years; she would perform the unpleasant task of informing them that their son had been killed.

When asked how long it had been since she'd seen her

brother, Marion said, "We haven't seen him for at least four weeks. Maybe closer to six."

"Do you know whether or not your parents have heard anything since then?"

"The last time they heard was a week or ten days ago. Said he was in Salt Lake City, his car had broken down, and he was wanting to borrow money to buy another car."

"Do you know whether or not they sent him any money?"

"No, they didn't. They didn't have any money to send."

"Did he say where he was going?" Pauling asked.

"Yes, he did. Said he was going to Idaho. They were having a large forest fire up there and he planned to help fight it. At least that's what he said."

That's what he said. Pauling felt as though Marion wasn't all that convinced.

"Mrs. Parker, do you know if any other family member has seen or heard from Glenn since he phoned your parents?"

"Yes. I heard that Avery saw him."

"Avery?"

"Our brother. Lives in California. Said that Glenn was by there Sunday morning."

"This past Sunday? August twenty-seventh?"

"Yes, this past Sunday. Glenn had breakfast with Avery and Sara. From what I heard, he stayed two hours or so. Avery said he was driving an Oldsmobile with a Utah license plate."

Pauling considered what she had said. Somehow or other, Clark must have come in possession of another car. He wondered if they should be looking for an Oldsmobile, or if Terrie's description of a Pontiac was accurate.

"Do you know whether or not anyone was with him when he was at your brother's house?" Pauling asked.

"Not that I know of. Avery would have mentioned it if there had been someone else."

"Thank you, Mrs. Parker. I'd appreciate it if you would talk to other members of your family to see what else you can learn. I'll be in touch."

* * *

What day was it? Where was he? Regardless of his efforts, Jimmy couldn't pinpoint the date.

He did, however, manage to figure out where he lay sicker than sick. In Nicky's hotel room. He remembered awakening earlier and finding himself alone. After staggering into the bathroom and relieving himself, he'd dropped onto a floor pallet and fallen into a troubled sleep.

The snap of a pop-top startled him awake. A blurred Nicky stood nearby with a smile on his face and a can of beer in his grip. Jimmy's hand reached out.

"I don't know what you're running from but you have sure been wrestling that blanket all over the floor," Nicky said.

Jimmy swallowed a mouthful of beer. "Yeah. Well, it's a long story."

Nicky pulled up a chair. "How you fixed for bread?" he asked.

They were alone. "Got a little," he said. "Not much, though. I can pay my way if that's what you're concerned about."

"Now, Jimmy, you know better than that. I was just wondering about doing that little job we talked about earlier. Wondered if you wanted in on it. Little Ramona has an expensive habit."

"What kind of job?"

"A little robbery. You're not chicken, are you?"

Oh hell, Jimmy thought. What next?

The investigation was now forty-eight hours old. Their chances of finding "John" were further diminishing. This knowledge didn't lessen their efforts. They did have a few leads to follow. So long as they did, they would keep on looking. Glenn True Clark might not have been a model citizen, but he'd had the poor judgment to get himself killed in Jackson County. That being so, they would continue looking for his killer until doomsday, if that's what it took. Little did they know that it would take them nearly that long.

Detective Seuter spent the morning helping Pauling check out suspects. In the early afternoon he escorted Terrie to the county jail where three cards of her fingerprints were taken for elimination purposes. After that, Detective Porter took two stand-up photos of the young lady.

"Why are you snapping photos?" Terrie asked.

Seuter explained, "They're for the purpose of identification should additional witnesses develop."

And, perhaps, just in case she became a suspect.

Since Clark's body was scheduled to be sent to Florence for burial, Seuter and Porter made one more trip to the funeral home. This would be the detectives' last chance to get whatever they would ever need from Glenn. So, Porter took four full-face exposures and Seuter took two more sets of fingerprints. A most distasteful job. They walked away somber faced, finished forever with the body of Glenn True Clark. All they had to do now was find out who had put a bullet in the old boy's brain and caused them all sleepless nights.

"Jimmy, hey buddy, you with us?"

Jimmy was still somewhere in a foggy world. When sleep could no longer eradicate memories from some mountain top, when the madness rushed to the front, he drank beer in a futile attempt to pull a curtain over events too startling for his mind to comprehend. When beer failed, he turned to bourbon. Whiskey, however, was even more unkind to him than wine.

They'd helped him to his feet and onto the bed where he was sitting now, held in place by the inner wall. He recognized Nicky's voice. Some chick, must be Ramona, was seated at the scarred desk, smoke curling from a cigarette clamped between her pale lips while she filed her nails. Another man, with a stocky frame and long hair tied in a ponytail, stood near Nicky.

"That you, Eddie?" Jimmy asked.

"Sure thing, man. How you feeling?"

"I don't know yet. What's happening?"

"We're getting ready to do that job," Nicky said.

"What job?"

"Don't you remember? I told you we were going to hold up a store. We got it all planned out. Ramona's gonna be in Eddie's car. Have the motor running and ready for a fast getaway. Eddie, he's gonna have his rifle and be across the street."

"What for?" Jimmy said.

"To cover you—whichever one of us goes in. That'll be either me or you. We've studied it, man. When there's no customers inside there's one old fart in there by himself. He looks out and sees Eddie holding a rifle, he ain't gonna try no shit, is he?"

"Probably not," Jimmy agreed.

"Either me or you'll go in with a gun. The other one will wait just outside."

"I don't want anything to do with no gun," Jimmy said. The sounds of gunshots pierced the fog that surrounded his brain. A raw forearm was a grim reminder of what had happened the last time he'd had a gun in his hand.

Nicky was offended. "You ain't backing out on us, are you, Jimmy?"

"Besides," Eddie said, "there's a fifty-fifty chance that it'll be Nicky going in with the pistol. That gun's just for show. I'll be right across the street with a rifle. He ain't gonna try nothing. Tell him to look my way and he'll break his arm handing you the money."

"This late in the day, he oughta have several hundred inside," Nicky said.

Jimmy thought Ramona looked bored with it all.

"What we're gonna do is flip a coin to see who goes in and who stays outside," Nicky said. "Flip it, Eddie, and Jimmy can make the call."

While the quarter was in the air, Jimmy said, "Tails."

Eddie caught the coin, lay it on the back of his left hand, and removed his right. "Heads," he said. "You lose."

It wasn't until later, when he'd had the opportunity to sober up, that Jimmy realized he hadn't seen the coin after it had been flipped. Maybe he had lost, and maybe he hadn't.

"Let's go," Nicky said. "The guns are in the car."

Eddie drove. Jimmy, still in a dazed state, sat with him in the front seat while Nicky and Ramona occupied the back. He wondered where the Oldsmobile was that he'd abandoned today. Or was it yesterday? Perhaps even the day before. He wasn't sure. Nor did it matter. He had a more pressing problem. Like what was he getting himself into?

He didn't need money that bad. There was still enough left, or so he thought, to buy a bus ticket to somewhere. Anywhere. That's what he would do. As soon as they were finished. Tomorrow, at the latest. Get out of town. Away from the car. Far away from a cursed mountain. Go somewhere where he would never be found. Now that Seattle was out of the question, he might go see his folks again. Yeah, it was time to go home.

Eddie was parking the car. It didn't seem as though they had driven far, not more than two or three blocks. Jimmy wondered why if they were going to do such a fool thing, why not pick on some place farther away from the hotel. Well, he supposed Nicky knew what he was doing.

They sat in silence for a moment and then Nicky said, "Now, is everybody clear on what they're going to do?"

"Let's do it," Eddie said.

Jimmy half emerged from his distracted state. "No matter what happens, don't you shoot that rifle," he said. "I don't want to get shot and I don't want to get picked up for any murder."

"Keep cool, man," Nicky said. "Ain't nobody gonna get shot. Eddie's just here for a little insurance, that's all."

They were about as inconspicuous as a marching band as they took their places. Slapstick comedy, San Francisco style. Ramona slid under the wheel. Eddie stood beside the car, rifle held at his side. They handed Jimmy a .38 snub-nosed pistol which he put distastefully into his back pocket and, along with Nicky, crossed the street.

"Go on," Nicky said. "Nobody in there but the man. I'll wait here."

Once again, Jimmy had been thrust into a situation where he began to sober up in a hurry. Although he had recently vowed that he would never touch another pistol, his friends had made it clear you either go along or else. On unsteady feet, Jimmy walked through the door of the store.

Only one clerk was inside. As Jimmy walked in, a short and chubby man came up from the meat counter, wiping his hands on an apron. He eyed this new customer with suspicion.

"What can I help you with?" he said.

Jimmy said, trying to keep his voice confident, "You can give me all your money."

The man froze and frowned as he saw the gun come out of Jimmy's pocket. "There's a rifle on you from across the street, man. Just open the register and hand it over. I'll be out of your way then."

The man looked through his front window and saw the rifle. He then studied Jimmy as though memorizing his face and details of his clothing. Without another word, he marched to the cash register, punched a key, and the door opened.

Jimmy picked up a paper bag and handed it to the man. "Put it in there, please," he said.

The man obliged. When the register was empty and there wasn't all that much in the bag, he closed the drawer. Not that much money for the risk they were taking. Maybe Jay had been right: you want money, rob a bank. Naw, he didn't need that kind of trouble. He didn't need this kind either. How the hell had he gotten to this point? He'd better get out quick.

"Stay right where you are," Jimmy said. "I'm walking out the door, but the rifle's staying on you."

Once he was outside, he and Nicky ran to the car. Ramona

was gripping the wheel, anxious to feed gas to the engine as they jumped in. As soon as Eddie was inside, she burned rubber. As soon as they roared down the street, Jimmy handed the revolver to Nick, who hid it under the seat.

Nicky took the bag from Jimmy, counted out the money, and handed a small amount to Eddie. "Not much," he said. "I got enough here to get Ramona high, and that's about it."

Jimmy, who had taken the most risk, didn't get a penny.

They took the long route and pulled up in front of the hotel. "I'm going to make a buy while Eddie parks the car," Nicky said. "You two go on inside. Play it cool."

When they were in the lobby, Ramona said, "Come on up."

"I'll wait down here."

"We got a little time before Nicky gets back."

"I'll wait right here until he does."

"You're chicken," she said, and turned to the marble stairs.

The hotel was old, with high windows and marble steps. Wing chairs were scattered about. The lone clerk stood behind a high counter, eyeing Jimmy with suspicion.

For the next half hour Jimmy paced the floor, sat in a chair, thumbed through a magazine, and kept an eye on the door. He expected to see cops come for him but as each minute passed he thought that the chances of this happening were diminishing. He wondered how far it was to the bus station. He didn't even know how to get from here to there. He could always catch a cab. As soon as Nicky came back, he'd go. Catch a bus. Get out of San Francisco. Besides, he needed to put as much space as possible between himself and a certain mountain.

"What you doing waitin' down here, man?"

Lost in thought, Jimmy hadn't seen Nicky come in and started.

"Where's Ramona?"

Before Jimmy could answer, Nicky said, "Oh hell! She must have had some stuff I didn't know about."

Jimmy turned at the sound of a scream and saw a woman falling down the stairs, bouncing, trying to catch herself and unable to do so. The screams continued until she hit the lobby floor with a loud thud. She lay as still as death. Blood trickled from her mouth. She wasn't dead. Her moans told them she was still alive.

It was Ramona. The two men rushed over. Nicky glanced at the clerk and then at his chick. He couldn't take a chance on being caught, not with what he had in his pocket. "I gotta get out of here," he said, and ran for the door.

Jimmy fought the impulse to run after Nicky and instead knelt beside Ramona. She opened her glassy eyes. She was stoned. He called to the hotel clerk, "I'll take care of her."

The clerk picked up the phone. "Don't move her. Help's on the way."

"I know CPR. I can handle her."

"No, leave her where she is."

Even as he knelt beside Ramona, Jimmy knew he should have left with Nicky. This chick was bad news. All chicks had been bad news for him since he'd left San Francisco with Jay. He should go, but he couldn't. Not until help came.

Instead of ambulance attendants, it was three policemen who ran through the door. Jimmy trembled as his heart quickened. He stood as they approached. They were three grim and determined men, but a smile touched the face of the man in front as he studied Jimmy.

"Look what we got us, men," he said. "I'd say the old boy at the store gave a good description."

Jimmy's hands were wrenched behind his back and handcuffs were snapped on his wrists. As he was shoved out the door, an ambulance pulled up to the curb.

10

COLD TRAIL

As the days passed, the sheriff's officers began to build a profile of the victim, Glenn True Clark. Although it was obvious that Mr. Clark was less than a model member of society, he had come to a violent end while in their jurisdiction. They were nearly as anxious to catch his killer as they would have been had Glenn True been an upstanding, conscientious citizen who obeyed most of the rules most of the time.

Nearly.

Although he certainly had no way of knowing of the eventual consequences, Clark had, during his brief encounter with Terrie, cast out remarks that were as red as any red herring. These she passed on to the investigators as though they were the gospel according to Miss Tidwell, causing the officers to turn down many a wrong trail with little to show for their efforts.

Even though Terrie was sometimes inconsistent and often stated she was not one hundred percent sure of what she was telling them, hers was the only story in town. All they had to go on other than her testimony were a few fingerprints. And a horseshoe cleat footprint.

Terrie repeatedly claimed the three of them had been riding in a Pontiac, a metallic, bluish green Bonneville. She insisted that the make and model came from Glenn; the color was what she had seen. Of course, the only time she'd had the opportunity to see the exterior was during the late evening or night. Jimmy, who rode in the car all the way to the top of Dead Indian Mountain and then drove it back to San Francisco, always believed the car was white or off-white. If so, they more than likely had been in the Oldsmobile Clark had stolen in Salt Lake City. Unfortunately, Jimmy wasn't there to tell this to the officers while they were attempting to put it all together.

As a result of Terrie's statement, the lawmen were looking for a Pontiac with an opening under the glove compartment, one that would accommodate an air-conditioning unit. The 1960 Oldsmobile Jimmy claims they were in had no such compartment.

Although Terrie thought the speedometer was round instead of rectangular, the instrument in the 1960 Oldsmobile was rectangular with rounded corners. Terrie had other, more pressing matters on her mind that night than remembering the shape and size of speedometers.

Avery Clark, Glenn's brother, informed Pauling and Armand that, when Glenn visited them on the Sunday before his death, he was driving a 1960 Oldsmobile with a Utah license plate. He described it as being cream or off-white in color.

As they continued the investigation, the detectives learned that Glenn had been writing hot checks and using credit cards to finance his escapades through most of the western states, British Columbia, and Mexico. They suspected he had also used burglaries and armed robberies to finance his travels.

The lawmen eventually concluded that Glenn had been driving an Oldsmobile when visiting his brother. When the credit card invoices started coming in, they discovered that on the day of his death Glenn used an Atlantic Richfield credit card in Sacramento and at that time the car he was driving had a Utah tag. Later that day, as the car moved upstate, a purchase was made at Yreka and the license was a California number: IVX-380.

It was subsequently learned that this California tag had been stolen from an abandoned car near Glenn's brother's house, the same brother Glenn had visited only days before his death. The question now became, what car had displayed the tag?

Since they believed Terrie's description, the lawmen assumed Glenn had ditched the 1960 Oldsmobile after leaving San Francisco and stolen the Pontiac she described, even though they never knew who had owned the car or when Glenn had made the swap. If they disputed Terrie on this, then they would be forced to consider that the little lady might not be too accurate in her assessment of other matters.

This they didn't want to consider since it would have led down even murkier paths.

Ironically, the next time California license number IVX-380 came to light it was in Los Angeles on a 1965 two-door white Pontiac. However, this particular vehicle had been stolen from San Francisco on September 18 by three people who were out looking for a good time. At the time it was taken, the Pontiac had been legally tagged with California plates: CZP-908. So then, how did tag number IVX-380 end up on the stolen car, since this was nearly three weeks after Jimmy had ditched the Oldsmobile in San Francisco?

They learned that a San Francisco cop had, on September 16, ticketed an Oldsmobile with license number IVX-380 for parking the wrong way on a one-way street. The cops eventually decided that the three thieves must have stolen the Pontiac and then stole the tag off the Oldsmobile sometime after it had been abandoned by Jimmy. By the time this assumption had been made, the three car thieves had been released and were long gone.

Back in Jackson County, they knew Glenn had switched

tags somewhere between Sacramento and Yreka. They knew that this same tag, IVX-380, was later found on the same Oldsmobile in San Francisco that they eventually concluded had previously been stolen by Glenn True Clark. That being so, whoever murdered Mr. Clark must have returned to San Francisco, removed the tag from the Pontiac and put it back onto the Oldsmobile. It didn't make sense, but if it was a Pontiac Terrie had been riding in, there didn't seem to be any other explanation.

Some time later, the detectives learned that the Oldsmobile had been towed away as an abandoned vehicle. It had been registered to a man in Salt Lake City.

Captain Barnard of the Salt Lake City Sheriff's Office was called upon to help. He reported back that this vehicle had been stolen from Harry's Auto Sales in Salt Lake City on Friday, August 25 of this year. Clark was a suspect. He would investigate and report back.

Another suspect who came to light that neither Glenn nor Terrie was responsible for in any way was Seth Davis. Pauling pursued Seth on a hunch after observing suspicious actions on the man's part.

On Saturday, September 2, 1967, the day after Jimmy had been arrested in San Francisco for armed robbery, Pauling was entering the courthouse and saw a man walk past who fit the description of their suspect.

Then, about one-thirty that afternoon, Pauling saw the same man walking in the opposite direction. He pulled him in for questioning. The suspect had a scar on his forehead and a series of scars on his left hand, quite similar to those Terrie had described on the head and hands of the killer, old John. Seth was advised of his rights and from the beginning was uncooperative in answering questions. He stated that he was employed at the Pacific Plywood Mill. Pauling knew that Clark had once been employed at this same mill.

It was learned that Davis was on federal parole for having violated the Dyer Act. He had also had run-ins with the Medford Police Department and so they provided a photograph. Terrie studied it and said she didn't think he was their man.

When Davis came up with an alibi for the night of the killing, they turned their attention elsewhere.

From the information passed on to them by Terrie, they felt that Glenn and his killer got together the day before the old man met his death, somewhere between San Francisco and Sacramento. However, they also believed that the two had traveled together previously.

Pauling learned from Avery and Sara Clark that Glenn had last been at their home on the Sunday morning before his demise. He claimed to have gotten into town about one in the morning and didn't come by then because he didn't want to awaken them. When he arrived at their home, his whiskers had been scraped off and he smelled of aftershave so they assumed that he had spent the night at a local motel.

The last time Glenn had phoned them before this was August 12. He said then that he was in Salt Lake City and that his Pontiac station wagon had broken down, adding that he and a friend wanted to report to a job the following Monday morning. To be able to do this, he was in need of fifty dollars. They refused to send the money.

Both Avery and Sara thought that on this occasion Glenn's parents had sent him a hundred dollars.

Before this, on July 23, Glenn had come to visit and had stayed until the thirty-first of the month. At the time, he had been driving a Pontiac station wagon with a Utah plate. During his visit, he would be gone all day, supposedly looking for work in the area.

Avery quoted Glenn as having said that he often picked up hitchhikers, but he wasn't afraid since he always carried a revolver.

Pauling also learned that Avery and Glenn's brother, Robert, was serving a long term for being a habitual criminal. So Glenn wasn't the only black sheep in the family.

As Pauling searched for more information about the dead man, he found Glenn had two teenage daughters who lived with his first wife, Mandy Wade, in Wyoming.

Relations were thought to be cordial enough since Glenn had visiting privileges.

It was Gayle, Glenn's last wife, who feared for her life. Glenn had been looking for her and had told several people that when he found her he would hurt her bad.

Pauling phoned Harold R. Prentiss who was with the Consolidated Company. Prentiss verified Clark had a credit card that was in the hands of collectors.

On September 6 Pauling and Armand packaged the evidence for shipment to the FBI. Boxes containing items that might have the killer's fingerprints had been built by Pauling. In a letter that accompanied the shipment, fingerprint cards of Terrie Trina Tidwell and Glenn True Clark were sent. They told the federal investigators any prints they might find other than these should be treated as belonging to the suspect.

In addition to the prints, the two detectives sent two wine bottles, one from the roadside park and one from the scene of the crime.

Four empty beer cans were in the shipment as well as one that was still full. What Jimmy wouldn't have given for that one on his ride back to San Francisco.

The bullet taken from Glenn Clark's head was also in the package.

As well as casts of the suspect's shoe print and heel print.

And Clark's clothing, including his jockey shorts.

Even the clothes Terrie wore the night of the killing were to be analyzed: jeans, tent dress, and panties. The FBI was asked to examine these for any semen specimen or any sign of sexual assault.

Finally, the detectives wanted the federal officers to examine Clark's clothing for menstrual blood or any other evidence of sexual intercourse with the witness, Terrie Trina Tidwell.

Meanwhile, Pauling and Armand continued their own information gathering. They widened their contacts, interviewing more of Glenn's family. It was becoming increasingly clear that Glenn Clark was a braggart who delighted in showing off around others, especially young women.

More information about the victim soon came in from many sources. From Maria, Avery's daughter, Pauling learned that Glenn had kept a rifle wired to the underframe of his car. Glenn had shown Maria his revolver, which she described as a .38 with the barrel sawed short. He confided in her that he had a friend in Salt Lake City who operated a small garage and specialized in transmission work. This friend had a pet coyote and a boat on a nearby lake.

Around Salt Lake City Glenn was known as "Okie" Clark.

He had even shown Maria his Texaco credit card and she had seen the hand-carved wallet made by his younger brother in prison.

One of the family members said that Glenn always wore a gold wedding band. Others said that he had a yellow gold watch.

The ring was gone, as was the watch and wallet. If this wasn't murder one, then the category simply didn't exist, the lawmen concluded.

At Pauling's request, credit card slips signed by Glenn True Clark were received from both Consolidated and Texaco. These covered all of June and July 1967. During this time he had made purchases in California, Oregon, Utah, Nevada, Idaho, and British Columbia. So far as anyone knew, he hadn't worked a day at any of these places.

On September 7 Brent Porter of the county sheriff's office hit the road to see what he could dig up. He started with Terrie's ex-roommates, Carol and Alicia. They had been her schoolmates as well, and both stated that Terrie seemed to be a nice girl. Neither of them had seen nor heard from her since the day she'd left for the weekend with her boyfriend, Greg.

Porter found Greg Winslow. Yeah, he'd taken Terrie to Eugene. No, there was nothing permanent in their relationship. They were just good friends. "Hey, man, this is the sixties," Greg observed.

The next day Porter found Marion Parker, Glenn's sister, who was visiting in Portland. He learned that Glenn had usually dropped by their parents' home every two weeks or so to pick up his mail. Marion had seen a bill he had from Texaco for two thousand dollars. Glenn told his sister that he was living and traveling on credit cards.

Since Glenn's death, she had received a phone call from a loan company in Denver concerning two thousand dollars he had borrowed.

She said also that Glenn had, ever since getting out of the service, carried a handgun. He always wore a gold watch with a gold expansion band. Because of a 10 percent service-related disability, he received a small pension from the government every month.

On September 9 Porter traveled to Wyoming to talk with Glenn's first wife and mother of his two daughters, ages fifteen and seventeen. Their mother said that Glenn had been real good about sending child support money until the first of the year.

Around Thanksgiving, Glenn had dropped by and the two girls had been allowed to shoot both his revolver and rifle. They didn't know the caliber of either.

They did know that he always wore a gold watch with a gold expansion band.

The last time their daddy had come by was in March or early May. He'd come from the Elks Club and was staggering drunk. They had fed him dinner and he'd taken off, telling them he was heading for Alaska.

On the eleventh of September Pauling and Armand went to visit again with Avery and Sara. In the exact spot on the gravel drive where Glenn had stood on his last visit Avery had found a piece of credit card some one-inch square. Yes, Glenn had pulled his wallet out. All that was visible on the small chunk of card was the name "John" followed by the numbers "423."

The card was from Bank of America. The lawmen checked with an official from that organization but learned little. They simply didn't have enough information to identify the card holder.

Any man with a criminal record and first name John became a prime suspect.

On the fourteenth of that month the two lawmen took a break to attend the Western States Burglary Investigators' Conference at Las Vegas.

There they were assured of the cooperation of other lawmen in their search for the killer of Glenn True Clark.

Captain Pete Barnard of the Salt Lake City Sheriff's Department phoned Detective Armand and reported the results of his investigation. Glenn's younger brother was serving a long term in the Utah State Penitentiary for second degree burglary and also for being a habitual criminal. The billfold he had made for his brother was approximately four years old, hand-carved brown leather, flower design, lined with pigskin, well-worn lacing, and the name "Glenn" on front.

Also, on February 9, 1967 Glenn had been caught trying to smuggle narcotics into the prison. He was accompanied by someone named Bill Colt.

Clark's friend in the transmission shop was named Marvin Rogers.

On October 17 an article in the *Medford Mail Tribune* newspaper spiked Sergeant Armand's interest. Vernon Mathis, twenty-one years of age and from Phoenix, Arizona, had been arrested in Roswell, New Mexico, on murder charges. Mr. Mathis was accused of the fatal shooting of Frank Jimenez in the chest on the first day of that month. The article indicated that the two men had apparently been involved in an argument prior to the shooting. Sounded somewhat similar to a killing on Dead Indian Mountain.

On October 24 a reply to an inquiry was received from the chief of police in Roswell, New Mexico. Once the detectives read that Mathis was a black man, Armand eliminated him from their list of suspects. Terrie couldn't be that mistaken.

Thanksgiving came and went, as did Christmas and the New Year. For the most part, the attention of the lawmen was turning in other directions. Crime does not take a holiday, and it seemed as though they always had new cases to work.

By now, instead of actively searching, they were either waiting for new leads to come to them or working what little research they did in with other duties.

Another lead came to them in January. At Salem, Oregon, a confidential informant by the name of Walker told Sergeant Serota that a friend, whose name he would not reveal, had told reporters that John Camp had killed Glenn Clark. Camp had told the friend that he thought the police were after him and he was hiding out at his parents' home. Camp's parents were supposedly living in a trailer park outside of Huntsville, California. Mr. Walker told Sergeant Serota he personally knew both John Camp and Glenn Clark and knew the two of them had left Mattson, Washington, together prior to the murder.

Walker described Camp as thirty-five years of age, six feet two inches tall, one hundred sixty-five pounds, blond hair, balding, and blue eyes. He didn't come close to fitting Terrie's description in any aspect.

Another suspect out the window.

On March 8 Seuter was dispatched to Riverside, California, to pick up a prisoner. It was decided that while he was in the general area anyway, he would stop and visit with Terrie once more.

He phoned Lee Tidwell, Terri's stepmother, and was advised to report to her husband's office the next afternoon. Seuter did so and Mr. Tidwell escorted him out to his house where Seuter could have a supervised interview with Terrie. Now that they were on Tidwell's turf, he set the ground rules.

In answer to Seuter's questions, Terrie said, "Since so much time has passed, the details are no longer clear in my mind. But I'm sure that if I ever saw John again I would be able to make a positive identification.

"As for the car, my recollection is still vague. I am positive that it was definitely blue in color. Officers here have taken me out to various places in an attempt to identify a similar automobile. I don't know why, but there was a Pontiac that looked as close as any.

"No, nothing out of the ordinary has happened that would indicate that John knew where to find me. I have not received any anonymous phone calls nor have I seen any individual that reminded me of John in any way.

"I am not certain about Seattle. These things do stand out in my mind though. I do definitely remember them talking about a new Riviera that John totaled about two weeks prior to that time. They did say that they had been traveling together since the death of John's fiancée some three months earlier. And they both said that they had been mining in Idaho.

"I can really recall nothing further to tell you concerning Slim or Virginia or the ranch or the singing group."

When Terrie was shown photographs of various suspects, she felt that John Allen Rawls of Crescent City, California, bore a strong resemblance to the man she'd known as John.

To Seuter, it sounded promising.

At that time Terrie was attending classes at a local college and working part-time as a stenographer in a law firm.

After returning home, Seuter learned that John Rawls had been arrested earlier that month in Portland, Oregon, for larceny in connection with an automobile. His California rap sheet warned that on all previous arrests Rawls had a record of violence.

The month of May came and they hadn't heard another word from Captain Barnard of Salt Lake City. Since Detective Mike McLaughlin of the Medford Police Department was scheduled to attend a Western United States Crime Conference in Salt Lake City, he was asked to check out a few leads for the sheriff's office.

When Mike checked with Captain Barnard, it seemed

as though not too much promising investigating had been done. All the captain had to offer was a manila folder full of notes. While sorting through these, Barnard discovered a piece of paper with the names "J.O. Smith" and "Sherry Rose" written on it. No, Barnard didn't recall the significance of these names but he gave them to McLaughlin, feeling as though they must in some way or another pertain to the case.

They did. These were names that had been found on scraps of paper in a 1960 Oldsmobile found abandoned in the Portrero Heights district of San Francisco. Pauling had requested that Barnard check them out, but the other man had either forgotten or not gotten around to it.

McLaughlin checked the phone directory and found that there was a Dr. J.O. Smith in Salt Lake City. He felt it was possible that this physician had treated Clark for his gonorrhea.

There had been a phone number on a scrap of paper found in the car with the name "Thomas" scribbled on it. McLaughlin called the number, but, without tipping his hand, was unable to get the identity of the person who answered.

McLaughlin asked about Bill Colt. Barnard said they had been unable to identify the suspect. McLaughlin went directly to the sheriff's office files and had the clerks pull the information on any person with a similar name. The first name up was William Marvin Cattsman.

William Marvin had been arrested a couple of times and had spent time in prison.

Next was Robert Gary Robertson, alias Gary Roberts. He was a convicted felon who was in the Salt Lake City area just before Clark's murder. He was five-feet, nine-inches tall and weighed a hundred and thirty pounds. Brown hair and eyes. Possibly part Indian.

The lawman was ecstatic. It all fit. It did until a fingerprint comparison was made. Start over.

McLaughlin learned that Barnard had, shortly after the murder, made contact with an elderly male clerk at the

New York Hotel in Salt Lake City. This clerk said Clark had registered a short time before his murder and that he was with a dark-complexioned fellow. Since Barnard had not made any follow-up, McLaughlin insisted that they do so now.

"Can't do," Barnard said. "The hotel has changed hands and the clerk is long gone."

McLaughlin went to the hotel and asked the pony-tailed clerk to see the registry for last August. "Sorry, sir, the former owners must have it."

After contacting them, McLaughlin was told that the registry slips were in a locked drawer of an old desk. "You want to force it open? Help yourself."

The name Glenn True Clark did not appear on any slip. It was assumed that he had used an alias.

McLaughlin turned his attention to the auto theft. The Oldsmobile had been stolen from Harry's Auto Sales on August 24. The suspect was a white male who fit Clark's description and, when shown a photo, the salesman said it sure did look like the person he'd seen.

On the day before the car was stolen, a man thought to be Clark drove it out of the lot and kept it for some time. Long enough that he could have had a spare key or two made. The next night the car disappeared.

While he was in the city, McLaughlin checked out the owner at his garage. Supposedly the owner was out of town, but McLaughlin thought that his garage looked like a shady operation.

McLaughlin returned to Medford with a wealth of information. It certainly wasn't his fault that most of it led up false trails.

Although time was marching its inexorable march, Armand wasn't giving up.

In the April issue of *True Detective*, on sale at news-stands for fifty cents a copy, the lead article was titled, "Oregon's No. 1 Murder Mystery." It was written by Bill Gould, a reporter for the *Medford Mall Tribune*.

This article skipped over many of the details, such as

Terrie's earlier statement that she had been picked up at a coffee shop in Medford instead of while hitchhiking. Gould depicted Terrie as seeing the killing and opined that she was held in protective custody after witnessing an execution-type, cold-blooded murder. This scenario seemed to be the general consensus of the lawmen at the time.

A photo of the investigating lawmen appeared in the article as well as one of the Oldsmobile after it had been stripped down and impounded. The only photo lacking was one of John.

As a result of this article, letters began arriving naming suspects. Many of these were from ex-wives. They all stipulated they were, of course, only seeking justice.

In March of 1970 Detective Armand accompanied Pauling to Crescent City where Carl Seuter, the officer who'd been first on the killing scene, was working as a deputy sheriff.

They just couldn't turn loose of John Allen Rawls as a suspect in the killing. Even though the FBI had said that Rawls's fingerprints didn't match, everything else did, and so they decided to pursue their alleged culprit a little further.

On the evening of March 4 they interviewed Susan Martha Berk, who had once been married to Rawls. During that time, he had been living in Portland, sometimes with his wife and at other times with a girlfriend.

Susan Martha told them that Rawls once had both a Buick Riviera and a girlfriend named Kathy. Quite possibly the Riviera had been involved in Kathy's death. She also thought that her ex had once given a pair of white go-go boots to a girlfriend who had been a dancer in a nightclub.

The lawmen were elated once again. If all this was true, they had enough evidence to justify hanging old John Allen from the nearest tree. Perhaps, just perhaps, the fingerprint comparison had been flawed.

The next morning they interviewed their suspect. He wasn't hard to find. At that moment he was a prisoner in the Del Norte County Jail. Within moments, their bubble burst.

He had not given any girlfriend a pair of go-go boots, white or any other color. He had never had a car that had been involved in a fatal accident. He had once had part ownership in a Buick Riviera, but the other owners had taken off for parts unknown quite some time ago.

Detectives in Portland had questioned his ex about these same points and so she had knowledge of them all. After the Jackson County detectives traced his whereabouts, they decided it would have been physically impossible for him to have been with Glenn on the night he was killed.

Rawls agreed to take a polygraph test, but none was given.

For a while the investigation cooled. So much time had passed since Clark's death that new clues were becoming scarce. And then, in December, the investigators got a new lead on an old suspect.

The Jackson County Sheriff's Office was once more advised by the Crescent City Sheriff's Office that they had a person of Indian descent in custody who had previously been a suspect in the homicide of Glenn True Clark. John Allen Rawls had done it again, gone and gotten himself arrested.

The reason the Oregon lawmen were notified was traced to Reba Louise Rawls, who was John's most recent ex-wife. "I was only wanting to do my duty and help the lawmen in anyway I could," she said.

Detective Andrew Matson and now Undersheriff Armand drove to Crescent City. Before talking to John Allen, they talked to Reba.

According to Reba, John had said he had wasted two people near Medford and would also kill her. She said Rawls had a .357 Magnum that had probably been used in the crime in Oregon.

Armed with this information, they went to the jail to visit with their suspect. When they asked him to take a polygraph test, he agreed to do so.

During the polygraph, John Allen answered all their

questions willingly and showed no signs of deception. The test indicated that Reba had led them down another false trail. Once they were through, the lawmen positively concluded that John Allen Rawls had absolutely nothing to do with the death of Glenn True Clark. They hoped he would have the good sense to stay away from his ex-wife.

11

CRAZY MAN

If you're a seasoned cop and forced to take a ton of crap from a horde of invaders to your city, as was happening in San Francisco in the 1960s and 70s, it is necessary to let off a little steam now and then. When the policemen arrested Jimmy, they had no idea that they had a killer on their hands. However, he was of the right age and temperament to be a hippie. To them he was just another wacko who was messing up their city.

Jimmy was dragged out of the hotel lobby while a crowd of spectators looked on. A tight grip on his wounded arm caused him to yelp. No one bothered to ask why or say, "I'm sorry." There were three officers in escort. To Jimmy they were the most intimidating men he had seen in some time. But he tried to act confident. Don't give the cops a lot of crap, but don't let on that you're afraid either, was his deep belief. You do, and you're dead meat.

Outside, he was thrown against the patrol car, head slammed against the hood, while a massive forearm pressed against his neck. He was searched amidst a steady peal of laughter. Cop humor. And, just for good measure, when his head turned, a night stick whacked him above his right eye. The crowd fell silent as blood trickled.

After Jimmy was forced into the back seat of the cruiser and sprinted off to jail, the cops didn't tell him what they knew from having talked with the grocer. Nor did they kill him with kindness. When you got the chance, you gave your licks. These men were experienced. They were accustomed to tossing homesteaders out of houses and experienced at throwing hippies into the slammer for shoplifting as well as running them in for sniffing, ingesting or mainlining illegal drugs or other mind-bending substances.

Although Jimmy didn't have the beard or long hair favored by many of the cops' adversaries, he was of the correct age, and he sure as hell had pulled an armed robbery. There was no doubt about who had robbed the store. This was an opportunity to get in a few licks for law and order. So what that their prisoner had a cut above one eye and a few new bruises. When they reached the station, nobody asked how it had happened, nor did anyone bother to call in the watchdogs from the Civil Liberties Union. This was just one more weirdo off their streets.

Jimmy was photographed and fingerprinted. There was the inevitable lineup and a positive identification by the grocer.

Held in jail, Jimmy knew never to ask for help. The arm bleeds, who cares? Doctor it yourself. Run cold water over the wound, pack it in toilet paper and hope it heals. When it fills with pus, keep repeating the treatment. Nobody gives a damn. If you die, they'll carry you out and drop you into a hole. The death certificate will swear to natural causes being the culprit. His injury could have been caused by the arresting cops. Best not to ask.

When interviewed from her hospital bed, Ramona cut a deal. Did a little plea bargaining on her own. Let me go free, and I'll finger the real culprit. Yeah, old Jimmy engineered the job. Hadn't been for him, it would never have happened. The rest of us were kind of forced to go along.

A quick guilty verdict and sentencing. Swift justice. One year in San Bruno, and, if you're a good boy, two years suspended. Jimmy knew enough about jails and the American way to know that you did your time, kept your mouth shut, and didn't take any crap off anybody.

No money, no friends. There were only two ways to survive and Jimmy wasn't about to bend over and grab his ankles. If the soap fell to the floor, he let someone else take the risk of reaching for it. He did work for other prisoners in exchange for cigarettes and a candy bar now and then. He knew he had been set up and there wasn't a damned thing he could do about it other than try and stay out of trouble and do his time.

Jimmy was allowed to make a collect telephone call. He needed help from the one person he could always count on. When Yuma answered, he said, "Hi, Mom. Guess where I'm at?"

His mother did what she could. She sent a ten-dollar money order each month. Enough to buy roll-your-own. Bull Durham, maybe, along with a pack or two of cigarette papers and a little candy.

Jimmy was high up, on the sixth floor. His cell number was six, south, eight. Eighth cell on the south wing, sixth floor. He thought it sounded like a hospital address.

His home was a small enclosure. He lived alone, surrounded by neighbors. Each morning the inmates were let out to scrub the floors in the corridor. Then it was clean your toilet bowl and make certain that your home was spotless. Once this was done, Jimmy was free to do whatever he wanted to do. Within limits, of course. Once these limits were applied, there wasn't a heck of a lot left to do.

To his surprise, the wounded arm eventually healed.

Whether or not Jay was dead, Jimmy didn't know. Nor did he have any idea of what had happened to Terrie. He often thought of how she had run from him when much, perhaps even most, of what he had done had been for her benefit. She had reacted as though it was him and not Jay who was wanting to first rape her and then bury her where she could never be found. This scenario played over and over in his mind, but he could never understand the reason behind Terrie's actions.

Nights he lay awake, reliving that trip up the mountain and then the wild ride down. He heard the guns, saw Jay fall and reach for his weapon, and then heard that second shot erupting from his own revolver. The man had to be dead, had to be. Somewhere in northern California. In a state where they still had the death penalty. Where you're led into a chamber—forced in more than likely—strapped into a chair strong enough to hold Superman, and then choke to death on the poison gas.

Jimmy had read stories.

No, he didn't consider it murder, but the cops would. Jimmy had run and now he'd committed armed robbery. That would be damning. Too late. Too late. God in heaven, what can I do?

These thoughts took predominance over the sounds of his new environment. There was never a quiet moment in jail, not even in the middle of the night. All of his worldly possessions were gone forever. This was the least of his worries. There weren't that many possessions anyway.

Each day he spent in jail Jimmy expected to be asked about what had happened on that desolate mountain. He was certain that he had left fingerprints at the scene. He hadn't stuck around to remove the evidence.

To his surprise, not only did nobody talk to him about that night, but he didn't hear one word from another source. He had no access to newspapers that covered the story, nor to any radio or television news broadcast. So, of course, he did not see the article published in *True Detective* while he was a guest of the state. He wasn't aware of its existence until some twenty years after the piece was published.

Jimmy began to practice denial. So long as no one told him differently, Jay was very much alive. Probably still stealing cars and picking up young chicks on the highway. Passing on his crud without giving it a second thought.

Perhaps burying a young lady now and then in some dark and lonely place.

If Jimmy had killed him, maybe he had saved some chick's life. Maybe he had saved Terrie's. Nothing to do now but keep his mouth shut and hope for the best.

Just do your time, Jimmy kept telling himself. Don't make any waves. Be inconspicuous and they won't even know you're in here.

This policy worked until a homosexual propositioned Jimmy, wanting new meat. After beating the shit out of what he considered to be a pervert, Jimmy was forced to spend ten days in solitary. Then he had his jail term extended by ninety days. In his judgment, the satisfaction he gained was worth every extra minute. With time off for good behavior, even with the extended sentence, Jimmy would get out in just over nine months. The authorities needed his bunk.

Finally, the day of Jimmy's release arrived. Another year of his young life was gone forever.

Jimmy didn't dare drift back to his old hangouts. Nor was he going to ask for his old job back. Too many questions would be asked. Perhaps too many questions had already been asked.

As for Nicky and Ramona, Jimmy was afraid of what he might do if he would run into them. There wasn't much chance of that though. They didn't stay long in one place. For sure they would be gone from the hotel by then.

Within a few weeks of his release, Jimmy was tired of sleeping outdoors and working odd jobs for food and smokes and an occasional beer. A condition placed upon Jimmy when released was that he check with his parole officer at regular intervals. Mr. Mathison had his own ideas about folks who committed armed robbery. He viewed them as the scum of the earth.

More than once the old man had said, "You shouldn't be out. If I had my way, you'd still be locked up."

"Man, I didn't do anything that bad to start with."

"Anybody carrying a gun shouldn't be out."

"I don't carry any gun. All I do is work. Make my own living."

"You saying you didn't pull that robbery?"

"I'm not saying anything, except that I'm working any time I can now and minding my own business."

"First chance I get, Taylor, you're going back."

It was time to get out of town. Jimmy was certain that if he made Yuma, he could work with his dad. So he phoned Mr. Mathison and said, "I have a job waiting for me in Arizona."

"You can't leave the state!"

"Mr. Mathison, I sure hope you give me the okay, because I'm gone. Soon as I hang up here, I'm leaving town."

"You'd better not!"

"Well, I'm gone."

"Oh hell, go on. Get out of California. I just hope you never come back."

You can go home again, but seldom is it the same. Jimmy rode a freight part of the way and then hitchhiked to Yuma with a little better luck than had Terrie Tidwell in her attempt at begging a free ride. It had been almost two years since he had seen his parents.

Chris Taylor hadn't heard one word from or about her middle son since he'd told her to stop sending the monthly money orders to San Bruno Prison. When she heard the knock, she expected to see some salesman standing there. She pushed open the screen door. Jimmy stepped through and gave her a big hug. "Good to see you, Mom."

If there was one person in this world Jimmy could count on, it had to be his mother. Chris had often acted as buffer between her sons and their father or any other problem the boys had.

Now Chris pushed her middle son to arms' length and studied his face. "You don't look well," was her conclusion. "You're too pale; you haven't been eating too good."

"I'll be all right. All I need is a little home cooking. Dad at work?"

Chris led the way into the kitchen and sat Jimmy at the large table. She sat across from him and said, "He's at work. We've all been wondering what's been happening to you. Your sisters keep asking, 'Where's Duke?' I didn't tell them that you was in jail in California. And I've been wondering where you've been since they let you out."

"I've just been getting on."

The two of them spent the next half hour sipping iced tea and making small talk. Chris brought her son up to date on other family members. Jimmy was thankful that his baby sisters were doing okay. He had little to say about where he'd been or what he'd been doing since the last time he'd been home on leave. It was enough that his mom knew that he had been in jail. He wasn't about to tell her what had happened on that mountain.

"My husband wouldn't go fishing with his sons," Chris later said. "He wouldn't go hunting with them. He wouldn't do anything. His music and his drinking and his going off—one time he went to the store to get cigarettes and he didn't come back for three months. I swear to God. I couldn't believe it. And here I'm stuck over there in Tennessee with six kids. Went off and got him a job. I didn't hear from him during that time. Not one word. Didn't know whether he was alive or dead, or what.

"His mother used to go out on the porch, and I'd cry myself sick all the time. I knew I could go back to my mother. And finally I did. I went to work and then he— he had been down in Florida. He'd met up with another adventuresome somebody, you know, and he went off with him."

Jimmy's younger sisters returned and they had a happy reunion. But then Andrew came home from work and the mood became wary, suspicious. Jimmy's dad, Andrew, greeted him with, "So you decided to come home, did you?"

Jimmy had never had the relationship with his father he'd enjoyed with his mother. None of the kids did. Andrew Taylor had his own idea of what life should be. For him there had been a time when he was more interested in playing music with a band than he had been in raising a family. Chris had the kids: she could raise them. All that was in the past, but kids remember. Even when they're grown up. Andrew's rambling days were over. Now he was as steady as they come. However, the damage had been done.

The old man looked at his son, nodded, and went to the bathroom to wash up for dinner. Not until the food was on the table and Andrew had taken his place at the head did the others sit down. It had been this way since Jimmy's earliest memory.

Jimmy knew he had to walk softly around his dad. Still, he wanted to spend a little time home with his mom while he decided what to do next. After dinner, Jimmy asked, "I was wondering if I could work with you for a while, Dad?"

Andrew looked up. "You'll have to work harder than you're used to working," he said. "You ready to do that?"

"I expected to."

The days fell into a somewhat boring pattern. Jimmy worked with his dad, painting houses inside and out. The hours were long and the pay meager. Andrew didn't believe in cutting his kids any slack. In fact, they had to work harder than anyone else and often for less money.

The nightmares wouldn't leave. Although he was back home, Jimmy had frequent flashbacks to that night on the mountain. Chris would hear him cry out during the night and know that some terrible memory was eating at her son. She supposed it had something to do with the war and his time in the Navy.

Within weeks, Jimmy knew he had to move on. Search. Go where he could find peace and forget what had happened. So one day he told his mom, "I'm sorry. I have to go."

She sighed. "Where to, Son?"

"I don't know. Maybe Los Angeles."

The next morning he began hitchhiking. Jimmy had saved his money, and so no longer had to worry about where his next meal was coming from. And he was a hard worker, so, if there was any work to be had, Jimmy could usually find it.

For several months he moved about over the western United States, working at whatever he could find. He hitchhiked or rode freights. Home was wherever he was at the moment. His love was whatever girl he might be sleeping with on a given night. Jimmy had no long term goals; just drift wherever the current flowed.

His money ran low, but so long as he had a few dollars he was satisfied. Stop at a grocery, buy bread and bologna, along with a six-pack of whatever beer was the least expensive, and hole up under a bridge. Hopefully, where there was the clean clear water of a flowing river. Try to wash himself clean. Try to forget. Throw down the sleeping bag. Maybe be joined by some chick on the move, and maybe not. No long term relationships. Over and over, he thought of a night on a dark mountain and wondered what had happened to Terrie.

Despite his attempts to forget, the scene kept playing in his mind. Some nights he would awaken, twisted in the sleeping bag, hearing the sounds of two pistols firing simultaneously. And then that final single shot. Jay falling. Seemingly lifeless. Upon awakening, Jimmy would grab his few possessions and run. Often leaving some girl to wonder what was happening. Run until he found another bridge, another six-pack, and then, when the money ran out, he would look for work.

The following spring Jimmy landed the best job he had ever had. Through a friend he was able to start work for a company out of Dallas which contracted for Consolidated Airlines, installing equipment and screens so documents could be reviewed on microfiche. Being a man with a record, it took intercession by his friend, Todd Hayman, to

Jimmy in Navy boot camp in San Diego.
(Photo courtesy of the U.S. Navy)

Jimmy and Jeannie with their children, Andy, Lynn, and Julie, at home in Wichita, Kansas, circa 1981.
(Photo by Mary Christine Taylor)

Jimmy and Jeannie with Andy, Julie, and Jimmy's sister,
Shirley Zink, circa 1989. *(Photo by Lynn Taylor)*

Jimmy at the
Guthrie home,
Christmas 1989.
*(Photo by Jeannie
Taylor)*

Daughter Julie standing beside Jeannie and Jimmy at home in Guthrie, circa 1989. *(Photo by Lynn Taylor)*

Jimmy standing beside his Farm and Home truck. *(Photo courtesy of Inside Edition)*

Jimmy and Jeannie in their kitchen, circa 1998.
(*Photo courtesy of* Inside Edition)

Jimmy and his wife at home, circa 1998. (*Photo courtesy of* Inside Edition)

Jimmy's wife Jeannie at home, circa 1998.
(Photo courtesy of Inside Edition)

Jimmy at home, circa 1998. *(Photo courtesy of* Inside Edition)

Jeannie and Jimmy with Julie, Andy, and Lynn circa 1998.
(Photo by Mary Christine Taylor)

Jeannie, Julie, Lynn, and Jimmy with Andy, taken at home
circa 1998. *(Photo courtesy of* Inside Edition*)*

Jeannie, Julie, Andy, Lynn, and Jimmy in front of their house, circa 1998. *(Photos courtesy of* Inside Edition*)*

Jimmy standing on his front porch, circa 1998.
(Photo courtesy of Inside Edition*)*

Jimmy standing beside his Farm and Home truck.
(Photo courtesy of Inside Edition*)*

vouch for him. They wanted an employee who wasn't afraid of hard work, and Jimmy wasn't. Good salary and all expenses paid. Able to sleep in a hotel now, instead of on the ground. Eat steak every day if he wanted. The company would fly their workers from one city to the other or pay mileage if they preferred to travel by other means. Jimmy preferred to drive. Buy an old car and head down the highway. Had God intended for man to fly, He would have equipped human beings with radar and landing wheels. Jimmy worked first in Salt Lake City, then Denver.

The job, with its constant change of scenery, suited him. Maybe somewhere he would stop having the same nightmare. Maybe.

12

MATING TIME

In any city where Jimmy worked for them, he knew that once the job was complete the company would then move on to another place. This became an accepted way of life. He drifted from town to town with the company as easily as he had done so alone in times past.

When he was moved to Boston for a longer stint, he rented an apartment. He was beginning to tire of stashing his things in lonely hotel rooms, of never having a place of his own.

It was during this time he also reached out for a permanent relationship, but after a fast courtship and an even quicker marriage to a more sophisticated woman who first cheated on him and then left, taking all their furniture, he was once again alone.

Less than a block from his apartment was a bar with pool tables inside. Jimmy loved to shoot pool and drink a few beers. He would come home from work, take a quick shower, and head for recreation. In the back room were booths where sometimes those underage were served drinks. This didn't concern Jimmy. He no longer had to show ID.

He had a friend, James Parker, and they spent many of their off hours together. One Sunday afternoon, engrossed in impressing the girls they were with, they'd been strolling near the freight yard when James dared Jimmy to lie on the railroad ties between the tracks and let a freight pass over him. Raise your head and you're dead. Jimmy threw the dare back and so they had to flip a coin to see who would be the daredevil. This time Jimmy won the toss.

Had James been sober, he would never have pulled such a fool stunt. However, while wearing a bandanna tied around his head and giggling nervously, he dutifully lay himself across the ties as a freight approached, bearing down on him at high speed. As tons of killing steel came roaring within yards of his friend, Jimmy began to sober up. He shouted for James to get off, but it was too late. There was nothing to do but wait. The ladies screamed all the while. The sound of screaming brought back terrible memories. They caught a glimpse now and then of deadly iron only inches from a pale face. Should James panic and raise up, his head would be gone. When the last car had finally passed, Jimmy and the two girls ran over to see if James was still alive. They expected to find a mass of mangled flesh. He sat up intact and said, "Fuck, I won't ever do that again if I live to be a hundred." The bandanna was gone, never to be seen again.

On one of their nights out though, it was not a dare but a look that drew Jimmy to the pretty young girl with dark glistening hair and big brown eyes shooting pool with her sister. He turned to Parker. "You see what I see?" he asked in a hushed voice. And promptly fell in love.

Jimmy walked over to her and said, "Do you shoot pool?"

"Sure," she said. "What about your friend?"

Jimmy shrugged. "James can find somebody to play with."

As the evening went on and on, they realized that each

was reaching out for someone. They seemed to click. Each time one began a sentence, the other nodded as if deep inside they already knew each other. Jimmy soon discovered that Jeannie was a good pool player. He liked her spirit, honesty, and lack of guile. He didn't give any ground but she held her own and won.

Jimmy walked Jeannie home that night. She stopped in front of her grandmother's house.

"This where you live?" Jimmy asked.

She nodded.

"I'll see you again," Jimmy said as he watched her go inside.

After their first evening together, neither could forget about the other.

Late evening, the day after she'd met Jimmy, Jeannie was at her grandmother's, sitting near the street window polishing her nails. When she glanced out, she saw Jimmy on the sidewalk. Her nails unfinished, she raced down the stairs.

"Jim, why did you come back?" she wanted to know.

"To see you."

Jeannie vacillated. She didn't want to become involved, and yet she finally said, "All right. We'll shoot a game of pool."

With all his other problems haunting him, had Jimmy known her troubled background or real age he might have run.

Jeannie was only seventeen but she had neither had a happy childhood nor a carefree adolescence. Her grandmother, Edith McAuley, had fought her alcoholic daughter for custody of Jeannie and her five sisters. One, Barbara, had died of a faulty heart valve not long after they'd moved into their grandmother's house in Jamaica Plain, near Boston. With only government assistance to raise the five remaining children, each day was a challenge.

For Jeannie the goal of that challenge was to find a way to escape. At fifteen and a half and immature, she had married an older man, but it hadn't worked out. Soon Jeannie was back living with her grandmother.

Within a week, Jeannie knew she was falling in love. She invited Jimmy to her grandmother's house. Although Edith was skeptical during his first visit, he soon gained her trust. She saw how happy Jeannie was and hoped the relationship would work. Jeannie's two younger sisters, Carol and Joan, fell madly in love with her new boyfriend.

After this, she would spend some nights in Jimmy's apartment, but Jeannie refused to move in. The next time she left her grandmother's house she was going to be very sure it was for good. She was drawn to Jimmy. But there were things about him that worried her.

"What are you afraid of?" she asked him one morning over coffee. He was dressed to go to work and she was prepared to return to her grandmother's.

"I'm not afraid of anything."

"Last night you were running from something. I don't know what, but you were sitting up and waving your arms and shouting something that I couldn't understand. I thought I heard the names, Terrie and Jay. Who are they?"

Jimmy shivered. Once again, he had relived that dreadful night on some dark mountain. It had been so real, as though they had all been together again and the guns were firing. He had shouted for Terrie, but she never did reappear. How could he ever tell Jeannie? He trusted her, but . . .

"It wasn't anything," he insisted. When Jeannie didn't reply, he added, "There was something that happened a long time ago. It still bothers me. Somebody might have gotten hurt. How bad, I don't know. It could still get me in trouble, I suppose."

Jimmy didn't volunteer any more information and Jeannie did not press for more.

It was a good time for them both. Carol and Joanie, Jeannie's sisters, often visited. During his time off from work, Jimmy often took them all fishing so they could escape from the city and spend some time with nature. Jimmy seemed comfortable with the outdoors. And the girls all felt safe, so long as their "Duke," as they called Jimmy, was around.

They had little but each other, but they needed nothing else. Here they stayed until they left Boston together.

13

DON'T LOOK BACK

In the early autumn of 1972, not long before the Oregon detectives were questioning John Allen Rawls for the last time, Jimmy began worrying that he had stayed in one place too long. He'd been in Boston longer than he'd ever been anywhere in his adult life. Even longer than he had been in San Bruno, and there he'd had no choice other than to stay until he was released. Now there was nothing to prevent his going. Nothing other than the woman he loved. Jeannie had already indicated that she was willing to go when he went.

Saying her goodbyes wasn't as easy as Jeannie had always thought it would be. It was especially difficult to leave her sisters behind. They couldn't believe that she was actually making the break. "You will be back soon," they both said.

"No, I won't be back to live. I want to be with Jimmy."

Her grandmother took her aside and said, "Jim's a good man, Jeannie. I'm happy for you both. I do hate to see you go so far away though."

Jeannie hugged the only mother she had known. "I love him and wherever he goes I want to be."

Edith knew that was true. "God bless and keep you, child."

And with those words still ringing in her mind, Jeannie left the boundaries of Boston for the first time in her young life. With Jim, she climbed aboard a bus that would take them not only across the city but out of the metropolitan area, out of the state, and across a country that was as foreign to her as the moon. Most of what she knew of the world she had read in newspapers or magazines or seen on television. But she was young and eager and in love.

Had Jimmy been traveling alone, he would have been willing to hitchhike, but Jeannie refused to even discuss the possibility of traveling in this manner.

It was November when they rolled into New York City, into the Port Authority Terminal, and laid over until they caught the bus that would take them down through Pennsylvania and eventually to Tennessee. Had Jimmy not been with her, Jeannie would have been even more frightened of some unsavory characters who prowled the terminal. She didn't relax again until they were in Pennsylvania.

Jimmy wanted to visit Tennessee. His roots were there. His parents had migrated to Arizona when he was a small boy.

"I want to stop first and see Uncle Charlie and Aunt Lucy," Jim said. "You're going to like them, Jeannie."

Jeannie didn't care where they stopped. At first she couldn't see enough. Looking out the bus window, she attempted to absorb every sight her eyes beheld, from Amish farmers to coal mines to mountains to cornfields. "I can't believe it, Jim. I really can't believe it."

To Jimmy they were merely moving from one point in the country to another, farther and farther from that dark mountain.

By the time they reached Ridgetop, Tennessee, Jeannie was homesick. She resisted telling Jim that what she wanted now was a bus ticket back to Boston. For both of them to head for her comfort zone, back to their apartment.

Jim could find work in Boston as well as anywhere else. He had before. She had hoped they would travel together for a while, then settle somewhere and have kids. They could raise a family in Boston, couldn't they?

But she didn't tell him this. They got off the bus in the little town of Ridgetop and caught a ride out to the Charlie and Lucy Taylor home, suitcases and all. Here they were greeted by coon hounds in a pen, greeted with a bark foreign to Jeannie. Almost frightening. Their low mournful bark reminded her of ghosts and graveyards.

They arrived at a house that showed signs of having been built onto and yet was small and in need of a paint job. The metal roof was rusty. A barrel was under an eave, placed in a strategic location to catch water from the roof when it rained. A round and rusty tub that had once been galvanized hung on a nail outside the house. The weather was turning cold. Overhead, geese honked and winged their way south, sounding with an urgency, as though realizing they had waited longer than they should have waited to begin their journey to their winter home.

The barking of the dogs brought an old couple who were lean and lanky hobbling out of the house. Jim made the introductions. To Jeannie, they were ancient but very cordial. Aunt Lucy was wearing a long dress and apron and had biscuit flour on her hands. Uncle Charlie was wearing old overalls and dragging one leg.

After "Howdies" and hugs, Uncle Charlie said, "Come in, come in. Make yourselves at home. Me and you sure know how to pick the pretty girls, Jim Boy."

"We sure do, Uncle Charlie. Jeannie picked me as much as I picked her. Aunt Lucy, you making a pan of biscuits for me?"

"Just like I knowed you was coming. I'll mix another batch and there'll be plenty. Charlie just come in. He's been out makin' wood."

Jeannie had never thought it would be possible to enter the home of strangers and yet feel as though she belonged. However, within minutes of their arrival, she felt as though she had known Jim's aunt and uncle forever. At the insistence of the older folks, their suitcases were carried into the only bedroom. "We don't want to take your bed," Jimmy insisted.

"We're gonna sleep in the front room by the fire," Charlie said. "You and your wife can have the bedroom. Weather turns cold, you'll be a wishing you had our bed for sure."

Jeannie caught sight of the room where they would sleep. Cracks in the outside walls were large enough for snakes to slither through. It would be no barrier at all when a cold wind howled.

Light bulbs hung on cords from the ceilings. The floors were bare wood, smooth from wear. Heating and cooking were done with cut wood. Water was carried in from an outdoor pump, carried in two buckets that were placed on a washstand. A long-handled dipper was in one of the buckets. There was no telephone in the house. Jeannie wondered at all she was seeing. It was too much to absorb quickly.

Eventually she had to ask Jim, "Where's the bathroom?" She'd not seen anything that resembled one.

Jim couldn't help the smile that spread his face. "Come on and I'll show you."

He led her outdoors, out behind the pen of black and tan hounds, who pressed against the fence begging for notice. They strolled together until they reached a small weathered building with a sloped roof and sagging door. "Here's your bathroom," Jimmy said. "Don't try to flush it, because you can't."

"Jim, tell me you're joking."

"I'm not joking. You gotta go, that's the only place around here to do it unless you want to go off behind a tree."

Jimmy shivered as he recalled Jay suggesting that he go behind a tree as they rode up that damned mountain. When they'd stopped in the clearing on that dreadful night, he had done just that while Terrie had remained in the car— gone behind a tree.

Jeannie felt a sudden longing for Boston. She couldn't believe such archaic conditions still existed in this country. Reluctantly she opened the door and was met with such an offensive odor that she quickly closed it and stepped back, almost gagging. "I can't go in there, Jim."

"Jeannie, I've told you what your choices are. That's all I can tell you. You gotta go, right here's the only place. Either that or go out in the woods and sit on a fallen log."

Jeannie tried to hold her breath. She went inside, closed the door and sat her bare bottom on the smooth wood, where many bare bottoms had sat over countless years.

Jimmy was waiting at the pen of hounds, getting acquainted. "See, that wasn't bad, was it?"

She looked at him anxiously. "Jim, we can't stay. Let's go somewhere where they have a bathroom."

"Jeannie, we can't go now. What would Aunt Lucy and Uncle Charlie think? You wantin' to hurt their feelings?"

At the moment, Jeannie didn't care.

After they'd eaten and it was scarcely dark, the old couple decided it was time for bed. "We'll talk more tomorrow," Lucy said. "Right now we're plumb tuckered out."

Jeannie couldn't recall ever having gone to bed this early. Real country life was a lot different from what they showed on television.

Jeannie didn't visit the outhouse again before bedtime and this proved to be a mistake. She awoke during the night, dreading what she must do. She shook Jim.

"What's the problem?" he asked.

"I got to go to the bathroom."

"There's a flashlight on the stand. Go on."

"Jim, I'm not going out there by myself. Not at night!"

Jimmy sighed and rolled his feet to the floor. "I'll go with you this time. You gotta get used to going by yourself though. Either that or use a thunder jug."

Jeannie was afraid to even ask for the definition of a thunder jug.

They put coats on and slipped out the back door. As they passed the dog pen, the hounds stirred but did not bark. Near the outhouse, Jeannie heard scurrying sounds. The light from the flashlight Jim held caught red eyes that showed for a moment and then quickly disappeared. She stopped abruptly and grasped Jim's arm. "What's that?"

"Nothing to be afraid of. Just outhouse rats. You don't bother them and they won't bother you."

Jeannie wanted to scream. She wanted to go home. She knew though that she would have to go alone and, despite all the problems, she wasn't willing to go without Jimmy.

The only work Jim could find was in Nashville. Not having a car, he had to hitchhike back and forth the fifty miles each way. He worked at making shower stalls, laying on the insulation.

On weekdays, Jeannie was left alone with the old couple. Alone with them and the pen of hounds and the outhouse rats. Having little to do, each day was hours longer than any normal day should be. There was a black-and-white television set in the house, but Lucy watched only religious shows. When they were over, she switched off the set. "Need to give it a rest," she told Jeannie.

Jeannie pulled on a sweater and walked the narrow, rutted road with trees on either side, wondering if someone was going to run out of the woods and grab her. Drag her off into the dark void and do terrible things. The days passed. Once in a while, she visited a store in the small town and bought a Coke. Had a bus come by during one of her trips, she would have been tempted to hop on.

Jim came home in the evenings tired and covered with insulation. Jeannie's chore was to stop him on the porch and sweep him clean before he went inside. Even then he had to take a primitive bath and change clothes. Each day, Jeannie said, "Let's get out of here, Jim. I can't live like this."

"Don't you like Aunt Lucy and Uncle Charlie?"

"I like them, Jim. They're wonderful people. If you want me to, I'll even say I love them. I just don't like the way they live."

Their baths were taken in the galvanized tub hanging on the outside of the house. Before taking a bath, it was necessary to bring the tub into the kitchen, heat water in pans on top of the wood stove, and pour it into the tub until only a few inches were covered. Then, hoping others respected her privacy, Jeannie would fold herself inside and bathe to the extent possible.

One Friday Uncle Charlie insisted on taking Jimmy coon hunting. After three consecutive nights of it, Jeannie issued an ultimatum. This time she meant every word. "Either you get me away from here, or I'll get me away from here. I can't take this any longer, Jim."

Jimmy knew when Jeannie had reached her limit.

They rented a furnished apartment in Greenbrier. Jim found work with a company that made heels and soles for shoes and boots. Jeannie discovered that she was pregnant. Though she felt it was too soon, she was excited with the prospect of being a mother. She would be a far better parent than her own mother had been. More like her grandmother. Jeannie took seriously the responsibility.

Soon after Christmas, when Jeannie told Jim he was going to be a daddy, she added, "I don't want to have my baby here. I want to go back to Boston, Jim."

"Sure, Babe. We've been in this place too long anyway. I don't like the winters back there, but if that's what you want, we'll go."

They packed their suitcases. Jeannie took their luggage on a bus while Jim hitchhiked. Even though she'd had to change buses and had suffered through layovers, she couldn't believe that she beat Jimmy to her grandmother's house by four hours.

They rented a small apartment near Jeannie's family, but, unknown to her, Jimmy was worried about staying in one place too long. Through correspondence with members of his family, he knew about a job in California. "I'm going, Babe."

"Don't you want to be here when your baby is born, Jim?"

His face clouded over. "Jeannie." For a moment he wanted to confess, tell her about his demons, but looking at her, happy and expecting their baby, he stopped. "I'll be back before then. When the weather gets warm, look for me, but I have to go now. Why don't you move in with your grandmother?"

Jim left Boston early one morning with a few dollars in his pocket and a pack on his back. First he hitched his way south, away from the cold. With his experience and road savvy, he could choose his route as well as though he had been driving.

Jimmy's job in California was making Pepsi bottles. When Jeannie could no longer stand to be separated, she flew out and they had a joyful reunion. On May 31 their daughter was born. Edith Lynn was named after Jeannie's maternal grandmother. Jeannie was content. Although they were a full continent away from her family, she was anxious to build a life of her own. If Jim was satisfied with living here, this is where they would make their home.

But, as each day passed, she could see Jim growing increasingly nervous. His eyes darted here and here, and he jumped at sudden noises. "Why are you so nervous?" she continually asked.

He never answered. Jim was having nightmares. Scenes from a dark night on a desolate mountain kept gnawing at him. He wanted to tell Jeannie of his horrible experience. She was his wife now: she had a right to know. He'd tried to but just couldn't. Maybe she would even tell the cops. He vacillated back and forth, telling himself over and over that Jeannie had a right to know. A man shouldn't keep major secrets from his wife. But what would he tell her? "I shot a man," or, "I killed a man"? What if she felt as though this act was so terrible that she left him? Or, would she be angry that he had waited all this time to tell? She was everything to him. He had nothing else. He just couldn't take the chance.

"It's nothing, Babe," he said.

Jimmy bought an old Chevrolet panel truck. It had no frills. No heater or air-conditioner, no radio. Not even a gas gauge that worked. He began equipping it for the road. He put a mattress in the back, a small crib for Edith Lynn behind the passenger seat. Late that summer of 1973 Jim came home from work and announced, "I quit."

"What ?"

"I quit my job."

"Why ?"

"We're leaving. We been here too long."

Jeannie didn't argue. She had been hoping they would move closer to Boston. "Where do you want to go?"

"Let's go back to Tennessee. See what we can find there."

Two mornings later, they loaded what possessions they had in their old Chevy panel truck. Food was in a cardboard box and portable ice chest. The mattress was on the floor. They pulled out, mother, father, and baby.

They headed for Yuma where Jeannie met Jimmy's folks for the first time, and the grandparents were introduced to Edith Lynn. Chris thought the baby was surely the grandest creature in God's world, while Andrew seemed to hardly know what to make of it all.

"You planning to live around here?" Andrew asked. Jimmy noticed a change in his dad. He was more tolerant now. Maybe he was finally accepting his son as an adult.

"No, Dad, we're on our way to Tennessee. Probably stop and see Uncle Charlie and Aunt Lucy again."

"Give them our love," Chris said. "There's times when I wish we had never left there. Had to for my lungs' sake though."

"Sure, Mom."

They only stayed a few days, long enough for Jimmy to put shocks on their old Chevy. Although this was supposed to help the ride, Jeannie could feel little difference.

While in Yuma, at Jimmy's insistence, they adopted a dog, a large German Shepherd who'd been a police animal, by the name of Major. Although Jeannie was apprehensive because of the baby, she soon discovered that Major was very protective and loyal. Not only would he not allow anyone near Lynn, but he protected the truck as well.

When they arrived back in Tennessee, they found that Charlie and Lucy had moved to Greenbrier, into a small house with a bathroom inside. Gone were the pen of coon hounds and the outhouse rats. The only place for visitors to sleep was in a small room tucked into one corner of the attic. They accepted this space gratefully but knew the house was really only big enough for two.

Within weeks, Jimmy and Jeannie moved out and into a rented mobile home. Even before they were settled, Jimmy was anxious to leave.

"Where do you want to go now?" Jeannie asked.

"I don't know. Anywhere."

"We have a baby now, Jim."

His face darkened. He looked away self-consciously. "Aw hell, Babe, babies travel too."

They made another trip to Boston. Jeannie was able to visit her sisters Carol and Joan and bring them up to date on her travels. Duke took them all fishing. They loved the baby.

"I named her after you, Grandma," Jeannie said one afternoon when alone with her grandmother. They were sitting at the table and Edith was holding her namesake.

"I'm happy about that," Edith said.

"There's something I've been wanting to say to you."

"What's that?"

"When I was growing up, I gave you too much trouble. I don't know how you stood having me around."

Edith shrugged and smiled at Lynn. "All kids give their families trouble."

"I just want you to know I'm sorry," Jeannie said.

Edith patted the baby. "I hope your children are perfect like you. I just hope your kid never gives you trouble when she gets older. Probably will though. Kids usually do. It's part of growing up and you love them anyway. Just like I did."

This response reinforced Jeannie's belief that her grandmother was a remarkable woman.

From Boston they moved back to Tennessee where Jim went to work for his Uncle Harold who was doing heavy construction. Julie was born in Memphis on August 8, 1975.

For the next ten years the Taylor family were often nomads, seldom staying long in one place. For some of those years, Boston was their home base but Jimmy was not content to settle anywhere. There were times when he would leave Jeannie and the kids and hit the road alone, though he always stayed in touch and sent back money regularly.

For Jeannie it was becoming harder. She enjoyed traveling and seeing new places but she thought of Boston as home. And her kid sisters were just crazy about Jimmy. They saw in him the father they had never known. He was their protector. Nobody dared mess with them so long as Duke was around. Besides always being ready to listen to their problems, he would take them fishing. Away from the apartment and the noisy streets and out into the peace and quiet of woods and lakes. But even they knew that sooner or later he would pack up and move on. Leave and then come back. For whatever reason, Jimmy could not stay long in one place. Jeannie would usually return first and then Jimmy would not be far behind.

While he knew Jeannie preferred living in Boston, Jimmy didn't. For a while they made their home in Wichita. His brother Ronnie and Ronnie's wife, Sandy, were living there. They'd bought furniture and were living in a rented house when Andy was born in November of 1978. Jimmy worked for Vulcan Material Company. Not long after this, they sold everything and lived once again in Boston.

During another stay in Wichita, Jimmy worked for a company, building and erecting large signs for along the roadways or to place in front of businesses. Both jobs paid good wages, but after a while Jimmy felt the ghosts within him stirring. He had to move on.

Jeannie became an expert at buying and selling used furniture. One late winter day when they decided to leave Wichita, she sold all they could not haul to a neighbor across the street. They loaded the kids and what possessions remained into their little car and left the city, going to they knew not where.

Before they were out of the city limits, Jimmy had a change of mind. "Let's stay in Wichita," he said.

Jeannie sighed. "I wish you'd make up your mind."

But he had been thinking perhaps this once when he'd thought that he was being chased by the past he'd responded to a false alarm. They returned to the same house, made do for the night, and the following day Jeannie bought everything back from her neighbor. The lady was very understanding. She was certain that before much time had passed Jimmy would once more be plagued with the wandering fever. She would wait until then to get the furniture.

While in Wichita, Jeannie's youngest sister, Joanie, flew in from Boston to visit. For her it was the experience of a lifetime. She saw what a contrast the much newer city was from old Boston, the only home she'd ever known. When Duke took them fishing in nearby lakes, Joanie fell in love with the place. It was all so peaceful. She could be content to remain here forever.

Her most memorable experience on this trip though was when Jimmy took the whole family to a rodeo and provided them with front row seats. Joanie couldn't get over the huge animals and the men who dared to ride such creatures.

She was sitting on the edge of her seat when a bull got loose on the far side of the arena. Suddenly, it charged directly at them, as though meaning to maim the Boston visitor who scrambled up two rows before the crash. But then the city girl was in for a surprise.

When it came time to ride the bulls for the $1500 first prize, one of the riders was Duke. He had paid his entry fee of twenty-five dollars, and for the first time ever climbed aboard one of the massive beasts. Cowboys helped wrap the thong around his hand and offered encouragement.

Jimmy could feel the power beneath him as though he was astride a great machine ready to explode. When the gate opened, the bull knew the routine.

He leaped into the arena, twisted and arched his back, all in one motion. Jimmy went flying through the air, twisted, and landed on his backside. Luckily, with only his pride hurt, he ended his bull-riding career.

A sad moment in Jeannie's life came while living in Wichita. She received a call from her sister Carol informing her that their grandmother, Edith, had passed away. "Babe, do you want to go?" Jimmy asked.

Dismayed, she shook her head. "I can't." Finances were extremely tight for the Taylor family and she could not afford to return to Boston for the funeral. Jeannie cried, and so did Jimmy.

In between moves, the Taylor family took short trips together. Jeannie and Jimmy wanted the children to see the country and to bond together as a family. They might eat a meal in a restaurant or buy some food from a grocery store. Often they slept in their car or outside in a tent, depending on the weather. Usually these trips were during the summer. When it was time for school to start, the family settled down again. Although he never once during this time used a fake name or a fake social security card, it was as though Jimmy knew he had to stay on the move. Running, always running. From what, he would never say.

As long as they could all be together, Jeannie went along. Jimmy was her stability. But the kids were getting bigger and each move was becoming more of a hassle. It was difficult but, if he didn't want to stay, she didn't.

And Jimmy showed no sign of settling down. Back in Boston for a few months one April, he loaded the five of them into a mustard colored Ford Maverick. They left with no particular destination in mind. However, Jeannie sensed that Jimmy was about to move again.

He drove out of the city with an urgency. They traveled to the Texas coast and stopped a few days at Galveston and then visited Houston. The next day they were in

Arkansas and two days after that, Tennessee. They stopped and visited friends, stayed the night and left early the next morning. After stopping for a brief visit with other friends, they hit the highway again in late afternoon. It was after sundown when they crossed the Mississippi River at Memphis. Heading west.

Heading nowhere.

14

HOME AT LAST

During the early night of April 16, 1985 those who drove on Interstate 40 in eastern Arkansas experienced one of those rare moments of light traffic on a major highway. The Taylor family had passed through Memphis and crossed the Mississippi. Jimmy was pushing the compact car to its limit. All of their worldly possessions were either packed in the small trunk or piled around them in the car. The kids were huddled together in the back seat. They were asleep, weary of traveling, and certain that a tiring trip lay ahead.

Jeannie, too, felt tired. When was Jimmy going to be ready to settle down, she wondered. These past few months had been such a mixed-up time. After their longest stay ever in any town, they had run from Wichita again. "We'll move back to Boston," Jim had said. She had known before they'd ever returned to her home city that Jim wouldn't stay. She ached for a place where they could put down their roots and she could say to Jim, This is it. We're not moving again.

She sighed heavily watching her husband's face in the semi-darkness. On this night Jim seemed once again to be absorbed in thoughts of his own. Jeannie checked on the children who, though it was only eight o'clock, were exhausted from the travel and frightened by the uncertainty that surrounded their parents. She turned the radio on and spun the dial, searching for comforting music, something to help her and them relax. Suddenly, Jeannie became aware of headlights coming up fast from behind, reflecting off the rearview mirror. Jeannie realized with sudden horror that something was wrong. She looked at Jimmy and saw pure helplessness. Even fear.

He managed to say, "Oh my God!" and that was all. The next thing Jeannie knew was the sound of crashing impact from behind. They had been hit. Their little car jumped across the grassy median, spinning slightly until their lights illuminated an eighteen wheeler. Her body flew up. Her head bumped the car top.

She saw the big truck stop and a black man hurrying towards them, trapped in the sweep of their headlights. A white man with blond hair climbed dazedly out of the driver's side of the truck.

"Is anybody hurt?" the black man asked.

"I bumped my head," Jeannie said. "I don't know about the kids."

Oh God, were they even alive? Jeannie was afraid to look.

"Kids? Wait here. We gotta move the truck and then I'll see if we can help."

He hurried back, spoke to the driver, and both men climbed inside. A few seconds later smoke poured from the stack pipes as the truck roared away on the interstate, headed west, away from the damaged Maverick, away from the woman with a bump on her head and away from children whose exact number and condition remained unknown to the two outlaws.

Jeannie was too stunned by the actions of the truckers to move. How could any person leave the scene of an accident? Jim was getting out. He showed no sign of injury. Jeannie turned and anxiously asked, "Are you kids hurt?"

"No," said Lynn and Andy.

"I bumped my head, but I'm all right," Julie said.

Jeannie breathed a sigh of relief.

Jim came back and poked his head through the open door. "Anybody hurt?" he asked.

"We're all right," Jeannie said.

"I can't believe those guys left us here. We're smashed in pretty bad in the back. I'll have to tie the trunk shut. Lid won't catch but I think I can still drive. The car being loaded like it is probably saved us. Looks like the driver was swerving at the last minute, trying to miss us, but couldn't do it. We can thank God that nobody was badly hurt."

Jeannie did silently thank God that her kids were not seriously injured, but she thought perhaps God was sending them a message. The Taylor family had been on the road too long. It was time to find a home and settle down. Somehow she would have to convince Jim. He would have to quit running.

They headed west in the crippled car. Jimmy drove slowly and on the shoulder until he was convinced that the steering had not been adversely affected. They had no insurance and no money to have the vehicle repaired. And they had three kids in the back seat who were lucky to be alive. They all were lucky.

On this dark night traffic was now flowing freely in both directions. They had seemed to be alone on the highway before the accident, but now they were surrounded by cars, trucks, and buses. People were all around them. And yet the Taylor family had never felt more alone than at this moment, as they huddled together and contemplated how near they had come to death's door.

At their first stop Jim was advised to call the law. And so he made a phone call to the Arkansas Highway Patrol. A trooper came who was polite and thorough, and a report was made out. With what the lawman had to go on, little could be done.

Jimmy stopped at every truck stop to look for the truck that had bashed them and run. People didn't do things like that. Not truck drivers. He knew. He'd driven a truck. Not across country, but he knew about truck drivers. He couldn't imagine one of them ramming into a car and driving off. It damned sure took a certain kind of lowlife to do that.

The only description he had to offer those who would listen was one young black man and one middle-aged white man with blond hair.

Before daylight Jimmy brought two cups of coffee to the car along with a bag of doughnuts. "Compliments of the guys inside," he said to Jeannie. "Good people. They're ashamed of what happened. Kind of a black spot on truck drivers. Hadn't oughta be though since it wasn't their fault."

"Don't wake the kids just yet," Jeannie said. "We'll save some doughnuts." They sipped coffee, munched doughnuts and counted their blessings. They wondered what this new day would bring.

The crash had been a catalyst for Jeannie. She was not only weary but she was sick of traveling, of not having a home to call her own. Never knowing where they would spend the night or where Jimmy would find his next job. They had the children to think of. More of their education had to start coming from schools and less from the hands-on study of geography.

"I can't do this anymore," Jeannie said.

"Do what?"

"Stay on the road. Wondering when the next truck's gonna hit us. We've got to settle down."

"Yeah, I know what you mean, Babe. After what happened, I feel the same way."

"The next place we stop, that's where we have to stay."

"The next place I can get a decent job, that's where we'll stop and stay."

"The kids and I are about through traveling. We don't have much money left, Jim."

"Enough, Babe. Let's catch a few hours sleep before we go."

The sun was well into morning when they used the

bathroom facilities at the truck stop and the kids devoured the leftover doughnuts. Jimmy filled the car with gas and then they drove on, heading west. Late that evening they reached Oklahoma City.

They dipped into their meager funds and rented a motel room. Their supper was hamburgers. A six-pack of beer and a pack of cigarettes for the parents, Cokes and candy for the kids. Jimmy bought a newspaper. They both searched the help wanted ads. Even as desperate as they were, there was little available or the jobs advertised were those for which Jimmy was not qualified. Jeannie knew that he would work at almost anything so long as his wages could support their family.

The next morning they headed west once again, still traveling on 1-40. They pointed their little car towards California. The children in the back seat had recovered from the shock and were boisterous, as kids often are when traveling. Being rear-ended by a truck was becoming something for them to joke about.

Not for their parents. For them the event had been traumatic. Before this they had told themselves what the kids missed in school they had to a certain extent made up for in personal experiences. But now Jeannie, at least, had come to believe the dangers outweighed any benefits. Jeannie knew this had to be their last trip across the country. She had no idea where they would land. This she would leave to Jim, so long as he decided soon. As the family provider, he had the right to choose. Of course, she retained the veto power.

They stopped at Amarillo around noon and bought bread and bologna. Jeannie made sandwiches that they washed down with Cokes. And then they moved on.

Forty miles or so farther on, Jimmy suddenly pulled off the road.

Jeannie asked, "What's wrong?"

Jimmy drummed his fingers on the steering wheel. "How'd you like Oklahoma City?" he asked.

"It was okay."

The kids started to voice their opinions and were told to keep quiet. They didn't have a vote in these weighty matters.

"Why don't we make our home there?" Jimmy asked. "I don't know what we'll do, but we'll find something."

Jeannie felt relieved. Her feelings towards Oklahoma City were neutral. It wasn't as cold as Boston or as dry as Los Angeles. If that's where Jim wanted to stop, it was fine with her. Just so they got off the road before they were hit by another truck. They couldn't count on their luck holding another time. "Okay by me," she said.

That evening they checked back into the same motel. For days Jimmy searched for work. As always he was willing to do anything, paint stripes on roads, haul lumber. He wasn't proud, as long as it was honest work. And then they faced the harsh fact that their money would soon run out.

For the first time since they'd been together, Jimmy and Jeannie had to accept charity. They were forced to move from the motel to the Ark, a family shelter sponsored by the Catholic Church for those who were down on their luck. They told themselves it was a roof over their heads and food to eat. And you didn't have to be of the Catholic faith to receive these benefits.

Of necessity, the Ark had to limit the stay of any family. It was not intended to become a permanent residence but instead was a temporary shelter until tenants could get on their feet. Thirty days was the limit. Then, whether or not their finances said they were able to do so, it would be necessary to move on and make room for another family. Almost always there were those waiting to get in.

Space at the Ark was limited. The Taylors, as did each of the families, had a room of their own. This is where Jeannie, Jimmy, and the children slept or could join together at any time. They were expected to not only keep their quarters clean but help out with the chores, the cooking, and the cleaning of the common rooms. The kids were enrolled in a nearby school but the parents knew that the thirty days would pass in a hurry.

The days fell into a pattern. As the calendar pages

turned, Jeannie began to wonder if there was any way out. Perhaps they should have continued on to California. When they weren't in school, the kids would play with others who lived in the Ark while she worked in the kitchen or helped with the cleaning. Since she always believed in keeping everything squeaky clean, Jeannie loved the work.

Unlike some of the men who seemed content to wait for good fortune to come to them, Jimmy arose early each morning and drove to the Peak-Load employment office. There he took whatever day work he could find. Some days Jimmy worked a full shift but usually only an hour or so on any particular job. He was becoming more and more discouraged.

Help sometimes comes from the most unexpected source. The Ark was receiving donated items for a rummage sale. The proceeds were to be used to help offset expenses. Dana Swalley, a lady who was ebullient and bubbling over with enthusiasm, and never seemed to run down, was the daughter of Joe Reale, owner of Farm & Home Termite & Pest Control. Darla came in early one morning to drop off donations for the sale. She was in a hurry, since she and her dad had another objective that day. They badly needed someone to help them in the business and were visiting the employment agencies in the area.

Jeannie, working in the kitchen at the time, happened to hear Darla say to the person in charge, "My daddy could use some help. The man has to be willing to work hard though if he wants to get ahead."

Jeannie stepped forward and said, "My man is a good worker. He isn't here now. He's either out working or looking for work."

"My daddy has a pest control and termite company, but he only hires someone who's able to work and willing to work hard. We're looking for someone who wants to work his way up."

Jim returned while Darla was still on the premises and came into the kitchen for a word with his wife. Jeannie told him of the opportunity in Darla's father's business that might be available.

"It's very hard work," Darla said. "But if you want the job, call my dad."

"Of course, I'll call him," Jim said. "I don't know how to thank you."

Darla wrote down the phone number. "Be there when he says to. If you're late, you can forget about ever working for my daddy."

Jimmy made the phone call and was told to be at Joe's house at eight the next morning. He was not late; in fact, he was more than an hour early. Joe sized him up and sent him out with Les Swalley, his son-in-law. The reports Joe heard on this new man for the next few days were all good. Although Joe never told Jimmy the job was his, the whole matter sort of evolved. Joe knew he had found a man not afraid of hard labor, a man who was a self starter and one who did not require a boss to watch over him at all times.

"I remember that first morning Jim came," Joe later said. "He had been told to be here at eight, ready to go to work. I looked out not long after six-thirty and there was his car. He was sitting there in that little yellow car with the rear end smashed in and the trunk tied shut. It looked like the devil but all he wanted was to go to work."

Not only was he willing to crawl under houses or do whatever else Joe wanted but Jimmy soon became adept at concocting formulas to wipe out spiders, termites, and all sorts of critters.

The family moved out of the Ark and into an apartment they could call home. Jeannie was almost content. An apartment was not a house, but still it was better than living in their car or hopping from motel to motel. It was now obvious that Jim had a steady job. The work day was often long. When Jeannie would start to complain about his working such late hours, she would recall how it had been when he wasn't working at all. Then she would count their blessings.

Much of Jimmy's work was out of town, north and west

of Oklahoma City. Joe decided it would be better for all concerned if Jimmy lived closer to his work. His son-in-law helped them rent a small but comfortable house. By now Les and Jimmy had taken a liking to one another. Having been born in the same year, they had much in common. Neither knew then how important that relationship would be when disaster struck the Taylor family.

Les, like his wife, Darla, was a bundle of energy. Slender and wiry, he was like an instrument wound too tightly in the morning which won't run down until late at night.

Jim and Les worked well together and shared an avid interest in hunting and fishing. As time went on, they became close friends and Jimmy began to confide in Les.

Once Jimmy even started to relate events that had transpired that dreadful night on the mountain. They were riding in Les's van on their way to a deer hunt when Jim said, "There's something else. I shot a man once. He was trying to kill me. I don't think anything will ever come of it though."

Les waited for Jim to say more, but his friend had said all he was going to say on the subject. Les didn't press him.

For Jeannie their home in Guthrie brought contentment. The house was old, but so long as they paid the rent it was theirs. She began to think about them finally buying their own home. As Jimmy became more and more part of the company, she started to relax and stopped worrying that he would insist on moving on.

That first summer the kids all made new friends and then in the fall they were enrolled in school.

A year after Jimmy began working for Joe, a young man by the name of Matt Swenson was hired. Affable and not afraid of hard work, he was teamed with Jim while Les usually worked alone. A special camaraderie evolved among these three men. If any needed help, on or off the job, the others were willing to pitch in.

After they had been in their house three years, Jeannie was certain that nothing bad would ever happen to them again. In Guthrie Jimmy's only problem had come from an expired inspection sticker on the car. That was all.

Jimmy too seemed content. His nerves had calmed. He no longer seemed to be looking over his shoulder as though running from something. Whatever had been haunting him all these years, Jeannie was certain had disappeared.

Yes, Jeannie decided, the Taylor family finally had things going their way.

The only bad thing that happened during this time was that Jim's father died. Even as Jeannie had not been able to attend her grandmother's funeral, they couldn't afford to make the trip to Arizona. They mourned in silence and prayed for the family. God and church were becoming increasingly important in their lives.

15

ELECTRONIC COP

During the years that the Taylor family stayed on the move hiding from ghosts of the past, it is ironic that no law enforcement officers were actively pursuing them.

In 1987 Detective Jay Armand retired. Twenty years had passed since he had begun the hunt for the elusive John. As time slipped away, he was realistic enough to know that cases as old as that one seldom got solved. Nonetheless, being a first degree murder case, it could not be swept under the rug and forgotten. So long as no state passed a statute of limitations against first degree murder, the case was still technically alive.

The evidence gathered long ago was still in storage. Clothes and photos and autopsy reports and the moulage of a knee print and another of a footprint had all been labeled and kept. There were also grocery bags and fragments of a bullet taken from Glenn's head. And there were eleven fingerprints thought to belong to the suspect: fingerprints that hadn't changed one little bit since being lifted from two beer cans and two bottles that had once held wine.

Since Armand was leaving, Peter Jones—Detective Jonesy, as the nameplate on his desk announced—inherited the file. A tenacious man with an easy sense of humor along with a doggedness that wouldn't allow him to accept defeat graciously, Jones soon began looking for new ways to pursue the old case. He knew if it was to be solved, the solution would come through somehow matching those fingerprints from the scene with those of the killer.

Jones joined the Jackson County Sheriff's Department a year or so after Clark's killing. Until then, he had only been on the fringes of the investigation. Armand's retirement changed this. It needled Jones to think that somewhere out there was a cold-blooded killer who had been flaunting the law for so many years.

Once a year the department reviewed their unsolved crimes. Jones studied the list of known suspects in the killing of Glenn True Clark and eventually discarded them all. Most of these had been hashed and rehashed until nothing new could be turned up. Either they had an adequate alibi or else they had been eliminated by matching their fingerprints with those left at the crime scene.

Fingerprints! He kept coming back to this clue. The killer had left them behind in abundance. If the case was ever to be solved in his lifetime, Jones was convinced that fingerprints were the key to a successful conclusion.

But how? There was no way this side of eternity that he or anyone else could plow through the tens of millions of fingerprints on file with the FBI, or even those retained by the State of Oregon, and hope to make a match.

An answer had to lie somewhere within the electronic age.

Before Armand retired, the two men had discussed the new innovation that would soon be available: the Automatic Fingerprint System. Perhaps that would be what eventually cracked the Clark case, thought the detectives.

When Jones heard that Bart Higgins, a state patrolman, was going to Sacramento for training on California's new Automated Latent Print Computer, a multimillion dollar machine that could scan latent images and make a match if a print was on record, Jones thought it was worth trying. It was reported that the computer could compare prints you loaded into its file with more than three million it had stored, but in all probability the prints of whoever had murdered Glenn True Clark were not among them.

Jones decided to check anyway. A long shot, sure, but it was a card he could play. If their killer had a criminal record in California, his prints should be on file. Perhaps Bart could take a print from the crime scene of 1967 with him.

On April 19, 1988 Detective Peter Jones asked Higgins to assist in obtaining photos of the fingerprints the FBI had developed from evidence the Jackson County Sheriff's Office had submitted on the Glenn True Clark murder in 1967.

On April 22, the same day that Jim and Jeannie were celebrating the ninety-ninth anniversary of the Oklahoma Land Run, Higgins wrote a letter to the FBI requesting photographs and negatives of the prints left at the scene. The FBI promptly sent the requested information. Higgins left for his training carrying the prints. The lawmen were careful not to let their expectations soar too high too soon.

On July 5 Detective Jones returned to his office to find a brief message from Trooper Higgins. After eight minutes search, the computer had been able to do what men had failed to do in all this time. Higgins's message was, "It's a match!"

Jimmy's prints, taken after being captured and charged with armed robbery in 1967 shortly after his trip down the mountain, were of course on file in California. Along with millions of others, they had been fed into the computer. And so the electronic marvel had spewed out the name Jimmy Dale Taylor, along with his social security number.

Jimmy had no way of knowing, but the trap was being set. This was during a summer when both Jimmy and Jeannie thought that their biggest problem was two daughters who were acting like the teenagers they were.

The following day, on July 6, Samuel Crimmins, legal

keeper of the records for the Bureau of Criminal Identification, Department of Justice, State of California, compared Jimmy's fingerprints with those sent by the FBI and declared that their computer had done a fine job and that Jimmy was indeed the culprit. He had left a fingerprint on a wine bottle and this was the one identified.

Jones now had a name and social security number to work with. He had no idea where to locate Taylor.

Bulldog Jones went to work. If Taylor hadn't had the good sense to use a fake social security number, he might be onto him at last. A check was made of Taylor's criminal history, and it was determined that he had been arrested on September 1, 1967 for armed robbery in San Francisco. Clark's car was thought to have been found abandoned in San Francisco about that time.

July the eighth was a busy but productive day for Jones. He contacted Ted Stein of the San Francisco Police Department by phone and asked Mr. Stein to check his files for information on Taylor's arrest in 1967. San Francisco didn't have such records, for they are destroyed after ten years, Detective Jones was told. "However, we do still have a mug shot of Taylor if you want it." Jones wanted it.

The pieces were falling into place. Jones was on a hot trail that was getting hotter. He spoke to Terrie by phone and brought her up to date. He advised Terrie that, if they could locate Taylor, it was possible they might need her help. Although this was surely a situation that Terrie would have rather seen buried and forgotten, she agreed.

That same day Detective Jones used another modern tool that was available to law enforcement. He made a nationwide inquiry on Jimmy's driver's license through the National Law Enforcement Telecommunications System. The results of this inquiry produced a driver's license for a Jimmy D. Taylor in the state of Tennessee which expired on July 18, 1976. Since this license had been out of date for some twelve years, Jones pressed on.

A second response was received from the state of Kansas, showing a driver's license to Jimmy D. Taylor that expired on July 18, 1986. This lead too was eliminated because of the passage of time.

A third response was received from the state of Oklahoma. Bingo! The state had issued a license to Jimmy Dale Taylor in August of 1987. This one had not expired. The license number matched Taylor's social security number. Height and weight were recorded and were near enough to their suspect. According to the record, Taylor had to wear corrective lenses.

Best of all, the Oklahoma license showed an address for Taylor in Guthrie, Oklahoma.

Detective Jones was thorough. He wasn't about to allow this lead to slip away. The following week, on July 11, he sent a letter to the FBI requesting that they compare the fingerprints they had on file from the crime scene to Taylor's prints.

On July 15 Jones received the photograph of Taylor from San Francisco. He compared the photo to the sketch drawn by the police illustrator in 1967. With Terrie's help, he concluded there was a strong resemblance.

The following Monday Jones phoned Paul Homan at the Oklahoma State Bureau of Investigation. He asked Paul to verify that Taylor was still living at the same address in Guthrie.

Homan called back the next morning. "The electric power for the address in Guthrie is indeed being billed to Jimmy Dale Taylor. Also, Mr. Taylor is now working for a pest control company in the area," Jones was told.

The trail was changing from hot to scalding.

The pieces continued to fall into place. Don't rush things, Jones kept telling himself. Be methodical. You're too close now to risk making a mistake.

He had to cover any loose end that might still be out there. Who knows what might have happened to the evidence on a crime this old. San Francisco had destroyed their records after ten years. Did Jackson County still have all the items from the crime scene? He was relieved to find notes and evidence still in the original box that had been returned to them by the FBI.

Yes, all of it was there. From the sack dress Terrie had been wearing to the grungy shorts that had been taken off Clark.

On August 15 the FBI responded. They had ten finger-prints from the scene that matched those of Jimmy Dale Taylor. Nearly twenty-one years after Clark had been killed, Jones was elated. They were closing in on the suspect.

The time had come to get Armand back in on the case. "Is it possible after all these years we're actually going to get our man?" he asked when Jones called him.

On a Tuesday in mid-August the two men drove the road that had been so familiar to Armand those many years back. The drive on Dead Indian Highway was peaceful now, almost pastoral, as was that on Shell Peak Road. A large log had been dragged across the entrance to the logging road. They parked beside it and walked the short distance to where Glenn True Clark had fallen.

This trip wasn't necessary for the capture of Taylor, or even for the trial that would follow. However, Jones wanted to familiarize himself with the scene of the crime. He lis-tened carefully as Armand described the scene at which Glenn True Clark had been shot to death one August night.

All Jones had to do now was convince a grand jury that they should issue an arrest warrant for Taylor.

Another month would pass before this opportunity presented itself. On Thursday, September 22, Peter Jones along with Armand, Bart Higgins, Terrie Tidwell, and David G. Davis, the attorney who had represented Terrie twenty-one years earlier, all testified before a Jackson County Grand Jury. The result was an indictment handed down for the crime of first degree murder on defendant, Jimmy Dale Taylor.

The indictment read:

The above named defendant, on or about the twenty-ninth day of August, 1967, in the County of

Jackson and State of Oregon, then and there being, did unlawfully and purposely and of deliberate and premeditated malice kill Glenn True Clark, a person, by shooting the said Glenn True Clark with a handgun, contrary to the statutes in such cases made and provided, and against the peace and dignity of the State of Oregon.

During her testimony Terrie failed to mention that Clark had been attempting to rape her and that she had screamed for help.

The following day Morgan E. Collins, the district attorney for Jackson County, requested a warrant for the arrest of Jimmy Dale Taylor. Judge Thomas Hodges issued a warrant the same day that read in part:

This is to command you forthwith to arrest the defendant and to bring the defendant before the Honorable Thomas Hodges, Judge of the Circuit Court of the State of Oregon for the County of Jackson, or if he is absent or unable to act, before the nearest or most accessible magistrate in the same county, or if no magistrate is available then deliver the defendant to the custody of the jailer of the County aforesaid.

Security is set in the amount of $ *None*.

No bail.

It was decided that Armand would accompany Jones to Guthrie so that he might be in on the arrest. After all these years in pursuit, this was only appropriate.

Before flying to Oklahoma, Jones made one more trip up the mountain. He drove District Attorney Morgan Collins and Deputy District Attorney Steve Donlevy to the crime scene. Before prosecuting, they wanted to be as familiar with the case as possible.

On September 29 Peter Jones and Jay Armand flew to Oklahoma City. They were one day away from making an arrest.

16

WELCOME TO HELL

As soon as an agent from the Oklahoma State Bureau of Investigation had arrested Jimmy Taylor, Jones from Oregon had handcuffed Jimmy. He was placed in the car. No shootout occurred. Not even a good old fist fight or scuffle. Jimmy was as docile as though he was in Sunday school. Perhaps because he was stunned beyond belief, absolutely shocked, feeling that there was no way in God's world this could be happening.

The lawmen had hoped to transport Jimmy to the jail with little or no commotion. Of course, it doesn't hurt to hope.

Like it or not, his family was traumatized. Jeannie had run out onto the front porch screaming, "What are you doing with my husband? Where are you taking him?"

Jimmy's daughter Julie was close behind her mother, wailing. Once she had realized something terrible was happening, she had charged out of the bedroom where she had been talking teenage talk to her sister to see her father handcuffed. Her first reaction was to feel guilt. Was it because of Lynn and her that the cops were taking

Daddy away? Treating him like a criminal? "You can't do that! We haven't been that bad to take our daddy."

She flung herself at the nearest lawman, fists pounding on his back as she screamed, "Leave my daddy alone! He didn't do nothing!"

Their hopes for an uneventful apprehension of the fugitive were quickly dashed. Now what in the devil could they do? Just try to regain control if possible.

Julie had dropped to the ground hysterical. "Bring my daddy back! He didn't do nothing!"

An agent took Jeannie to the end of the porch and said, "Keep your kids quiet. We don't want anybody getting hurt."

"How can they keep quiet when you've taken their daddy? You've got to tell me what's going on."

"He's under arrest for a murder he committed in the state of Oregon twenty-one years ago."

Disbelief swept over Jeannie. Her mouth flew open. She staggered from the shock. "What did you say?"

"I have nothing to discuss with you." The agent turned away.

"Wait a minute," Jeannie said. "What do you mean, you have nothing to discuss with me? I've been with this man for nineteen, almost twenty, years and he's been good and loyal."

"Then you didn't know him when it happened," the man said and started down the steps. "For your sake, I hope you don't know anything about it."

Neighbors were at their windows now. Those exceptionally brave stepped outdoors for a better view. They saw Jimmy Taylor being herded into the car, Julie being subdued, and Jeannie on the porch locked in a heated discussion with one of the lawmen. Straining, they caught a word now and then, but none had any idea what was being said. They only knew their tranquility had been violated.

Other than when a Santa Fe train rumbled by, First Street was a quiet neighborhood. The road bent to the right less than a block north of the Taylor home so cars that traveled this residential area usually moved at a speed between slow and moderate. There was, of course, the occasional hot-rodder who accepted the challenge of a short strip and sharp turns and gunned his car's motor.

Otherwise, sounds that one might hear were predictable. Could be crows as they cawed their way along the creek, or children as they called out one to another. Listen and you'd hear a car door slamming, people laughing, or a baby crying. A television playing too loud; rock and roll music even louder if teenagers were home alone. Most of the time, peace abounded in Guthrie, Oklahoma, then and now.

But on Friday, September 30, 1988 the street was filled with police cars that had roared in and slammed to a stop. Men were out of their vehicles, guns drawn. Deputy sheriffs' cars blocked the alley. The lawmen had covered all bases in the event their prey had charged out the back door of his home tossing grenades or running like a scared rabbit. When making an arrest on a first degree murder charge, you don't take chances. The fact that the crime, or alleged crime, had occurred twenty-one years ago was of little consequence. Murder is murder.

Inside the house, Lynn sat on her bed, eyes wide, trembling, listening. She couldn't believe this. Was it something she had done that had caused all these men to come after her daddy? There had to be some mistake.

Little Andy ran in from the back yard, away from the lawmen who had congregated there, and sought refuge in the big chair in the living room.

Jeannie stayed on the porch until the last car was out of sight. She felt numb. She had no idea why they had taken Jimmy. All she knew was the lawmen had made a mistake and she had to find out why and what this was all about.

Except for Julie's sobs, a silence settled over the street.

Jeannie stepped off the porch and helped Julie to her feet. "Come on, Honey, let's go in."

Andy still sat in the big chair, gripping the arms tightly. Lynn slipped into the room, fighting back tears. "Mamma, what happened? Why did they take Daddy?"

"I don't know. They arrested him, that's all I know." Jeannie was not about to say anything to her children about any murder charge. That was crazy.

"What did he do?"

"Nothing. I don't know. Listen, you children be quiet now." For the first time in years, Jeannie knew that she had to make decisions alone. She and Jimmy had made most decisions together. She silently prayed: God, if You'll bring him back, I'll be a better wife and a better mother.

Fingers trembling, her eyes so blurred she could scarcely see the phone, Jeannie punched the numbers of Jim's boss, Joe Reale. After she'd rambled on for some two minutes, she said, "Jimmy's been arrested for murder."

Joe, not believing what he was hearing, said, "Wait for me, Jeannie, I'm on my way."

"She was so distraught over the telephone that I didn't even know who was calling," Joe said later to his wife. "All I could hear were the words 'arrest' and 'murder.' Finally she said, 'Jim's been arrested for murder.' There were lots of people who ran through my mind at that time, people who I thought might be capable of doing such a thing. Jimmy wasn't one of them. There had to be some mistake."

Joe ran out of his house in north Oklahoma City and jumped into his company pickup. Close by was his daughter and son-in-law's home. He started to stop for Les, but then remembered that, along with their son, Anthony, Les and Darla were at a high school football game. He stopped in Guthrie to pick up Matt Swenson, who had been working with Jimmy that day. Quickly, he related Jeannie's story.

Matt, too, could not believe what he was hearing. "Not Jimmy."

Some twenty minutes after he'd left home, Joe got to Jeannie's, picked her up, and got back in the car. They headed for the jail.

Matt got out of Joe's pickup and into the company pickup he shared with Jim. He followed them.

* * *

Before Jeannie had hung up from talking with Joe, her neighbor Helene came in, waiting to hug her friend. As soon as she had terminated the call, they embraced and Jeannie told her all she knew, which at this point wasn't a lot. Of course she couldn't tell Helene without the kids hearing.

"I don't know what it's all about," Jeannie said. "That one man said it had something to do with a murder in Oregon twenty-one years ago."

Now the kids knew, too.

Everybody shared her disbelief. They gathered in the living room, the children not wanting to be alone. One parent had been taken without warning; they felt the need to stay near the other.

"What do they mean?" Helene asked.

"I don't know. Jim never said anything about trouble like that. They must have the wrong man. I've lived with him so long; surely I'd know if anything like that had ever happened."

Jeannie knew she had to tell Jim's family. God, but she hated that chore. She dialed a number in Yuma and talked to Jim's recently widowed mother. Chris was shocked by the news. "There has to be some mistake," she insisted.

Jeannie heard Joe's truck pull into the back and asked Helene if she'd care for the kids while she went to check on Jimmy. "We'll lock up and go over to my house," Helene said immediately. Jeannie ran out the back door and climbed into Joe's pickup.

"Get them cuffs off that man. He's not going nowhere."

Meryl Hawkins, the town sheriff, was a tall man with a thunderous voice. He and everyone else knew it was Sheriff Hawkins's jail; so even though the lawmen weren't convinced that Jimmy wouldn't make a run for it, they unlocked the cuffs. Jimmy rubbed his wrists, trying to restore circulation.

"All right if we use your office, Sheriff?" asked Detective Peter Jones.

"Sure. Go ahead."

The Oklahoma State Bureau of Investigation agents had done their job. So had the Guthrie police officers. They began to drift away, as did most of the county deputies. For all practical purposes, Jimmy now belonged to the state of Oregon. There was the matter of extradition still remaining, getting him from here to there, either with his permission or by a court order, but it was inevitable that eventually that's where he would go.

Jones and Armand escorted Jimmy into the sheriff's office and sat him on a chair. The first words Armand spoke to the prisoner were, "Let's see the bottom of your shoes."

"What?"

"You heard me. Let us see the bottom of your shoes."

"What for?"

"Do you wear horseshoe cleats?"

Jimmy lifted both feet so that they could see. He was wearing lace-up work shoes, not anything that would resemble prints left on Dead Indian Mountain, prints of cowboy boots along with horseshoe cleats. "No. Why in the hell are you asking me that?"

"We want to talk to you about a murder that took place near Medford, Oregon over twenty-one years ago," Jones said. "Now, we know you did it, so you're only wasting our time if you claim to be innocent."

Jimmy, who had always thought the mountain was in California, had a momentary feeling of relief.

"That's crazy. I've never been to Oregon in my life. If that's what this is all about, you've got the wrong man."

"Yeah, why did we know you'd say that? Let me tell you something. We've got so many of your fingerprints that there's no chance we've got the wrong man. Fingerprints aren't all we have."

"Is that why you were looking for horseshoe cleats?"

Armand shrugged. "Could be."

"Do you think that whoever did it would be so stupid he'd be wearing the same pair of shoes twenty-one years later? Even if he was, I'd like to find the pair of shoes that would last that long."

"All right," Jones said. "I'm going to ask you again. Have you ever been in the state of Oregon?"

"No. Never."

"Have you ever used the name John?"

"John?" Oh, oh. Beads of perspiration appeared on Jimmy's lip. What was going on here? His earlier feelings of relief quickly vanished. "Hell no!"

"Did you ever know a man by the name of Glenn True Clark?"

Jimmy swallowed hard. "Never heard of him."

"How about the name Jay?"

"I think maybe my brother had a friend by that name."

"I got ten of your fingerprints left at a crime scene in Oregon."

"I can't tell you anything except what I've already told you, and that is I've never been in Oregon in my life. You've got the wrong man. I ain't got time for this. Hell, I got a family out here I gotta take care of."

Jimmy was informed that he did have time. From now until he was found guilty (a mere formality) and his sentence was served, his time belonged exclusively to the state of Oregon.

Jones then showed Jimmy the photo he'd received from the San Francisco Police Department, as well as the composite drawing of the suspect made in 1967. "Do you recognize the man in the photo?" he asked.

Jimmy glanced at it and said, "That's an old photo of me. It hasn't anything to do with what you're asking me about."

When the two detectives were convinced Jimmy wouldn't confess, they took him back to the holding area. As they did so, Joe and Jeannie came in. Matt followed close behind.

When Jeannie started to move towards Jimmy, she was told, "Don't approach the prisoner."

"He's my husband. Don't tell me what to do." By God, she

would approach him or touch him or anything else. Strangers couldn't just jump into your life and tear up your world without a good reason. She took another step forward.

"Hold on, Jeannie," Joe said. He turned to Sheriff Hawkins. "There must be some mistake here. Taylor has worked for me over three years, and I know him well enough to know he's not a murderer."

"They had a warrant for his arrest," Hawkins said. "We'll have to wait and let the law sort it out."

"That'll take time. What would it take to bail him out?"

"No bail." Hawkins shook his head. "He'll have a hearing and the judge will tell us what can and can't be done."

"We want to search his house," Jones interjected.

Hawkins turned to Jimmy. "That's up to you," he said. "You'll have to sign a consent form first. If you don't, they'll have to wait and get a court order if they can."

"I have nothing to hide," Jimmy replied tersely. "There's just one thing you gotta promise me before I do though."

"What's that?"

"I don't want any of my family in the house."

"No problem," Jones said. The lawmen didn't want them in there either.

"I'll personally see to it that your family is not bothered," Sheriff Hawkins said.

His hand shaking, Jimmy signed the form. Matt agreed to accompany the lawmen to the Taylor home. Jeannie handed him the key, then watched helplessly as they took Jimmy away through a steel door. She rushed up to the two Oregon detectives and said in a grieving voice, "Why are you doing this to us?"

"Because he murdered a man," Jones answered sharply. "What can you tell us about it?"

Tears rose to Jearmie's eyes, but she refused to let them fall.

"I can't tell you anything about it. I've been with him for a lot of years. Don't you think I would have known if he had ever killed somebody?"

"This happened before you knew him," Jones said. "It

was over twenty-one years ago. What I want to know is, what has he told you about the crime?"

"He hasn't told me a thing. There was nothing to tell."

Jones's voice tightened. "You trying to tell me you've lived with him that long and don't know nothing about what he did?"

"That's exactly what I'm telling you. The reason I don't is that there's nothing to know."

Jones asked her some more questions, but Jeannie, thoroughly frightened and numb, kept shaking her head, afraid not to answer.

Joe took her arm. "Come on, Jeannie. Let me take you home. There's nothing more we can do here."

"Those lawmen knew all about me and my family," Jeannie said to him later on the drive back to her house. "They knew every place we had ever lived for any length of time as well as where and when all my kids were born. They even had social security numbers for us all. It was scary, like they were going to arrest me and the kids."

Jeannie felt that, other than having a stranger violate her body, perhaps the most humiliating experience she could ever know was finding men she had never seen before that day in her home telling her she had to stay outdoors while they searched through every nook and cranny. Sheriff Hawkins and one of his deputies had accompanied the two Oregon detectives so that they could witness any discovery that might be made. Perhaps also to see that the family wasn't harassed.

Matt sat in his company truck watching helplessly. Helene and the children came, and they all gathered outdoors. And waited.

The men began a systematic search. They poked inside every cabinet, through every drawer. Backs came off stereo speakers. Not even the kids' rooms were sacred. Every little trinket the girls owned was handled or viewed by the lawmen.

Through the open back door, Jeannie could see an officer sitting at her kitchen table looking through every magazine and newspaper that Jimmy, an avid collector of old reading material, had neatly stacked.

Each time one went out or in, Jeannie asked what they were looking for; none of the lawmen would say. Her first thought was that they were looking for a gun or some other weapon that might have been used to kill someone. The man had said "murder." But then she decided that nobody would keep a gun around that long if they had killed somebody with it. She wondered if they were looking for papers. Clippings, stuff like that.

When they had searched everything inside the house, Jeannie was called in. Jones pointed at a spot on the kitchen ceiling and said, "What's that?"

Jeannie wondered if he was joking. When she saw that he wasn't, she said, "I suppose it's where it rained in, don't you?" She was escorted back outdoors while one of the cops climbed into the attic and poked around. Moments later they all left, empty-handed.

The remaining Taylor family went back inside. Backs were still off the stereo speakers. Items were out of drawers. Their poor little house seemed as wounded as they felt. It had been violated. For days, when they touched any personal item, the thought entered their minds that it had recently been in the hands of strangers.

At 8:00 P.M. Pacific Time on the same date that Jimmy was arrested, the Jackson County Sheriff's Department, Medford, Oregon, released a statement to the press. The news was broadcast nationwide. It told how on that date Jimmy Dale Taylor of Guthrie, Oklahoma had been arrested on a Jackson County Circuit Court Warrant charging him with first degree murder for the August 29, 1967 slaying of Glenn True Clark, then forty-six years of age.

The release went on to detail how Taylor had been trapped by a computer that had identified his fingerprints. "Jimmy Dale Taylor is being lodged in the Logan County

Jail while awaiting extradition proceedings to Oregon," the statement read.

It did not tell about how Jeannie and their three kids were left to cope the best they could.

Jimmy found himself thrown into a dungeon-like environment, a large basement room with concrete walls and no windows, where human odors offended the nostrils. Inside this huge concrete tomb were two steel, as the inmates called them, "tanks." Each of these was subdivided into cells. Rusty floors sat above the concrete.

There were steel ceilings as well as steel walls on two sides of each cell, each side having double-deck bunks. An aisle ran down the center of each tank. Walls that faced this aisle, as well as the walls that faced out towards the concrete walkways that surrounded the tanks, were bars. Doors on the ends of each aisle were locked down for the night. Doors to individual cells were left open, other than for an isolation cell or two holding drunks who were in for overnight or someone who had stepped too far out of line. Prisoners were free to wander throughout the concrete tomb during the day and within their tanks during the night.

There were no tables or chairs. Those who were fortunate enough to grab a plate of gruel or the fish sandwich of the day either stood or sat on the floor or on their bunk to eat. They spent their time talking, arguing, shouting, fighting, or maybe playing a card game with a makeshift deck that had been torn out of cardboard or paper. Their card table was the concrete floor. Jimmy's basement home had no windows. Not a hint of natural light found its way inside. Contraband was often smuggled in either by visitors or through the trusties. A man could crawl up on one of the steel tanks with the steel ceilings and smoke a joint until it burned his fingers. Get high. Try to forget where he was. Maybe swing on overhead pipes while he was there.

The only time the dungeon was ever cleaned was when

some of the inmates asked a trusty for a broom, dustpan and mop. These occasions were rare.

When space allowed, the inmates were segregated by choice other than by command. Even so, the blacks migrated to one tank, the whites to the other. So long as there was a numerical balance, this system worked.

Women prisoners were housed beyond a wall, past a locked door that led down a hallway where they could not be seen at any time. Conversation between the sexes was possible by standing in an area near this door and yelling. It happened. This added to the maddening din, sounds that came close to driving a man crazy.

Unless asked, Jimmy stayed alone and kept his counsel.

Jimmy was accepted, even looked up to by some. Convict Code: You kill a man, no big deal. The bastard probably deserved to die. Child molester or a child killer though, you'll be lucky to get out alive, man.

Jimmy observed the antics of the others, the braggarts and the showoffs, the challenges and the fights. Friends and families from the outside brought in cigarettes, more than he could possibly smoke. These he shared freely with the other inmates.

The place was dingy and dirty. Ancient painted pipes ran overhead. For exercise, or just to show off, some inmates would climb atop the steel cages and swing on these. They wore blaze orange coveralls, "carrot suits," the prisoners called them.

These were human beings thrown together in an environment that brought out their base behavior, their animal emotions. There were no security cameras. Guards seldom entered the dungeon area other than to take a head count. Let the beasts fight it out among themselves and settle their own differences was their philosophy.

Jeannie came every visiting day. She and Jimmy talked on telephones as they stared wistfully at each other through little glass windows. So near, and yet they could not touch. Believing their calls were surely monitored, Jeannie held intimate written messages near the glass for Jimmy to read instead of speaking the words. Jimmy's brother and his wife came down from Wichita. The preacher came when he could. So did Joe, Les, and Matt. They all asked what they could do.

Jimmy's reply was, "Get me the hell out of here!"

They were all helpless to do so.

A court lawyer had been appointed. He, too, seemed inert.

As the days began to melt one into another, Jimmy's assessment of his new environment as hell was only reinforced. He was lonely, despondent, and fast losing hope.

Mostly though he felt lonely. It was the reality of never being alone which got to him. Jimmy was a man who enjoyed moments of privacy. It would be a long time before he would have another moment when he would feel as though he was truly alone. His world had shrunk. Still, he felt a responsibility for his family that he knew he could not fulfill, might never again be able to fulfill, and this deepened his moroseness.

Despite his predicament, Jimmy had respect for Sheriff Hawkins and his deputies. He was never mistreated by any of them. He knew they did what they could with what they had. They didn't believe in pampering criminals, but they were not sadists either.

Jimmy's arrest made the news nationwide. The Associated Press reported that a fugitive hunted for twenty-one years was caught in eight minutes by computer technology. In Guthrie where he lived his arrest was hot news and not only the local newspapers but word of mouth spread the story. Those who knew him and heard what had happened couldn't believe the stories. Not Jimmy! There was no doubt that they had arrested the wrong man. You hear about it happening all the time.

Those who didn't know Jimmy supposed that what they heard and read was bound to be the gospel truth. After all, fingerprints had been left at the crime scene and, from what was being said, they matched Jimmy's. And the Oregon officials called it murder. Would they send officers halfway across the continent to make an arrest unless they were sure?

In one paper, an official from Logan County was quoted as saying, "Since Oregon didn't have a death penalty at the time of the crime, he is only facing life imprisonment."

Only! This pronouncement brought a further shiver of fear to Jeannie when she read it. They couldn't execute Jimmy, but they could ruin all their lives.

In the *Daily Oklahoman* the following Tuesday Jimmy's arrest hit the front page. On Wednesday the papers reported that bond had been set at one million dollars. This was done on Monday, October 3 in the courtroom of Harold Morgan, Jr. Jimmy requested a court appointed attorney. Making bond was out of the question and there was very little any attorney could do since the warrant came from Oregon. His next appearance was set for October 14. For Jimmy all that remained to connect him with the outside world were very limited visitations and letters. The question of whether or not to fight extradition weighed on his mind, but he was afraid to discuss the matter.

On Saturday Jimmy wrote Jeannie, "I'm not sure how to write this short letter but I am going to try anyway. First, I don't know if this is hello or goodbye because I don't know when they are going to take me to Oregon or what is going to happen when I get there."

He ended by asking her to take the children to church on Sunday and to read the Bible each day. Jeannie wept as she read it.

Between an office that houses sheriff's deputies and the jail itself is a wall with several hooked shutters about eye level to an adult of average height. Open any of these and you can see through a small glass into a jail that isn't well lit. Iron bars are visible, as are inmates milling about inside. On either side of the wall are phone handsets that can be activated. So, with a visitor on one side and on the other a prisoner, a conversation can take place. This is how Jimmy received visitors.

As for extradition, Jimmy could not make up his mind whether it would be good or bad. He refused to discuss those events of long ago, certainly not with the lawmen. He feared that if he even tried to relate what occurred that night to anyone else his words would be distorted or someone could use the disclosures against him. Jimmy felt as though his only chance of ever regaining freedom was to not admit to anything. And as badly as he wanted to tell Jeannie, he was afraid that whispered conversations would be overheard or his letters would be read by others.

At this point he felt the real truth might never be known. All he wanted was to know that somehow or other his family would be cared for. Although Jeannie had worked for a brief period of time, his salary had for most of their days together been their only source of income. However, state aid was soon approved for Jeannie and the kids and so that major problem was at least temporarily solved.

After two weeks of living in hell, with Jeannie's urging Jimmy decided to sign the extradition papers. "The sooner you go to Oregon the sooner you'll get this settled and we can get back to normal," she said. He wasn't as sure that things would ever be okay again, but on the morning of Friday, October 14 Jimmy appeared in Judge Morgan's court and an extradition hearing was set for the first day of November. Later that same day he appeared in the courtroom of Judge Ronald P. Barnes and signed the extradition papers. His waiver of extradition was approved by the court, and the Sheriff of Logan County was exonerated and directed to surrender the defendant to the Sheriff of Jackson County, Oregon. Even so, it would be twelve more days before he would make the journey west.

Not knowing when or if Jimmy would agree to extradition, the two Oregon detectives had long since returned home. Now they seemed to be saying, You made us wait; we'll do the same for you. Enjoy your stay. Eat well and sleep tight.

On the evening of Tuesday, October 25 Jeannie made a visit to the jail. To her surprise, she didn't have to stare at Jimmy through the glass or talk to him on the phone. Sheriff Hawkins had arranged for Jimmy to be brought out. Jeannie and Jimmy were allowed to sit with their arms locked around each other on a bench outside the sheriff's office.

Of course, two guards watched them constantly and were close enough to hear what was being said. But they could touch. Hold hands. And talk. God, but it felt good. They both felt a sincere debt of gratitude to Sheriff Hawkins.

"Have they told you when you'll be going?" Jeannie asked.

"No, they haven't said."

"Jim, I don't know how, but if they take you to Oregon, I'm going to find a way to go, too. Maybe get an apartment for me and the kids. I'll get a job and we'll make it somehow. Families should be close together when there's trouble."

"Let's wait and see what happens," Jimmy said. "Maybe they'll forget to come after me."

Jeannie doubted that the Oregon lawmen would forget about Jimmy. As to when he would be taken away, she didn't know what to expect. Jimmy knew. He hadn't been told, but an inner sense told him it was about to happen. They didn't allow this kind of visit unless something was up.

17

ANOTHER JAIL

Early in the morning, before daylight, Jimmy was awake when a Logan County deputy came to his cell and said, "Jimmy, it's time. They're here."

Although no one had ever said, "This day or tomorrow you are going to Oregon," Jimmy knew who was here and where they were taking him.

No handcuffs this time. They helped him place an orthopedic brace on his left leg. This steel restraint fit from ankle to well above the knee. When sitting, a release was pushed, allowing the leg to bend in a near normal manner. When standing, the brace locked and the wearer was forced to walk with his leg straight, making escape all but impossible. Even had he been inclined to do so, there was no way he could have outrun the lawmen.

Once this device was in place and the few possessions Jimmy was allowed to carry were secure in a paper bag, the three of them climbed into a rented car and left Guthrie. There were no goodbyes from family or friends. The only folks who saw him go were his fellow inmates and the few personnel on duty at the jail early in the morning.

Although he had thought of Peter Jones as his primary adversary during their previous time together, Jimmy now saw the officer's human side. Not being forced to suffer the humiliation of wearing handcuffs was the first sign that the man was considerate. When they reached Will Rogers Airport at Oklahoma City, the veteran lawman even helped carry Jim's bag. Then they went into the airport restaurant and Jimmy was told to order whatever he wanted. He settled for coffee and a roll.

Though he was somber, he couldn't suppress a smile when the two lawmen were not allowed to carry their pistols onto the plane. Explaining that they were escorting a dangerous desperado back to Oregon had little effect on the airport personnel. "Check your guns or you don't get on. Period!" So, they checked their weapons.

Of course, once they were on the plane, Jimmy got neither the aisle nor window seat. He felt small and insecure wedged in between the two big men.

Jimmy forgot his fear of flying. He could not remember ever feeling lower than he did that day. If they crashed, they crashed. Other than for taking so many innocent lives, he didn't really care one way or the other. Or so he thought until he felt the plane's engines shudder and come to life. As the jet roared for takeoff, Jimmy said a silent prayer. They had three takeoffs and landings before he stepped out of the plane at Medford. He had the opportunity to do a lot of praying.

Late that same evening, they landed in a valley, a beautiful niche on God's earth, surrounded by mountains. Hereford cattle grazing on the slopes created a pastoral scene. Snow, although not with them yet, would turn the landscape into a winter paradise. Jimmy wasn't interested in the view.

Although Jimmy didn't know it at the time, several miles to the southwest as the eagle flies but many more if you follow the route taken by Terrie in 1967, lay Dead Indian Mountain, a ridge that got its name from Dead Indian Creek.

Carnivorous animals that might still be seen in the area

are black bear and wildcats and maybe, just maybe, a rare mountain lion. Grizzly bears once roamed the mountain but decades before Terrie's night of fear they had all been killed or driven off.

Trees that one might encounter on Dead Indian Plateau are fir and pine, including ponderosa. Had Terrie not stayed on Shell Peak Road that night, she might have found herself trapped in the thick undergrowth.

Jimmy was not aware of any of this as he was escorted from the airport to the Jackson County Jail, a new modern building that would put the old dungeon in Logan County to shame. Built of concrete and reinforced glass, the jail was tucked in behind the courthouse. Its exterior gave the appearance of a structure that might house government offices. An outsider could not easily guess that inside this building were criminals and suspected criminals accused of crimes ranging from petty theft to first degree murder. Many of their deeds were drug-related.

Jimmy arrived with no more fanfare than had been evident upon his leaving Guthrie. It was after seven that evening when he was allowed to call Jeannie collect and let her know that he had arrived safely at his new location. He was given a receipt for what he'd brought in the brown paper bag. He was fingerprinted and locked away for the night.

It was to be a near sleepless one. He was in no mood to appreciate the beauty of the region nor to recognize that his living conditions had improved. All that crossed his mind was that he was separated from his family by half a continent. Each torturous moment seemed to increase his doubts that he would ever see them again. Jeannie had talked about coming up, but he didn't see how that would be possible. For now, he just wanted her to get away from Guthrie and be with her family in Boston.

Except for the officers who had accompanied him on his journey to Jackson County, he had no friends or acquaintances in this town. It was as though he had been carried away to some distant planet and suddenly found himself surrounded by aliens.

In Guthrie, Jeannie also was distraught. When should I tell the children he's gone? What about the upcoming murder trial? How can I ever explain it to Jim's family? What should I tell his mother, our neighbors and friends who thought this all was a mistake which would be rectified in a few days? And how do we survive?

These were the thoughts that churned over and over in Jeannie's mind as she sat on the couch in her living room after Jimmy called her to say they had taken him to Oregon. When she told them, the kids were silent and wide-eyed. Their shock was evident. Their eyes mirrored questions that they were afraid to ask.

That's when it really hit her that Jimmy wasn't coming home any time soon, in fact that he wouldn't be with them until God alone knew when. Maybe not ever.

She wondered if the lawmen had planned it that way.

They were all huddled together in the living room as though afraid to be alone. Had someone walked in without knowing the circumstances, they might have thought there had been a death in the family. In ways, this seemed worse. Had their husband and father been dead, as final as that might be, at least it would be something they could comprehend. Perhaps it would be easier to say, "He's dead," than to say, "They arrested Jim for murder and now they've taken him to Oregon for the trial."

"I've got to call Jim's mother again," Jeannie said to no one in particular. "I told her I'd call as soon as I knew something more."

"Mamma, what's happening?" Lynn wanted to know.

"Oh, Honey, I don't know," Jeannie said. "They've made a big mistake, that's all. It's just something that's going to take a while for them to realize."

The night slowly passed.

It was almost nine o'clock when Jeannie phoned Jim's mother, who was terrified by what she'd read in the newspapers. This time they talked for some thirty minutes while Chris was brought up to date on the situation. First degree murder. Twenty-one years ago. Locked up. No bail. Taken to Oregon. Jeannie didn't know much more than that. They agreed that a terrible mistake had been made and there was no doubt but what they had arrested the wrong man. Still, wrong men get convicted!

"Oh my God," Chris said. "That wasn't Jimmy. You know, that wasn't Jimmy, going out and killing somebody or something like that. How could they think anything like that happened?"

Jeannie had no answer.

Next, Jeannie phoned the one person in the world who was closer to her than anyone outside her immediate family, her sister Carol in Boston. Sister Joanie was visiting Carol that night. They'd also been reading of the arrest and didn't know whether to call her or not. They experienced shock and dismay. Not their Duke. Not the brother-in-law who had taken them fishing and watched over them when they were young and foolish. Jeannie's sisters offered to help in any way possible. What could they do? Pray, that's about all.

Thursday and Friday were no better. Go through the motions of living. Try to put on a front for the children. Don't let them see that you're being ripped apart by an obstacle that is too heavy to move and too wide to go around. She pushed herself to go on.

It wasn't until Sunday morning that the full impact of the past few weeks hit Jeannie. At four o'clock that morning she hit bottom. This was for real! It wasn't going away!

Jeannie crawled out of bed and sat numbly in the living room. Lynn, wearing her pajamas, came in crying. Taking her in her arms, Jeannie realized she couldn't share her own desperation with her kids. If you cry, you cry alone. When they're looking, force a smile.

The family had attended church fairly regularly while living in Wichita but upon leaving had quit. Since settling in Guthrie they had again felt the need to seek out religious affiliation. First they had tried a fundamental church with very strict ideas about worldly pleasures. The denomination didn't hold with television. It was thought to be the instrument of Satan and as such was not allowed inside their homes. But, while husbands were at work, wives would visit Jeannie and sit for hours watching her television, knowing all the while that this would be their only opportunity.

When the Taylors decided all this didn't really suit them, they began attending the Nazarene Church. Although they too had a number of do's and don't's, they were considerably more liberal than had been the congregation they left behind.

Now that Jeannie was alone with the children, she turned to the church for help. She studied the Bible and prayed often. Especially at night when the loneliness was worst.

Jeannie's sister Carol called. "Maybe you should come back to Boston. We'll be cramped with two families living together in one apartment, but at least we'll be together."

Jeannie wanted to go to Oregon to be with Jimmy. But how was she going to get enough money together so she and the kids could get tickets and make their first month's rent on an apartment? And, if she went alone and left them, they had no family here. There would be no one to leave the kids with, so whatever they did they would have to do it together. Unless she went first to Boston and left the kids there. Doing so was an option she decided to keep open.

Jim's boss, Joe, knowing Jeannie and the kids were in a financial bind, was already helping financially, but Jeannie couldn't bring herself to ask him for enough money to carry out her plan to travel to Oregon.

In her next letter to Jim, Jeannie wrote, "Sometimes I have a hard time dealing with the kids without you. When I do, I get mad, yell, say a prayer, and read my Bible.

"I talked to my sister Joanie. She said that if we come to Boston, Julie and Lynn could stay with her. Maybe we should go. Remember, your family is waiting, no matter how long it takes."

Despite Jimmy's being taken to Oregon surreptitiously, word got around the town that Duke was gone. In the house at 508 North First were an attractive lady and her two pretty daughters. Men and boys sat and contemplated. Some thought it would be easy pickings.

It was two in the morning the following week when Jeannie, lying in bed awake, heard a noise outside. She tiptoed through the house only to discover someone was trying to pry the screen off the bathroom window. "Dear God, help us," she whispered. Jeannie didn't have a gun in the house, but she did have three children.

She retreated to the living room and, using what little light penetrated the front windows at night, dialed the police station. The policemen were at the house before she even knew they were in the neighborhood. They had parked in the next block and snuck in, hoping to catch the intruder. Jeannie could see their flashlights as they checked outside. Whoever had been there had fled.

Two officers came to the door. They were polite and respectful. They were aware of her circumstances and knew that she was alone with three children. "Mrs. Taylor, we'd like to show you something," the older officer with graying hair said. She followed them around the house to where the policeman's flashlight beam picked up footprints outside her daughter's window. Jeannie was petrified.

"Go back inside and lock up," the officer said. "We'll patrol around here a little more often. Any time you need us, just call."

The following day Jeannie told Matt and Les about the incident. "I'm afraid," she said. "I want a gun. Somebody get me a gun."

Before the week was over, she had a .22 caliber rifle, but only four shells. Were the four shells an omen, she wondered. That same night, Jeannie was sitting in the living room smoking a cigarette, the rifle within reach. She felt so desolate, so isolated, so desperate. In spite of what others were telling her, she worried that Jimmy would never be free. He and her sister Carol both were urging her to take the kids to Boston. Jeannie still wasn't sure. What would await them there? She wasn't strong enough to raise three kids alone, here or in Boston. Sure, others wanted to help, but how long would that last? Would her sisters agree to keep the kids for God knows how long while she went to be with Jim?

Four rifle shells. They had left four shells. There was a way out for her. But if she went, she couldn't leave the kids alone to the uncertain mercies of others. God would carry them all off to heaven. They would be better off there than here. Four shells. She would have to do this while the children slept. No warning. Just bang, bang, bang! They would feel no pain. Save one for yourself.

She held the rifle, seeing in her mind how it would play out. But then she began seeing other scenarios. What if she missed somehow, or what if one bullet didn't kill a child? What if she only wounded them and they would face a lifetime of being a vegetable? Who would she kill first? After the first shot, the others might wake up and struggle or run. Should that happen, there might not be a bullet left for her. If the kids were gone, she would have to be dead also. Have to be!

For two days and nights, Jeannie, who had always been a fighter but now felt as lonely and desperate as Jimmy, agonized over the idea. She came oh so close to going through with this tragedy. And then Reverend Carter came by to see how she was.

Immediately he saw her distress and comforted her. "It's going to be all right, Jeannie. I know what you and the kids and Jimmy are going through. But I believe this will pass and before long now Jimmy will be free again. I want you to hold onto that belief."

Jeannie thanked God she had not yielded to the devil's strong temptation.

18

SURVIVING

The morning after he'd arrived at Medford Airport, they booked Jimmy and took his mug shot. He now realized that Jay had been shot in Oregon, not California. Not only shot, but killed. He knew, too, that he wasn't going to talk to any person about it. Nobody! Not even his lawyer, whoever that might be. If one were ever appointed, that is.

During the day they moved him into the maximum security section of the jail. This was a four-man tank. Most of the men there were in for the crime of either murder or manslaughter.

The only personal item he could have was his body. He was issued a green uniform, a "surgeon suit," as named by the inmates. These were collected once a week for laundry and replacements handed out. All items of clothing had to be accounted for.

In this quad, each man had his own small cell. Steel doors and electric locks dampened any thought of escape. During the day, unless they had a lockdown for whatever reason, the doors to the cells were open and the inmates could step out into a day room. The four of them had a shower stall they shared. There was a specific time of day when they were allowed to use it.

On the second tier was the guard station (or guard shack, as it was referred to by the inmates). The walls of this room were glass so that the guards could stand and look directly down into the day room or into the cells when the doors were open. The lockdown was eleven at night.

Jimmy spent most of the time in his cell having little to say to other prisoners. However, one night he wandered out into the day room and saw himself on television. The mug shot wasn't all that complimentary. The commentator was telling how Jimmy had been arrested for a murder that had taken place some twenty-one years earlier. The newsman went on to say that no local lawyer would take the case.

Jimmy felt even more alone and isolated. Was there no chance that the truth about that night would ever be known? Did everyone believe him guilty?

Jimmy lay on his bunk in the darkness, agonizing about the past, worrying about the future. Now and then he heard a distant sound. Periodically he heard the electronic door leading into the day room open. A guard often came by and shined his light into each of the tiny cell windows to see that all was quiet.

Also, periodically, guards would search the cells. Prisoners were not allowed to have any item like a paper clip, rubber band, or piece of string. They could have disposable shavers, pencil and paper for writing letters, toothpaste, and aftershave lotion. There was a metal mirror in each cell.

Jimmy was given what the Jackson County officials called a "Prisoner Information Manual" which the prisoners called the rules booklet. Consisting of an index, plus twenty-three pages, it laid out rules and regulations, explained schedules and activities, and spelled out the penalties for misbehaving.

If a prisoner was held accountable for three minor violations in a one-week period, he would be referred to the jail commander and face possible disciplinary action under the major rules infraction guidelines.

Three minors equaled a major rule infraction.

Now the booklet listed thirty-six possible minor rules infractions—a violation of any might start you down the road to ruin. Inmates could not refuse to clear their cells or make their beds. Another rule forbade insolence towards a staff member.

A total of thirty-two major rules infractions were listed. Number four, "fighting with another person," would eventually haunt Jimmy who didn't like to start a fight but had never in his life backed away from one.

There was a chance that failure to conform might be referred to the District Attorney's Office for criminal prosecution. There were a lot of rules to learn. Of course, there was plenty of time to memorize them.

Unless a guard came into the day room or unless there had been a rules infraction that cost privileges, each day was predictable.

Jimmy was quick to learn what he could and could not do.

Prisoners were told that incoming mail would be opened to check for contraband but that outgoing letters would not be opened. Still, Jimmy did not trust the officers to the point where he would write anything that might later incriminate him. Consequently, even had he then wanted to, he could not tell Jeannie why he had been arrested.

He wrote his first letter to Jeannie on October 27, the day after he arrived.

In the letter he told her that he went to court that morning and they were going to give him a court appointed attorney.

He wrote Jeannie as often as he could and called collect perhaps more often than he should have.

But, in his isolation, Jeannie and his children represented his only tie to sanity, in fact to life.

* * *

Around Thanksgiving, Jeannie decided to send the girls to Boston on a bus. Doing so tore at her heart, but her options were limited. At least they would be with her family and away from the gossip about their father.

The Taylors' phone was soon disconnected for nonpayment and when this happened Jimmy lost his only means of speaking to his wife and children. Jeannie hadn't wanted to tell him how desperate her own situation was becoming. In a letter to Jim, Jeannie said, "I'm sorry I couldn't let you know I was sending Lynn and Julie to Boston on the bus. I was worried, too. If things work out like I hope, I will be leaving on Tuesday the sixth." The journey for her and Andy would be delayed.

Before Jeannie and Andy could follow the girls, she had to store most of their possessions. She had a yard sale on a cold and wet day to dispose of what remained.

On the day that Les took Jeannie and Andy to the bus station, Jeannie had walking pneumonia. As they rode the bus to Boston, she decided that Les was right. Whatever happened, they would never come back to Guthrie. Why return to a town where you had lived when your family was torn apart?

Jeannie had a happy reunion with her daughters as well as with her sisters and their families. Finding everyone in good health and even Lynn being well cared for, she felt that they had made the right decision.

This euphoric feeling soon dissipated. There was no way she could leave the kids here and go on to Oregon herself. The city of her childhood had ceased to exist. Conditions seemed so different from what they had been during their last visit less than four years earlier. It seemed as though the neighborhood was plagued with robberies and drugs and guns. Right on the street where Carol and her family lived. Jeannie prayed, "Dear God, I don't want my kids to be raised in a large city."

Jeannie began to lose hope of being able to be with Jim.

There were three reasons why she couldn't be with him in Oregon while he went through this terrible ordeal. The reasons were Lynn, Julie, and Andy. When faced with the terrible choice, her motherly instincts told her that the children had to be her first priority. For now, they were all trapped.

Even though Julie and Lynn were staying with Joanie, there were eight people living in Carol's apartment. Jeannie began to realize what sacrifices Carol, her husband, and children were making. The pressure of being confined to a small area with so many people from whom they had been separated for so many years by time, space, and custom began to wear on them all. For the most part, the outdoors was off limits, so this apartment became a prison for Jeannie and two of her children.

Carol instructed Jeannie on how to dress before leaving the apartment. "Hang your purse over your shoulder first," she said. "Then put your coat on and be sure to button it. If you don't, somebody is going to snatch your purse."

Julie was enjoying her visit, but Andy felt as though he was as much a prisoner as was his dad. He hardly got to leave the apartment, not even to go to school. He spent most of his time trapped in the one room he shared with his mom, helping her make plant holders. Andy ached for the opportunity to go outdoors and romp.

Lynn's feelings were a mixture of relief and sadness. She had been anxious to leave Guthrie and the swirling gossip, but, like her brother, she felt trapped. It didn't really bother her that she was not sent to school, but she did want to get out. Because she was fifteen and the neighborhood was dangerous, Jeannie kept a close eye on her. For the most part, Lynn's excursions out of the house were limited to an occasional trip to the mall with her cousins.

Carol had married a man from Puerto Rico and had adapted to his lifestyle and eating habits. Rice was a staple, and chicken was a regular meat item. Jeannie had Midwestern tastes. She had grown accustomed to red meat and potatoes. Food seemed so unimportant, and yet the strangeness of their diet only made things seem worse.

The two sisters who had been so close soon began to feel the pressure. Jeannie missed her things. She wanted *her* refrigerator to turn to and *her* stove to cook on.

Carol had thought Jeannie would come to Boston and find herself a job and a place of her own. That whether or not Jim ever got out, this would be home for her and the kids, but Jeannie was even more unhappy than she'd been alone far away. Realizing that Oregon was a hopeless dream, she soon discovered that there was no way they could all survive in Boston. Things were too expensive or too dangerous. There was little hope that they could have a place of their own.

Soon after the first of the year, Jeannie learned that Jim's trial was scheduled to begin on March 1, 1989, so, in a letter postmarked January 10, she wrote, "I told the kids we would probably be back together in March. I'm going to take the kids back to Oklahoma as soon as I can, very soon. Boston is a pretty bad place to raise the kids. Tonight a car smashed three other cars in front of Carol's house and the guy got out and ran. Andy went down there before I could stop him."

She added, "We have had all we can take. I'm not staying here any longer than I have to. I have the kids to think about. Right now they are hurting as much as we are, maybe more.

"I miss going to church and having time to talk to the Lord."

In addition to her other problems, the welfare office was putting pressure on Jeannie to put her kids into a school which she knew had all kinds of problems. If she stayed, or if the kids stayed while she went to Oregon, she would have no choice other than to send them.

And her financial problems had gotten so bad she couldn't even accept Jimmy's phone calls. Jeannie wrote, "I hope you did not get mad at me because of the phone, Babe, but I can't afford to pay Carol for the phone bill and try to save money to go back to Oklahoma. We have to go home. I hope you understand what we are going through. If you could see it for yourself, you would understand."

Not long after receiving Jeannie's letter, Jimmy wrote back, "Keep your chin up. I talked to Les. He said you could move back into that house. I am trying to talk Les into putting up the first month's rent and get the utilities for you. Also, he will try to get some furniture.

"Even if I go to prison for the rest of my life, I will never forget you or the kids. I will love you forever. I know it is important for you to have your own place. I never should have told you to leave.

"If something does happen and I am gone away for a while, are you going to wait for me? I am not afraid of going to prison, but I am afraid of losing you and the kids."

Sure, Jim was getting paranoid. He could no longer phone Jeannie and if he didn't receive a letter a day he felt deserted. He was facing a trial date of March 1 and his fears were multiplying. *They didn't spend all that money to find you and bring you up here just to turn you loose. You're going to prison, maybe for a long time—maybe for the rest of your life!*

But just in case he didn't, Jimmy needed to hold onto what was important in his life: his family. He prayed and he tried. On January 13 he wrote to Jeannie saying, "I get depressed thinking about this mess and what it has done to our family. But we are not beat! Our family will be stronger than it was. I will spend more time with you and the family than I did before, I promise."

For better or for worse, Jeannie and the kids wanted to return to Oklahoma. Thanks to Les, they were able to move back into the same house. Thanks to Les, they had enough furniture to make do. Thanks to Les, who sent five hundred dollars by Western Union, they had enough money to buy bus tickets home.

On February 10, Jeannie's birthday, they arrived back at the same house they'd left what seemed so long ago. She tried to get the phone turned on using her maiden name, but the telephone company saw through her ruse.

Several days later Jeannie wrote, "Sorry it took so long to get this letter off. Have been running around trying to get settled, putting the kids back in school, getting some of the bills in my name.

"The kids are doing well so far. They are glad to be back and back in school. I have been tired and kind of worn out, mind and body.

"The house is the same old house. It feels good to be back in it. Andy is so happy now. He can go out and play like a little boy should.

"As the day for your trial gets closer, it gets real scary, but I know our love and God's is going to see us through all this, and at least the kids and I are home."

Yes, Jeannie and the kids were home. She had given up all hope of going to Oregon unless Jimmy was convicted and would be kept there a long time. Then she would find a way to go and take the children. Meanwhile, all she could do, like Jimmy, was wait. And somehow survive.

19

THE DEFENSE

Though locked in his cell, Jimmy could see outside. However, it wasn't as though he had a panoramic view of the town or countryside. In fact, the lone window in his cell was made of thick reinforced glass and so high in the wall that it was not intended to be used by inmates to admire the scenery, but to let in a little light. Jimmy was not content with this.

Each day he climbed onto his bunk, stepped up onto his sink, and watched cars and people go by. Dreaming of what it would be like to be free and outdoors.

He could look out and see down into the outer edges of a parking lot. He could see a road and a row of houses, and that road climbed into the far mountains. Pristine beauty! He could see a path and cars coming down, but where they went he could not tell. He stood on his sink at night, after lights out and his cell was dark, just to watch them. Just to look out. Wanting to reach out and touch.

What Jimmy couldn't see or know was that he had already been tried in the minds of many of the natives of Oregon and found guilty. In fact, although few of the locals could actually remember the events that had happened in 1967 on Dead Indian Mountain, much less claim any remembrance of the victim, Glenn True Clark, they took pride in the fact that such an old case had been solved by using modern technology. The general consensus was a combined sigh of relief— this should send shivers through those perpetrators who had committed a heinous crime in times past and now felt as though they were beyond the reach of the law.

Newspaper accounts had already provided titillating copy for those who were newcomers to the area and refreshed the memories of those who had trouble recalling details of events more than two decades past. Most accounts failed to mention that Clark had been a lawbreaker living on plastic cards and fictitious checks; or that he was in possession of stolen guns as well as a stolen car; or that he had left a trail of crime across the western states; or that he had been about to rape a young girl, knowing he had gonorrhea. How could they report what they did not know?

Nor did they know that Clark had threatened to bury the young hitchhiker he had picked up where she could never be found if she didn't willingly submit to his advances. Even Miss Terrie Tidwell was not aware of his boasted outcome to her night on Dead Indian Mountain.

No, what the newspapers played was the computer angle. They celebrated the technology that after all these years had allowed the lawmen to locate a fugitive from murder. Although they did not actually refer to Jimmy as a murderer, their accounts left little doubt that he was guilty as charged. Fingerprints, they insinuated, did not lie.

Of course, all they had to base this assumption on were the reported physical evidence at the scene and the account of the woman who, at the age of eighteen, had been there. She was given credibility when quoted as saying that, while the two men argued, she was dragging her two suitcases out of the car. Then she saw "John" force "Jay" to kneel in front of the car, heard him order the older man to remove his shirt, and then was witness to the fact that with cold-blooded determination John shot his adversary once in the chest and then followed this with the coup de grace, a bullet in the brain.

Although in fact Terrie Tidwell, in her own statement, admitted that she did not actually witness the shooting, what was fed to the press or assumed by the press in 1967 as well as 1988 ignored this.

The Jackson County Sheriff's Office did nothing to discourage this line of thought. In a memorandum sent to other law enforcement agencies shortly after the killing, they said, "The circumstance of the actual crime was that the victim, accompanied by the suspect, was traveling north from California on Interstate Five in an apparently stolen vehicle. They stopped and picked up a young female hitchhiker near Talent, Oregon. They diverted from the highway into the remote area and apparently in preparing to attack the girl became engaged in an argument. This suspect brandished a thirty-eight-caliber revolver, commanding the victim to remove his shirt and assume a kneeling position for the execution, whereafter he was shot through the chest and the back of the head and all of his ID and personal effects were stolen."

Similar statements were released to the press. Even though the lawmen had Terrie's deposition by this time and she had made it clear that John had been polite and stated that he had respect for women, this didn't seem to carry much weight. Although she had also said that the two men had argued shortly before the killing, she had added that John had gone off by himself with wine and beer in hand and a gun in his pocket.

In the media release dated September 30, the same day as Jimmy's arrest, reporters heard from the Jackson County Sheriff's Office that "Clark and Taylor consumed a large quantity of beer and wine."

The release went on, "A confrontation occurred between Taylor and Clark when Clark made advances towards the female hitchhiker. Clark was shot at close range after he was made to kneel in front of the car's headlights."

These statements were only partially true. What was

damning was the omission of pertinent information that might have helped Jimmy Taylor's cause.

Even by the lone witness, Terrie Tidwell's, own admission, it was not until after she had screamed for help that John came running over and ordered Jay out of the car. During subsequent events she was crying and screaming and dragging her suitcases from the back seat and running off into the dark and frightening forest, crying her eyes out. Under such circumstances, it would take an incredible eighteen-year-old girl to make a credible witness. Although Terrie was no doubt as credible as the next person, she was also about as scared as it's possible to be.

The final and most important admission on Terrie Tidwell's part was that she had not actually witnessed the shooting. This being so, there was a lot of assuming going on.

This is the environment that awaited Jimmy when he arrived and was jailed in Oregon in late October 1988. Anyone who followed the news accounts would have to have some preconceived notion that Jimmy Dale Taylor had, on the night of August 29, 1967, shot Glenn True Clark in cold blood. After doing so, Jimmy had stolen all Mr. Clark's possessions and had even gone so far as to strip the victim of all identification. From the news accounts, they would have to assume that all that had saved the poor young girl from a similar fate was that she had, after taking the time to drag her suitcases out of the car, run off down the mountain.

Run for her life until she found refuge in a logging truck. Why, if those men hadn't found her the next morning . . .

This is the account given by the law enforcement agencies and passed on by the press. Jimmy first became aware of this in maximum security when he viewed the news broadcast on television.

That was when, in addition to being some fifteen hundred miles from home and family in a hostile environment, Jimmy began discovering first hand that he had another problem. Indigent and without funds to hire his own attorney, it seemed as though he was being prejudged as guilty and none of the local lawyers were willing to jump in and defend him from the charges he faced. This part of the television account was true.

There is a difference of opinion as to why this was so. One reason, voiced in and around Medford, was that the local attorneys were not willing to accept the case unless the fee was increased from the allowable thirty dollars per hour to a figure that would at least allow them a few dollars profit after covering overhead. To do justice to Jimmy's case would be time-consuming, and they would much rather bill their precious hours at a hundred dollars per than at only thirty.

Even the public defenders of the county were reluctant to step in for less than forty dollars per hour. The State said no. Thirty bucks and that's it. Take it or leave it. There were no takers. According to published reports, this was the first case in the history of the county where a local attorney could not be hired to act as a public defender. Knowledge of the situation only increased the desperation Jimmy Dale Taylor was already feeling.

Some seventy-seven miles from Medford over tortuous and winding roads lies the town of Klamath Falls. There, in modest upstairs quarters, was another public defender's office. This firm had a contract with the state requiring them to take on a set number of murder cases per year in the region of southern Oregon. One of the firm's attorneys later said that they were intrigued by the newspaper accounts and they asked for the case. Other law firms ran from the responsibility and yet these men asked for an opportunity! Following their initial visit with Jimmy, they soon questioned the wisdom of being so eager.

The three men who would work to free Jimmy were attorneys Myron Gitnes and Richard Garbutt, along with private investigator Paul Arritola. Although Jimmy knew nothing about them at the time, the trio eventually proved to be formidable opponents for the state's legal brains.

According to published reports, the same Medford attorneys who refused to take the case for the thirty-dollar fee just couldn't understand the logic of bringing in defenders from so far away.

Up until then, Jimmy's experience with public defenders had left him feeling deflated. In Guthrie a lawyer had been appointed by the court and was paid the grand sum of $150 to plead Jimmy's case and to do what he could for his client. He did nothing. Jimmy still had been extradited to Oregon. However, in truth there was little that any attorney could have done to deny Oregon's right to extradition and eventual trial. There was just too much evidence against Jimmy. The most damning of all were the fingerprints. It is understandable why the Oregon authorities had a "Gotcha!" mentality. They felt that this one was in the bag. All they had to do now was go through the formalities of a trial and then wait for the sentencing.

On Friday the fourth of November Jimmy met for the first time the men who would defend him. From the beginning, Jimmy had decided that he wasn't about to admit to a damned thing. These three men didn't change his mind. For all he knew, these guys might be spies from the district attorney's office. If he hadn't whispered a word to Jeannie about those events of long ago—and he hadn't—he wasn't about to confide in total strangers even though they claimed to have his best interests at heart.

On the ninth of November Richard Garbutt first appeared in court with Jimmy and entered a not guilty plea on his client's behalf. Jimmy was formally charged with first degree murder.

A stoic, soft-spoken man with a full head of dark hair and trim mustache, Garbutt entered the plea decisively but failed to impress his client. At the time no attorney would have impressed Jimmy.

Soon, all three members of the defense team were meeting with their new client, individually or collectively, grasping for any tidbit that might eventually help his case. After each meeting it became more and more clear that they didn't have a hope in hell of winning an acquittal, not with Jimmy's attitude and lack of cooperation. The state had the evidence for a conviction and all Jimmy would tell them was, "I didn't do it. They've got the wrong man."

Even Myron Gitnes, the dynamic lead lawyer in the case, who believed in Jimmy, began to wonder if they had been wise to have taken on this venture. Still, he had a gut feeling about Jimmy, and when he had that feeling he was a tough man to beat.

The third member of the team, Paul Arritola, had his office in the same building as the two attorneys. He played Paul Drake to their Perry Mason.

Paul, a stocky man with a quiet smile and ready wit, headed Arritola Investigations. He had spent more than twenty-five years in the business, specializing in criminal defense. Although he was the type of man most people usually confide in, Jimmy wasn't about to fall into that trap.

In addition to detecting, Paul had a small ranch where he lived, outside Klamath Falls. During a snowstorm, when he hadn't seen many of his cattle for some time, his philosophical outlook on life was reflected when he said, "Oh well, the coyotes have to eat, too."

This was the trio upon whose shoulders Jimmy's fate and future rested.

Jimmy was polite to them, often to a fault. It was always, "Yes sir, no sir, thank you, please." But he wasn't about to tell them a damned thing.

He wrote Jeannie, "The investigator phoned. He asked how long I've lived in Guthrie, how long on the job, married, how many kids, ages, have I been convicted of a crime in the past twenty-one years, ever been arrested in Guthrie, and so on.

"A woman from a local television station called here, wanting to talk to me. I didn't call her back. I'm glad that I didn't. The investigator said for me not to say a word to anyone concerning this case, not even to anyone in my cell block. Said they are known for putting snitches in here.

"I know the newspapers caused some hardship on you and the kids. If I had known this was going to happen, I would have come up here myself to straighten out this mess before it hurt my family."

This was the closest Jimmy had come to admitting it was his mess that needed to be straightened out. Even though he knew deep within that his only hope lay with these three strangers who were about to defend him, he kept silent.

Myron Gitnes said later, "Dick, Paul, and I would basically travel over there every Friday, all three of us, and talk with him. The first maybe three months here's this scared little guy from God knows where, in jail in Oregon, without the possibility of a pretrial release, with two lawyers and an investigator from out of county that he knows nothing about, appointed by the court to represent him. And what all three of us sensed from the very beginning was a lack of confidence in the system. Which we were part of.

"During the next three months we'd go in and say, 'If there's anything you'd like to tell us, then tell us.' And most of the time it was, 'No, I just don't understand about these fingerprints, man.' You know, this kind of stuff. So long as he maintained that attitude, we didn't have shit.

"This was an identification case. Were those his fingerprints on the bottles? On those wine bottles and beer bottles? Well, there is no question of how accurate fingerprint identification is. We couldn't challenge that. Then we found out they had the big honcho from Washington, D.C. who teaches this to everyone throughout the nation. So there was no question in the lawyers' minds where we were going to end up if this was the issue in the case. Jimmy was going to be convicted."

Those who knew Jimmy felt more and more helpless. Many were willing to assist him any way they could, but they were also stymied.

Joe Reale, his employer, tried. He wrote a letter to the Jackson County Jail in which he stated that in the three plus years he'd known Jimmy the man had been honest, trustworthy, and hardworking. In the last line Joe said, "I would rehire him immediately even if convicted."

Only his sister had the same wariness Jimmy did. When Jimmy talked to her by phone, Shirley said, "You'd better watch your attorneys. I called the district attorney up there, and he said that you're a very dangerous person. You can't have no bail."

Trying to help, she had only driven another wedge between Jimmy and his attorneys.

Jeannie wrote a letter to the Governor of Oregon, feeling as though he would understand the injustice that had been done and would use his authority to see to it that her husband was released at once.

Governor Neil Goldschmidt, or a spokesman writing over his signature, replied, "As governor, I do not have the authority to intervene in or to review criminal legal matters pending before the courts. Because of the Oregon Constitution's separation of powers between the legislative, judicial, and executive branches, I have no jurisdiction in legal matters. Due to the criminal charges Jimmy faces, I understand that your son is represented by legal counsel. I suggest that he continue to consult with his attorney to better explore his legal alternatives."

Son! Jeannie's son was safe at home. It was her husband she was concerned about. How could she expect help from someone who couldn't even keep the facts straight? As for Jimmy continuing to consult with his attorney, he had yet to even start such a relationship. He wasn't telling them a thing.

"My attorneys had been copying down about everything I'd been telling them," Jimmy said. "This kind of shocked me. I didn't know these people from Adam. I thought it was very possible that with all the money they spent they were trying to bust me."

Paul Arritola said later, "This was big history in the law enforcement part here. California had this new computer which coughs somebody up twenty-one years later. They were going to put a major follow-up on this one.

"Sacramento called all departments and told them to

send them the fingerprints on all murders and major crimes. They said, 'We'll put them in our computer,' and that's where they got this.

"As for Jimmy, he was such a mellow amicable client compared to what we're used to. He was one of a kind."

Myron Gitnes said, "Jimmy would go over the police reports in our absence and pick out one or two little things that didn't quite make sense and we'd talk about them. To him, the reports didn't prove anything against him, but we knew differently."

Finally the lawyers decided that, with Jimmy's refusal to speak, there was only one alternative.

"Because he wouldn't tell us anything, we were asking Jimmy's permission to go forward and seek a negotiation. We wanted to know if Jimmy would authorize us to see if we could cut a deal. We wanted permission because we didn't have a thing to go on. The state was not willing to talk to us about a lesser charge. The D.A. just said, 'Plead guilty and take the ten.' In Oregon, if you are sentenced to life, you do a minimum of ten years. If they can show that you're a bad guy, and in their mind Jimmy certainly was, they can add another fifteen to that. And that's without parole. So he'd do the twenty-five without parole.

"Oregon didn't have the death penalty when the crime was committed. If they had, this might have qualified if they could have inferred that he stole Clark's watch and wallet. Then it would have been a death penalty."

Jimmy wrote Jeannie, "I sure am lonely. Well, sweetheart, today we started the ball rolling on this mess. The attorneys seem like they are going to really try and help. Both attorneys and the investigator were asking lots of questions at the same time. It's so confusing.

"You can expect to see the attorney or investigator any day now. I don't know what day or what time he or they will be there and I don't know what kind of questions he or they are going to ask you. They want a copy of the newspaper clippings. Also, my discharge from the Navy. They will ask you a lot of questions, so don't be nervous."

Jimmy was of the opinion that a member of his defense team would soon visit Jeannie in Guthrie. Actually, that was never their intent. There was too much else to do. They only planned to talk with her by phone.

The attorneys and investigator all still felt as though they had a fighting chance if only Jimmy would finally level with them. For reasons that he felt were valid, Jimmy continued to refuse to do so. Other sources, those he was incarcerated with, concurred with his feelings of fear and offered different words of wisdom.

So far as the attorneys were concerned, the advice that he was receiving from these jailhouse lawyers was only making matters worse.

20

JAILHOUSE LAWYERS

One of the obstacles any criminal defense lawyer must contend with is negating the advice their client constantly receives from those self-proclaimed experts who have spent much of their life within various jails and have learned the system. However, when a prisoner, especially one who is far from home and who feels as though he's been separated from reality and his family by a judicial system that has gone amok, receives advice from his fellow inmates, he usually listens.

Three strangers, their salaries paid by the state, walked into Jimmy's life and said, "We're here to help. Tell us everything you know about this case and then we'll decide what defense to use."

Jimmy was looking for guarantees.

On their regular schedule, Jimmy saw his defense team one day a week and then only for a limited time. He saw his fellow prisoners day and night. Sure, his lawyers said they wanted to get him off, but so what? Words were cheap. They got paid their money whether he went to prison for the rest of his life or went free. Either way, they'd win. One way, he would lose. Not only lose, but lose everything.

The conflict here was that, to adequately represent a client, an attorney must know all there is to know about a case to have any realistic chance of success. Jimmy was afraid that if they learned the truth they would somehow use it against him.

Many of the inmates, however, had personal experience with the way the law worked. They had an "us against them" mentality, and their "them" included most if not all defense attorneys. Their comments increased Jimmy's distrust. To their way of thinking, court appointed attorneys were only interested in collecting money. Get their bucks and to hell with the outcome. It won't be them behind bars. Another argument they advanced was, "Hell, man, these guys can't be any good or they wouldn't have to drive all the way over from the next county to find clients."

Also, it was whispered that the real reason no local attorney would take the case was that it was a loser. This contradicted their other argument that attorneys get paid win or lose, but it added to Jimmy's fears. The reasoning continued that if they were going to lose they wanted to be paid more than just their expenses. To an outsider thinking rationally, none of the arguments made much sense. To Jimmy in his present distraught state of mind, they made all the sense in the world.

So, when three guys from the next county said, "Tell us what really happened. Tell us the whole story," he countered by withdrawing further.

Like hell he would. Whatever happened now, Jimmy was determined to hold his cards close to his vest. If he hadn't told anyone in twenty-one years, why should he now?

"There's nothing to tell," Jimmy repeated week after week. "I've never been to Oregon. They have the wrong man. Why don't they get out and find who they're really looking for?"

Next trip: "You got anything to tell us, Jimmy? Anything new?"

"There's nothing to tell. I haven't ever been to Oregon. They have the wrong man."

What, they all three wondered, would they have to do to gain this man's confidence? The only people Jimmy trusted at this point were his fellow prisoners—perhaps his worst enemies. The truth, his best friend, remained hidden.

In a letter to Jeannie, Jimmy told her, "A guy in here showed me a book you can order different legal forms from. I am going to order a book on fingerprint use in court. He also has law books about how they work in different cases in the state of Oregon.

"He is going to help me look up different laws on the use of fingerprints because the average person doesn't know that much on how different laws are written. Maybe the state is wrong on some laws. He told me that he had beaten some charges that way. Most people don't go back to the law books to check on the new laws, but we are going to try."

To Jeannie who knew him so well, Jimmy wasn't making sense. He seemed so different from the calm, gentle man she had known so long. Her greatest worry now was what was happening to him and how it would further complicate his chance of coming home.

In another letter, he said, "They just called me out to have another fingerprint test. They took my palm print, too. Maybe they are not too sure what's going on either. They say the ink they use now won't fade like it did years ago.

"If the prints they used twenty years ago are not good enough to read, maybe they can't do anything with them. Maybe that's why the machine put out my name. I sure would like them to tell me that they made a mistake. If they ask me to be printed again, I am going to refuse."

Looking in all the wrong places.

Grasping at any old straw.

Scraping the bottom of the barrel.

* * *

During the time that Jimmy was incarcerated in Jackson County, he saw many men come into his quad and just as many leave. He said in a letter to Jeannie that by the time he had been there for thirty-five days he had seen nine men pass through. Some he was close to. Others he wasn't.

In this same letter, Jimmy said, "I know a man now in here who has a real heavy cross to bear. He will probably be sent to prison for the rest of his life. He is fifty-five years old. They said he paid some people to kill his wife. If he is found guilty, his kids will hate him and he will lose everything. I don't know if he is guilty or not, but he does have a big cross to bear. At least I have twenty-one years of a good history. And a lot of loving people behind me. So you see, things could be worse."

Frank, the man accused of contracting his wife's murder, had told Jimmy and the other prisoners stories that caused them to further distrust the legal system in general and lawyers in particular.

"I'm a prosperous man who owned two houses before this occurred. The lawyers ate me up. I sold the two houses and it took the receipts from both as well as every penny I had to pay for my defense."

He was accused of hiring a cousin and cousin's friend to kill his wife. Supposedly, the cousin called Frank's wife from a truck stop and said he had car trouble. When the woman came to help, she was killed. The police caught the two killers, obtained a confession, and were able to trap Frank through a telephone call from his cousin.

Was Frank guilty? He insisted he loved his wife and he'd been framed. What was the truth? No one knew.

However, Frank's experience further reinforced Jimmy's belief that if a lawyer bought and paid for couldn't get you off, what chance did a man have with guys appointed by the court? Most cons were of the opinion that money bought freedom. They seldom talked about guilt or innocence. If you have enough money, you walk. Evidently the proceeds from the sale of two houses wasn't sufficient to buy yourself a lawyer who could get you off if a man was innocent as he said. Jimmy felt desperate. He didn't even have one house to sell.

While they were together, Jimmy did talk Frank into attending church services. Eventually he even had him joining in singing a spiritual song. As Frank sang, tears streaked the older man's face. Was he guilty as charged? Jimmy didn't know. Frank was convicted, but that didn't convince his fellow inmates. Maybe he just didn't have enough houses to sell so that he could hire better lawyers. You got enough money and get the right lawyer, you go free. Not though if you get some guys from another county who can't find work close to home, they confided to Jimmy.

As each day passed, and his anxiety increased, Jimmy turned more and more to prayer. Although he had brought his own Bible from home, he wasn't allowed to have it in his cell. The Bible they provided was torn, with pages missing. He asked the captain for his own.

"No," said the captain. "Prisoners are not allowed to have their own personal property."

In the jail library Jimmy asked the librarian for a Bible just like his own. The librarian, who liked the gentle, soft-spoken man, went so far as to check Jimmy's own edition and provide him with an exact duplicate.

Every Sunday Jimmy attended church services offered inside the jail walls, and every week he went to counseling. He tried to help other prisoners. Although he was no biblical scholar, Jimmy seemed to know the Bible better than did most of his fellow inmates, so they listened.

He read the Bible every day and said his prayers every night. Often he pointed to his Bible and said to his fellow prisoners, "Hey, man. Right here, man. It's all you need. The Lord God wrote it and it's true. He's guided me through everything. I'm not the most perfect man in the world, but He's guided me through. He'll keep my family safe."

Though his belief in God was strengthening, within

Jimmy was an earthly conflict, pulling him first in one direction and then in another. Soon the jailhouse lawyers were at work again. Now they were telling him to insist on a change of venue. "That's the only way you got any chance of getting a fair trial, man.

In early January, when his attorneys came to visit, Jimmy said, "I want a change of venue."

This they didn't need. "Why," Gitnes asked, "after all the work we've done would you want to change now?"

Taylor didn't give any answer.

Eventually Jimmy decided to stay where he was instead of taking a chance on a new environment. But he agonized over the decision.

Though Jimmy and Jeannie's families were spread across the land and some had not seen one another for many years, when Jimmy was arrested and charged with first degree murder the word spread fast. Whether rich or poor they gave sympathy and support to the man all knew as a giving and kind person.

His sister sent money and clothes for the children. In addition to talking to the district attorney, she also obtained copies of newspapers from Medford in an attempt to further understand what was going on. She wanted to make the trip to Medford, but, like Jeannie, financial difficulties put a stop to this consideration.

They were all convinced that Jimmy could not have killed anyone in cold blood. Perhaps, since they knew and loved him, this was to be expected, but he was terribly grateful for their support.

Several relatives, including his mother and Jeannie, sent money orders so that he might visit the commissary. Jimmy's brothers and sisters, along with Jeannie's siblings, responded with disbelief and a willingness to help in any way.

Still, even though he appreciated his family's belief and support, it was not enough to temper his despair.

On Tuesday, January 17 Jimmy wrote to Jeannie, "The

trial date is getting closer and closer. I'm glad. I'm forlorn, jumpy, and nervous but at least the waiting will be over and I will know what lays ahead, good or bad.

"If it is bad, at least I will know how much time I will get. It has to be better than this uncertainty. At least I hope it will."

With only two weeks remaining before his trial, Jimmy was becoming more confused. And more frightened. The advice from the jailhouse crew about new laws to be researched and a change of venue had yet to materialize and he was beginning to realize that it never would. In a few days his attorneys would come for their weekly visit. Should he level with them or not? He spent tormented days and nights trying to decide.

Jeannie, too, felt wretched not only about Jimmy's situation but about his failure to speak out. She wrote:

Dearest,

I know you are frightened of all these strangers but your only chance, *our* only chance, is to confide in your lawyers. Please, if you love us as much as we love you, tell them what happened. Tell them the truth.

Jeannie

On Friday, February 17, just twelve days before the trial was to begin, the three men arrived from Klamath Falls. Jimmy was escorted into the small conference room where they all three sat around a table while a guard waited outside the closed door. Paul Arritola was the first to speak.

"I saw Peter Jones," Paul said. "They're pretty confident. He says it's all over but the sentencing. Jimmy, it's my opinion only you can do something about it."

Jimmy stared at the two lawyers. They didn't contradict this assessment of his chances. He glanced at the closed door, afraid that the guard outside could hear. He would have to risk it. Jeannie was right; he had only one chance—the truth.

"I want to tell you guys something," Jimmy said.

"What?" asked Gitnes.

"I want to tell you what really happened back in 1967. The whole story."

A silence settled over the room. Jimmy paused as though he was reconsidering. None of the other men said a word.

Hesitantly, Jimmy began speaking. He told them how he'd met Clark only a few months after being discharged from the Navy. He told them about the car trip to Seattle when Glenn had spotted Terrie and went wild. He spoke of the trips to the convenience stores, the roadside park, and finally parking the car in the dark clearing on Dead Indian Mountain. Jimmy told how he had been warned to stay away from the car but had worried about Clark's boasting about rape and murder if Terrie resisted. How he had taken his gun to a nearby tree stump and sat alone drinking until Terrie screamed for help.

"That was when I told Clark to get out of the car. Terrie was screaming and crying, pulling her suitcases out and took off."

He told how he told Clark to go around to the front of the car and remove his shirt. "I knew he had a gun on him somewhere."

Jimmy had turned in an attempt to find Terrie. "When I turned back, Clark's gun was coming into view."

He described the shooting, leaving out only one detail. Thinking it wasn't important, he never did tell the attorneys that Clark fired a shot that had ripped a chunk out of his arm.

He spoke of his agonized trip down the mountain and return to San Francisco.

They all waited until Jimmy had stopped speaking, and then Gitnes said, "I wish you'd told us this three months ago."

"I just couldn't till now," Jimmy said, looking into the eyes of first one of his defenders and then the others.

"Don't breathe a word of this to another soul until I get you on the witness stand," Myron said. "We're going with self-defense."

As Jimmy was led back to his quad, he hoped and prayed that he had done the right thing. Soon he would know.

21

UNHAPPY REUNION

From the day that Jimmy Dale Taylor was identified through his fingerprints, the state of Oregon felt as though it had a strong case.

Terrie Tidwell, the only one other than Jimmy who had been there in 1967, had returned the previous year to testify for the grand jury and had agreed to testify against Jimmy at the trial. What she had and hadn't seen that night on the mountain is debatable. Even so, the prosecution had her deposition, given one night after the killing. This testimony had the potential to be damning for Taylor.

Soon after Jimmy was arrested in Guthrie, a deputy district attorney for Jackson County had filed a motion to withhold the address and phone number of witness Terrie Trina Tidwell from the defendant, Jimmy Taylor. Whether she was frightened of him or just didn't want to have to face Jimmy or his attorneys is unknown. Whatever, her whereabouts were to be kept secret from them all.

Even before Jimmy had disclosed his side of the experience to his attorneys, Myron Gitnes had filed an affidavit in support of a motion to require the state of Oregon to divulge Terrie's address so that he might interview her before the trial. The district attorney's office had told him earlier that Terrie could be reached through attorney David G. Davis; but when Myron inquired he was told that Mr. Davis had no information as to the witness's whereabouts. The state then offered to set up a conference call with Terrie so the defense could question the lady while an assistant district attorney listened in and recorded the interview. Because of these conditions, the defense refused.

Now that Jimmy finally had decided to confide in his defenders, there was little doubt that they would call him to the stand. Since it wasn't feasible to call character witnesses from Oklahoma on his behalf, they decided to call those who could best describe Clark's character. Arritola went to work and found folks who had known Glenn best: his relatives and Ted Ryder, who had once been a friend and neighbor. They all agreed to testify.

They needed to make Jimmy look presentable to both the court and the jury. Since the day of his arrest, he'd had one haircut and that was a botched job by one of the inmates at the Jackson County Jail. Garbutt inquired and learned that they had hair-cutting equipment at the jail but nobody who was qualified to give a decent haircut. Before he would be allowed to bring a barber in, that barber would be required to undergo a background check, a time-consuming endeavor. And so James filed an affidavit with the court requesting that a deputy take Jimmy to a shop in Medford on Monday, February 27, only two days before the trial was to begin. Judge Roberts issued the order to do so.

On that Monday afternoon, Jimmy was brought out of the day room and the officers secured him for the outdoors. He knelt on a low bench, his feet and ankles pointing back while he faced a wall, a very submissive and humiliating position. The leg shackles were placed first. Then he stood and his hands were cuffed behind his back. This was one of those rare times when Jimmy was allowed to go outdoors.

By now the three men from Klamath Falls were concentrating exclusively on defending Jimmy. His case and plight had touched each of them. They had rented a place outside of Medford where they would stay until the trial was over. Their other cases were put on hold. Despite their belief in Jimmy's story, it would be Terrie's word against Jimmy's. Who would the jury believe?

On Tuesday, the day before the trial was to begin, a pretrial conference was held, with Judge Edgar R. Roberts presiding. Jimmy sat at the defense table, knowing his future would soon be decided. Myron Gitnes wanted it on record that the defense had tried to locate Terrie so they could question her without being monitored and their request had been refused. Judge Roberts sided with the prosecution.

Next, the prosecution wanted to know whether or not Jimmy would testify. Gitnes claimed not to have yet made a decision. Jimmy was certain that he would.

Peter Jones was the only witness called. He described the arrest so that the judge would know it was all done in a legal manner. Rights had been read and no threats had been made. Jimmy couldn't deny what was said.

The next issue to be discussed was an important one.

Garbutt began, "Your Honor, I think we need to discuss at this point the reference to the armed robbery in San Francisco."

Roberts looked toward him. "Do you want to make a motion in limine, is that what you're suggesting?"

Garbutt nodded. "Yes, Your Honor, to exclude any references to the armed robbery. It can't be used under the evidence code, it's older than fifteen years, and I think it would be much more prejudicial than probative at this point. He can show the, the photograph; I still have to think that through, but at least the composite photograph. But anything, any references to an armed robbery, would be out of bounds."

Garbutt and the district attorney began to argue. Garbutt's voice hardened.

"This is just going to be something that blows up in front of the jury and makes him look like some kind of a runaway man going up and down the coast killing people and doing armed robberies, which isn't the case."

The district attorney matched his tone. "Well, at the very least, I think the state ought to be able to introduce evidence, if not of an armed robbery, that he was in fact, in San Francisco on September 1, 1967."

The judge nodded. "I don't have a problem with that."

District Attorney Dentoni added, "Without explaining the circumstances of his being there."

Garbutt frowned. "Well, that's fine as long as the circumstances . . ."

Judge Roberts discussed the stipulation and Garbutt agreed to stipulate.

Then Dentoni raised another thorny issue. "Another matter I'll raise now. I have no idea whether the defense plans to use it, but the eyewitness in this case had been hitchhiking. We're alleging that she had been hitchhiking before this occurred, and was picked up by Mr. Taylor and the victim while hitchhiking." He went on to say that in doing their background investigation the detectives had discovered other issues.

There was an unspoken agreement reached here that so long as the state didn't attempt to tell of the armed robbery, the defense would not raise questions about Terrie's past.

The following morning Jimmy dressed in his own suit and tie instead of wearing the outfit the state had bought. He was escorted to the court room and sat at the defendant's table, between his two attorneys. Jimmy searched through the spectators and members of the media. There was only one person he wanted there—Jeannie.

He knew she wouldn't, couldn't, be here, but still he looked. Not for the kids—he didn't want them to see him in this position, but these days ahead would be much easier to endure if only Jeannie was there with him. Even worse, he was, at this point, completely cut off from her. He couldn't even phone.

The entire day was spent picking a jury. They were sworn in at 4:57 P.M. These twelve citizens held Jimmy's future in their hands.

On Thursday morning, March 2 they were back in the courtroom. Still no Jeannie. No, of course she couldn't be here. But still he couldn't help hoping. Jimmy knew he was going to be seeing Terrie again for the first time in over twenty-one years. He looked around thoughtfully. Once court was in session, Gitnes moved to exclude all witnesses other than when they were testifying. Judge Roberts granted the request. After the judge instructed the jury, it was time for the prosecution to make opening statements.

Assistant District Attorney Daniel Dentoni's thin face was serious. He began by telling the jury, "The purpose of an opening statement is to kind of give you a road map to show you what we expect the evidence to show, not to go into detail about the evidence, but just to give you a general idea of what it is so you're not charging into it blindly.

"The State has to prove that Clark was killed with a handgun, that Mr. Taylor did it, that he did it on August twenty-ninth, nineteen sixty-seven, and that the act occurred in Jackson County, Oregon. And last, we have to prove to you the intent, what was going on in Mr. Taylor's mind. We have to prove to you that he purposefully and deliberately and with premeditated malice killed Glenn True Clark."

Dentoni identified some witnesses and gave the jury an idea of what each would testify to. Among them would be Terrie Trina Tidwell, Detective Carl Seuter, Detective Armand, Ted Porter, and Mark Thyson. Doctor Morgan would testify that the second bullet wound was right in the back of Mr. Clark's head. He described the physical evidence they had and told the jury a fingerprint expert from the FBI would testify. Then he described Detective Peter Jones's role.

Dentoni concluded by saying, "At the end of this case,

ladies and gentlemen, I'm going to ask you to find Mr. Taylor guilty of murder in the first degree. Thank you."

Jimmy had been warned by his lawyers not to show emotion in the courtroom, but he couldn't help but pull a deep breath when he heard Dentoni's somber intent.

Myron Gitnes told the jury, "There are two sides to the story that happened a long time ago and didn't quite happen the way the State said."

Gitnes then recited to the jury a capsule version of the story Jimmy had told his defense team only days earlier. He wanted them to feel and understand the revelation Jimmy had given as he and the others had received it. Although the prosecution was aware by now that Jimmy would testify, they were unaware that his defense would be self-defense. Gitnes began building his case carefully, thoughtfully: revealing to the jury that there were two guns in the car that day. How Mr. Taylor had meals that day while Mr. Clark didn't eat; all he did was drink. Of the three in the car, only Clark was familiar with the area. Gitnes told of the trips to the store and of the point where Jimmy showed the gun to Terrie. Myron described the scene on the dark isolated mountain, led the jury to the confrontation, then took them through the killing and what later happened.

He concluded, having come full circle, "Please listen to all the evidence. Thank you."

Neither opening statement was of long duration. At 9:49 that morning Terrie Tidwell, the first witness for the prosecution, was called. As she was escorted into the court, Jimmy sat very still at the defense table, looking straight ahead. "Don't show any emotion," Garbutt whispered.

Terrie took the oath, sat in the witness chair, and looked at Jimmy. Now Jimmy permitted himself to view her. The hippie look was gone. Jimmy saw the mature Terrie for the first time. Yes, she was still attractive but older. Her hair was styled in little curls and she was wearing glasses. She looked more like a suburban housewife and mother like Jeannie. This must be a difficult time for her, Jimmy thought.

Young, intelligent but a trifle self-conscious and glancing at his notes, Richard Samuels, who was working with Dentoni, spoke for the state. He said that recalling details from twenty-one years ago was a problem. Samuels noted that this witness, along with others, would need to lean on reports or statements from that time. He turned to Terrie.

"Are you aware of anything that would help make your memory more complete of those events as they occurred twenty-one years ago?"

She nodded. "Yes. I read a statement that I made twenty-one years ago."

Samuels nodded approvingly. "I'm going to hand you several sheets of paper, if you would look at those. Is that the statement to which you referred?"

Her voice was barely audible. "Yes, it is."

Samuels then took her through the sequence of events as she recalled them happening in 1967.

"And on either of those occasions, did you go in the store, if you can recall?"

"Yes, I went in."

"And what did you do when you were in the store?"

"I bought some food. I was hungry."

"Okay. Were you aware of what the men that you were with were purchasing?"

Back and forth the state representative and witness went. "Yes."

"And what was that?"

"They were purchasing beer and wine."

She purchased food; they purchased beer and wine! It became evident early on that what Terrie remembered often was in conflict with the statement she had made those many years ago. In time, Samuels asked:

"Other than the gun that you had seen John handling, were you aware of any others?"

"Uhm, no." She stuttered over the word then began again. "I never, I didn't see any other guns, no. And I, uhm, my impression, twenty-one years later, was that was the only gun they had. But apparently in the statement . . ."

Gitnes jumped in to object if she was referring to any statement other than her own. Terrie answered that she was referring to her own statement. She went on, saying, "In this, I guess someone had told me that—well, John had told me, because John and I were the only ones who talked about a gun—he told me that Jay had a gun also, that they both had guns."

Samuels continued taking her through that evening and led Terrie to the scene in the clearing on Dead Indian Mountain. According to her, the two men talked in front of the car, discussing something, as though whatever was about to happen they were in agreement. Then she spoke about after Jay had made his move on her. Samuels asked:

"And what did you feel his intentions were?"

"Well, I, I think I suddenly panicked and I figured that he probably wanted to rape me. And then I knew that they had a gun, there was a gun in the car, you know, and I, that I, you know—I guess I probably was concerned about the gun and being raped."

"Okay. What happened then?"

"Well, I screamed, you know, and I fought with all of my strength, uhm, you know, not to be pulled out of the car."

"What happened after—while you were fighting, what happened?"

"Uhm, then the younger one, John, came around to the driver's side of the car and held the gun to Jay and said," she looked self-conscious, "you know, 'let go of her.'"

"And what did Jay do?"

She made a doleful face. "He immediately let go."

"Okay. What happened after John had brandished the gun at Jay and Jay had let go of you? What happened between the two of them next?"

"Well, John was giving, you know, telling Jay, you know, what to do. He said, 'Get up here in front of the car and . . .'"

"What did Jay do?"

"He did. He was afraid of John. He was, he just put his

hands up, and he said, 'Hey, I . . .'" She turned to Samuels. "You know." He gestured for her to continue again as she looked at him. "You know, he was quite scared of John."

"Okay. What happened after they got around the front of the car?"

"Well, John told Jay to get on his knees."

"And what happened?"

"And Jay did. He got on his knees, and he, you know, just really, you know, said, 'Please don't shoot, please don't shoot.'"

"After John had ordered Jay to his knees, were you able to see what happened after that?"

"Yes. He said to Jay, 'Take off your shirt.' And I guess I thought that was kind of strange. I mean, I remember this some twenty-one years later. And he did. He took off his shirt, you know. And there he was on his knees in front of the headlight."

"Was there any conversation between John and Jay while Jay was on his knees with his shirt off?"

Her nervousness was visible. "Well, the only conversation I remember was Jay pretty much begging for his life and being quite afraid of John, just, you know—John was, you know, I mean, he, apparently Jay, in my opinion, was really afraid John was going to, you know, pull the trigger. And he was just trying to say, please don't shoot, don't shoot, I'll, you know, whatever you say, I'll do it, you know, just, hey . . ."

"Okay. Were you able to get your bags out of the car?"

"Yes. I got both my suitcases out of the car. And I was, you know, thinking about, you know, should I get out of here or not?"

"Uh-huh."

"Because, you know, I was way out in the forest and it was a decision I had to make."

"Now, during the time that Jay was down on his knees and pleading for his life, how far away from the two men were you at that time, as you recall?"

"I think that I was sitting in the back seat of the car, you know, watching him in the headlights. And I may have been standing up next to the back door of the car and they were in front of the headlights. They were like maybe three feet from the headlights, and I was either viewing through the window or standing up."

Samuels nodded, gesturing for her to go on. "Okay."

"I don't remember that exact detail, except that I do remember seeing him on his knees with his shirt off, distinctly, and the other guy holding the gun, you know, at him."

Samuels tried to get her to focus. "Where was the gun pointed, as you recall?"

"Well, I thought it was pointed towards his head or upper body, you know."

"Did John say anything to you during the time that he had Jay down on his knees?"

She shook her head. "I don't remember him saying anything to me. I remember that the two of them were having their own conversation, you know, up there."

Jimmy and Gitnes exchanged a somber look. Bitterly, Jimmy wondered what would have happened if he'd left her there to fight for her survival on her own. Then he let the thought go. He couldn't have abandoned her. He brought his mind back to the present.

"And, at some point, you decided it was best to leave?"

She gave a heavy sigh. "Well, you know, I, I don't know. I heard the shots. I suppose I was looking in that direction when the first shot went off. I didn't stop to see Jay fall to the ground or anything like that. As soon as I— as soon as I realized John had shot Jay, I skedaddled."

Terric claimed to have hidden behind a tree at this point and to have looked back and seen what was going on at the scene. She also claimed that for some three or four minutes John called out for her. And then the car took off.

Samuels continued with the questioning.

"What did you do after he left in the car?"

"Uhm, I had felt that I was out in the forest with— I knew that man was dead, there was no doubt in my mind.

And so I wanted to get just as far away from that body as I could get. I was, for some reason I was afraid of bears. I was afraid that I would, you know, run into a bear there along the road there. And of course there was—there were a lot of noises and crickets and, you can hear noises. But I was scared. But I decided to try to get up on a road where maybe I could get back into town, I could walk into town. And I wanted to get away from that body as fast as I could."

Terrie relived that night as she looked for help. "After finding the truck: well, I decided to pass on, you know, I went along, I passed the truck. And then I realized that it was just too dark, and I didn't know where I was going. And so I decided, my judgment was to go back to the truck and get inside of the truck for protection from whatever bear might want to come after me, so . . ."

After she'd told about being found by the loggers, Samuels said, "I'd like to go back to the time just before the shooting. As you remember it now, who would you say was in control of that situation?"

"During the shooting?"

"Just before."

"Just when John had the gun on Jay?"

"Uh-huh."

"Oh, John was firmly in control. And Jay was firmly afraid of John. I mean, he was really afraid of him."

Soon after this, Samuels said he had no further questions at this time. A recess was taken and then it was time for Gitnes to begin his cross-examination.

After a few preliminary questions, Gitnes asked about the document Terrie'd been referring to earlier in her testimony. Terrie admitted to having only read it twice, once the day before and she had skipped over quite a bit before the grand jury hearing. Quietly, deliberately, Gitnes inquired:

"Okay. Would you say that comparing your statement in nineteen sixty-seven with your recollection of the events today, without that statement, would be more true and accurate in terms of all of the full story, all of the details?"

"Oh, the statement would be more accurate. I mean, twenty-one years, any normal person would remember— I mean would forget some details. The statement would be more accurate."

After Terrie had testified that this statement was indeed the one she had given in 1967, Gitnes said, "Your Honor, I would offer Exhibit One Hundred Five."

Samuels objected, saying that Terrie had used this document only to refresh her recollection. Judge Roberts overruled the objection and Exhibit 105 became "Defendant's Exhibit 105" and was received into evidence.

There was no rancor in his voice, but Gitnes then asked if there weren't certain things she had told people the day she made that statement that were not true, such as having been kidnapped and having been picked up in a coffee shop. Terrie didn't remember. Many of her answers from this point on were, "I don't remember," or "I don't know."

Gitnes asked, "Okay. And they picked you up somewhere in Talent, correct, near Talent, Oregon?"

She shrugged. "I guess."

Once again he brought her back. "If you said that in your statement?"

Terrie sighed audibly. "Then it must be true."

Now that he had her statement in evidence, Gitnes continually referred back to this document. She had answered earlier that she didn't know who went in and bought beer and wine. Her statement identified this to be Jay. Time after time her statement answered questions that she either could not or would not. Though he felt sorry for the girl, he had to have the truth. His client's life depended upon it. Gitnes asked:

"Okay. Would you say that one or the other one was becoming more intoxicated than anyone?"

"Yes. I would say that John was more intoxicated than Jay."

"Now, who are you talking about, driver or passenger?"

"The passenger."

She nodded her head.

"Now, if you said something different back in nineteen sixty-seven, that Jay was the more intoxicated of the two, would that have been more accurate than your testimony here?"

"It, it probably would, you know, uh-huh. It was just fresher in my mind at that time, so. . . ."

In answer to another question, Terrie said she could recall "drinking a little bit."

Gitnes plowed through the same ground covered by Samuels, often being answered with, "I don't know," until he referred Terrie to her earlier statement and then there were many times she changed her answers.

Then Gitnes asked a telling question: "Didn't you, as the hours progressed, get the feeling that the passenger was the person who you could rely on more, was kinder to you, more respectful, who would tell the driver to quit using vulgar words, and so forth? Isn't that true?"

Samuels's objection was overruled by Judge Roberts, and Terrie answered, "That might be true."

Gitnes's voice rose, its resonant quality reverberating in the now silent room. "If you said it in nineteen sixty-seven, it would have been true?"

"Yes."

Later, after Gitnes had begun questions pertaining to the clearing on Dead Indian Mountain, he inquired:

"And doesn't John say—and I'm referring to page six, toward the middle—doesn't John say, 'I promise I'll shoot him if I have to?'"

"Is that what I said he said?"

"Well, I'll show it to you so you can show me. I can't testify for you, ma'am. This area right here." Gitnes pointed to the page.

"Yeah. Apparently that's what he said."

"And he said that a couple of times to you, did he not, and then Jay comes back to the car?"

Grimly, determinedly, Gitnes continued to compare her testimony with her statement, finding inconsistencies. And then he inquired, looking directly into Terrie's eyes,

"Did John direct Jay to get out of the car while he was holding the gun to his head?"

"Yes, apparently."

"And you were pretty panicked at this time, correct?"

"Yes." Her head was down.

"Okay. Didn't John ask you if you were all right this time?" Gitnes held his breath. What he wanted was the same answer. "Again, if you would like to. . . ."

"Does that say that on there? Then if that says that, then he probably did."

He faced her squarely.

"Okay. One more time, if I may show you a portion of your statement, read that paragraph there." He pointed to the place on the page.

Unhappily, eyes downcast, she said, "All right."

He said quietly, "Now John says to you, 'Are you okay?' Correct?"

"Yes."

"And what are you doing now? What is your reaction to everything?"

She paused, seemingly considering. "Well, I think I was shook up because he had grabbed me. I was shook up because one man was holding the gun to the other man. To this point, I had never even seen a real gun. I mean, this was scary."

Terrie admitted that she had said in her statement that the men were "kind of hassling." Also, that she didn't know what they were talking about. She insisted that John told Jay to get on his knees and remove his shirt and that the older man complied. After indicating that she had remained near the car and had not run until after the first shot, Gitnes's forehead creased in concentration.

"Now, isn't it true that in nineteen sixty-seven right after this event," he went on, "you told the police when you first heard the shots you were fifty to one hundred feet away?"

"Did I say that?"

"Yes," he replied firmly. "Did you?"

"Then I, you know, that must be true. I'm sure that that's true, but I certainly knew that he had, that the man had been shot."

"Was there any time between the two shots?"

"There might have been, but I just don't know."

"Okay."

"I know that I heard two shots."

His questions came rapid fire. "And when these two shots, you heard two shots, were you still walking, were you standing still, were you looking at any particular direction? What were you doing?"

"I know that I was looking in that direction. But when I heard the first shot, I began to go. That was when my first foot step, you know, I mean, I made a quick foot step and a quick decision happened."

Vigorously, Gitnes shook his head. "Okay. Then I believe you said that you went behind a tree for your own safety?"

"Yes."

"And you could still see these two men, or you could still see the scene where these two men were when you were at the tree?"

"Yes."

"And you could still see these two men, or you could still see the scene where these two men were when you were at the tree?"

"Yes."

"Yes?" he asked softly but decisively.

"That's what I recall now. However, the statement is a little different. And I don't, I don't think the statement necessarily conflicts. I remember hiding behind a tree and Jay calling for me and looking around for me."

He stared at her. "Okay. Now . . ."

"I mean, John, excuse me, John calling for me and looking around for me. And I remember thinking, should I make myself known, because there I was out in the forest. I was afraid of bears, and I thought, you know, should I stay out here or do I make myself known. And I chose to stay out in the forest."

Several times during his cross-examination, Gitnes referred to the date on Terrie's statement as being September 1, 1967 when it was actually August 30, 1967. Once he angled his head toward the witness chair and demanded, "What did you—well, isn't it true that on September first, nineteen sixty-seven you told the police that, after the shots, 'I turned around. I didn't run. I just walked real fast, I was screaming and crying while I was walking.' Do you recall telling them that?"

"Probably, you know, that's probably what I did. I can remember thinking, now I've got to get to a place where I can, you know, conceal myself."

Gitnes looked up at the judge thoughtfully.

"Okay. Let me approach the witness one last time, Your Honor. And this is the last time." He walked to the rail. "If you would just read for me down this way a little bit."

"All righty. Okay."

"Thank you. Isn't it true that on September first, nineteen sixty-seven, you told the police that, after you heard the shots, you started walking real fast, that you didn't stop, that you went to the main road and then you turned down the main road basically to get as far away from this scene as you could?"

"Yes." She nodded.

"That's what you told the police?"

"Yes."

"Isn't it true that the police asked you on that occasion, 'Did John call after you ever again after you heard the shots? Did he say anything to you?'"

"Yes."

He moved strongly now. His voice took on a cutting edge. "Is it also true that right towards the end of your statement, and that's on page ten, ma'am, the police were trying to have you, invite you to add anything to your statement, refresh your memory, or anything like that? And you tell them, 'I'm not really too sure about the shooting and I don't want to confirm anything about it. I was upset and I don't really know what I saw. I know that I was looking in that direction,' etcetera. And you say—isn't it true you say, 'All I know was that John was holding the gun and I saw Jay's skin'?"

"Yes."

Gitnes turned, glanced over at Jimmy and held his eyes for a moment. Then he stepped back from the witness box.

"Thank you very much, ma'am, appreciate it."

On his redirect, Samuels wasted no time in pointing out that the date on Terrie's statement was August 30 and not September 1. Then he went on to say:

"In terms of the alcohol that you consumed on the twenty-ninth of August of nineteen sixty-seven, how do you feel that affected you at the time?"

She took a deep breath. "I don't think that I had consumed too much alcohol, and that it had, you know, affected me. But I had a few drinks. I can't say I hadn't, knowing myself during that time. I. . . ."

"Were you intoxicated?"

"No."

Samuels made an attempt at damage control by asking Terrie once again if this was indeed what had happened. Terrie insisted, "Twenty-one years is a long time, and it is to the best of my recollection."

After a brief recross by Gitnes, Samuels had no further questions.

As Terrie stepped down from the stand, she and Jimmy eyed one another for the last time. As she headed down the aisle, out of his vision, he wondered if she actually did remember events as she had described them. How would the jury know the truth?

The court took noon recess, and Jimmy was removed to a holding cell outside the courtroom. A plate of food was brought, but he ate very little. Never had he been more afraid.

The first witness of the afternoon session was Doctor Tilton Morgan, the pathologist who had performed the autopsy on Clark. He testified that the victim suffered two wounds, one just below the clavicle or collarbone and the other in the back of the head. The head wound was three inches above the hairline and near center.

On cross-examination, the doctor admitted that the chest wound was horizontal. And that there were no powder burns.

David G. Davis, the attorney who represented Terrie in 1967, was only on the stand for two or three minutes. He was followed by Carl Seuter, who had been the first police representative on the scene in 1967.

Dentoni conducted the direct examination. After the preliminaries, he asked:

"Can you tell me what you observed when you first started walking down this spur road off Shell Peak Road? Did you see any indication that anybody had been there?"

Seuter nodded. "Yes, sir. We saw barefoot prints of a small size."

Dentoni, his voice pitched low and serious, asked, "What do you mean by bare? Could you see the toes or not?"

"Yes, sir. They were obviously shoeless prints."

"Did you see anything else?"

"Yes, sir. There were tire tracks coming out of the road."

Next, Dentoni offered State's Exhibit Number One, a drawing of the crime scene that had been made on the date Clark was found. This sketch showed where the car had been parked as well as the tracks leading in and out, where Jimmy had sat, where one knee print had been, where the body fell and where it had been dragged to. Unlike Terrie, Seuter had studied his reports and also used field notes he had retained.

Seuter pointed out that there was a white mark on Clark's left arm where a wristwatch had been removed, or had been worn and was no longer there. He also testified that they had found drag marks indicating that the victim had possibly fallen on his face and then had been turned over and dragged to a point about nine feet away, leaving a trail of blood marks.

Dentoni stated his questions carefully now. "Do you recall finding any identification or wallet on the body?"

And Seuter, a conscientious and thorough policeman, answered just as meticulously. "No, sir. There was no identification or wallet on the body at all."

"Do you recall finding a gun in the pocket of the body?"

"No, sir."

"Did you find any guns at the scene?"

"Nothing at the scene, sir."

"Did you find anything on the body that might indicate that a weapon had been on the body, such as a holster clip or bullets or shells or anything like that?"

The singsong pattern continued. The spectators angled their heads first toward the witness and then toward the lawyer. Jimmy stared straight ahead.

"No sir, nothing."

"And there was a wristwatch missing, is that right?"

"There was a mark that would indicate that he had been wearing a wristwatch, yes, sir."

"Did you find any money on the body?"

"No, sir."

"Did you find a wristwatch, a watch or a wallet or a weapon with Miss Tidwell?"

"Nothing other than her own, no."

After confirming that those items with Jimmy's fingerprints had come from the scene, Seuter testified that they had found prints of a narrow-toed Italian shoe or a cowboy boot with a horseshoe cleat on the heel.

Seuter later said that the car they had been riding in had been found in San Francisco and that it had been stripped.

Upon cross-examination, Gitnes asked:

"Why did it appear to you that this is a knee print? Tell me what made you reach that conclusion."

"It was a fabric print and it was round, and in the dirt at the front of where we would have to have presumed the vehicle was parked, and it tied in with the account that was given by Miss Tidwell, that Mr. Clark was placed on his knees."

"Exactly. Miss Tidwell told you that one person had the other get down on his knees, and you found a circular depression that looked similar to a knee print."

"That's correct."

"Okay. But you only found one, not two? You found one knee print?"

"I don't know specifically. The diagram so indicates, yes, sir."

Despite Seuter's precise answers, the defense scored several points: upon further questioning, Seuter admitted that they had no way of knowing whether or not Clark had removed the watch from his arm or perhaps another person did. When asked about the motor vehicle found in San Francisco, Seuter admitted he had never seen the vehicle but Pauling and Armand did. Referring back to his reports, Seuter admitted that Terrie had told him that when the men were standing in front of the car prior to the shooting, they were arguing over who had stolen the car. Also, John had told her that he had the gun and would protect her if necessary. The substance of Seuter's reports came much nearer to matching Terrie's statement given in 1967 than they did what she had said that morning.

On redirect, Dentoni tied up loose ends.

"Didn't she also say that the suspect, the person you referred to as the suspect, shouted to her, 'Don't leave, I'm going to kill him, turn out the lights?'"

"Yes, sir, that is a quotation."

"What was Miss Tidwell's state of mind when she talked to you the first time?"

"Initially she was almost in shock, she was afraid, she was crying. She made sure that everybody there was not who was fresh in her mind as having been involved in this situation."

Next, Detective Porter testified briefly and was followed to the stand by Jay Armand who had not only been in charge of the detective division at the time but had come out of retirement to accompany Peter Jones to Guthrie to arrest Jimmy Dale Taylor. Daniel Dentoni took him over much of the same ground that had been covered in depth by now. Armand's answers concerning the knee print and footprints were consistent with Seuter's testimony.

Also, he agreed that there had been no money or watch on the victim. In cross-examination, Gitnes asked:

"Now, taking a look at the knee print and the footprint drawn there, wouldn't that indicate to you that a person was down on one knee like this, sir, his left knee down like this and with his right leg like that?" Gitnes demonstrated. "Wouldn't that be the indication?"

"It would appear so."

Later, Gitnes asked whether or not Armand could see in a photograph of Clark's trousers whether or not a hip pocket showed any signs of having held a wallet. Armand could not tell. After discussing footprints and interviews with the loggers and Terrie, they moved on to Undersheriff Pauling. Pauling like Armand was retired and lived in Alante where he had his own cabinet shop.

He confirmed that, along with Armand, he had traveled to San Francisco and visited the neighborhood where the car had been stripped. During Pauling's testimony, Dentoni asked about the wooden boxes that had been used to pack those items sent to the FBI.

"Do you know who manufactured those boxes?"

"I was the manufacturer of the boxes."

"Why did you go to so much trouble to make these boxes to hold the wine bottles and beer cans?"

"We had elected to have the investigation of these articles for latent fingerprints conducted by the Federal Bureau of Investigation at their lab. In order to convey them in a fashion that would ensure protection of the articles, it was necessary, we felt, to construct these containers to hold them securely without having packing material or anything rub on the surface of the cans and perhaps destroy any latent fingerprints that might be present."

In cross-examination by Gitnes, Pauling admitted that he and Armand had not actually seen the car in San Francisco, but only the neighborhood. That the car had been traced through credit card slips and through a license tag stolen from a vehicle near Clark's brother's house, supposedly stolen by Clark and not Taylor.

After Pauling's testimony, Peter Jones briefly took the stand. After he'd answered a few questions concerning his early investigation, court was adjourned till the next morning.

After Alex Booth and Kenneth Michaels had testified briefly concerning fingerprints and palm prints, Graham Terbert, fingerprint expert from the FBI, was called to the stand. After Mr. Terbert had completed his testimony there was no doubt that the prints found on those items left at the crime scene as well as those left at the wayside park belonged to the defendant, Jimmy Dale Taylor.

Later that morning, Peter Jones was recalled. He told how Taylor had been identified through fingerprints and how the arrest had been made. He told about questions asked of Jimmy and of answers received. As with Terbert, Gitnes knew that little could be gained by attacking Jones's testimony. He asked a few questions and then sat down. On Friday, March 3 the State rested its case.

22

JIMMY'S LAST CHANCE

Pale and haggard with dark rings under his eyes, Jimmy sat in the courtroom waiting for the defense to begin its case. In the intervening weeks since he'd been arrested he had aged. All of his former buoyancy was gone and, in its place, only his hard-won faith sustained him.

Soon he would be called to testify, to spread his life before all these strangers. He looked at the jury members one by one. Each of them would have to decide who was telling the truth. He knew it would be difficult. He was not so naive to think that the truth would set him free.

No, it was these people who would or not. The pain of that thought struck him viscerally. What would it do to Jeannie and his children if he was found guilty? Trembling, he willed himself not to think of that now.

He focused once more on the courtroom scene swirling about him, and with a sense of unreality heard his name called. On unsteady legs Jimmy moved toward the witness box. It was only when the bailiff said, "Raise your right hand and repeat after me. Do you swear to tell the whole truth?" that Jimmy Dale Taylor knew his last chance was now.

Richard Garbutt conducted the direct examination.

Garbutt began back in San Francisco when Jimmy and Glenn first met. At first, Jimmy's answers were brief, almost hesitant. They discussed Jimmy getting the gun from Glenn. He led Jimmy through that day and into the evening.

Garbutt asked, "What kind of car were you driving at the time, or was he driving?"

"He was driving a nineteen sixty or nineteen sixty-one Oldsmobile, white."

"Okay. How far did you get that night?" Garbutt asked a few more questions about those first hours and then went on:

"Had you been in northern California before?"

"No, sir."

Jimmy told the jury how Clark had nearly caused a fight over a woman while they were in this bar and how they had slept in the car that night. They had stopped at a restaurant but Clark didn't eat. From here, Jimmy began to talk of that afternoon when Clark saw a hitchhiker across the highway and doubled back and invited her into the car, which she climbed into.

Garbutt went on, "What happened after that?"

"Well, I thought we were still in California. I didn't know I was in Oregon. After she got in the car, he said he was going to stop and get some more beer. So we stopped and got more beer."

"Were you getting nervous at all about this point? Did you have any reason to suspect there was something bad that was going to happen?"

"No. I was aggravated because I didn't, you know . . . I thought, well, why come all the way up here and then turn around and go back. He didn't know the girl, not that I know of. I'm sure he didn't."

Jimmy continued telling about how they had stopped for beer and wine and how Clark had asked Terrie if she wanted to visit some friends who owned a ranch or house or something. Clark hadn't asked Jimmy—only Terrie. He told how they had stopped at the wayside park and when

Terrie had seen his gun. Jimmy said, "I told her it was for protection."

Garbutt then turned to Clark's demeanor. "How much—how was Mr. Clark driving during the period?"

"He was scaring me. He was driving crazy, driving pretty fast, and up in the mountains. And I'm not used to mountains."

"Did you have any arguments with him about driving too fast?"

"No. He just told me, 'Don't tell me how to drive.' And, well, I wasn't too comfortable."

"Okay. What happened after you—driving around, where did you finally stop then?"

"Well, after maybe, he drove for quite a while. And, uhm, the lady between us, she passed out or went to sleep. Anyway, she was unconscious. And she was still drinking."

"Prior to her passing out or going to sleep, you mean?"

"Yes, sir."

"How long did you drive after she went to sleep?"

"Oh, fifteen minutes, twenty minutes, maybe."

"Was it still daylight out then?"

For Jimmy it was almost as if he was being transported back in time to that awful night. And the words welled up in him for so long began to come out. At first slowly, then in clumps and gradually like a waterfall cascading.

"No, it was dark. I didn't want to go to sleep. I was tired, too, but the way he was driving I'm not sure I wanted to go to sleep. So he was, I kept telling him to slow down and be careful, and he was barking back at me. And so, all of a sudden, he took this side road. And I think that's when she woke up, the lady in the middle. Miss Tidwell woke up then. And she asked what was going on. Well, I thought he was going to the rest room, too, so he pulled down this road so far, then he pulled off again onto this other little road."

After leading them to the point where the two men were out of the car, Garbutt asked, "So the two of you are now walking up in front of the car. What happened then?"

"Well, I got there before he did, and he told me to wait

a minute; so I stopped. And he walked up to me, and I can't remember exactly what it was, but he was drinking pretty heavy, both of us were. And he said, 'Well, right now is a good time and a good place. . . .'"

Garbutt queried, "Did he tell you what that meant?"

"Well, I thought it was about going to the rest room. And then he decided he was going to screw that girl."

"Did he use that word?"

"No."

"Use the word he used."

"He said he was going to fuck her, that girl, right now, here and now. So . . ."

The lawyer broke in, "How did you respond to that?"

"I didn't know what to do. I told him, 'Man, that's not a very good idea.' And, well, I knew he had a gun."

"How did you know that?"

"Because he showed it to me before."

"Okay."

"And he had carried it in that car." The bitterness within him also flared. "That's probably the reason he was so brave. But he carried it in there. So he told me he was going to screw that girl. And, let me see, there was no argument, but he told me to take a walk. He said, 'Don't go back to the car.' He said, 'Go on past the car. Take a walk for a while.' So . . ."

"What did—did you tell him that it wasn't a good idea or that you were going to join in, or what?"

"Yes. I told him I didn't want to have anything to do with it."

"Did you have your gun with you at that time?"

"No."

"What was his response when you told him it wasn't a good idea?"

"He just told me, 'Don't interfere.' So I told him, I said, 'Do you know what you're talking about, do you know what you're going to do, what could happen?' And I knew he was drunk. And he said, well—" Jimmy coughed self consciously, "well, first he said, well, 'I could have her down and done before she knows what happened.' And then I said, 'Do you know what—do you realize what could happen because of that?' And he said, 'Well, they would never find her here. Or, if they did, they would never identify her.' So I told him I didn't want anything to do with that, and then I started getting nervous. He told me to stay away from the car. He said, 'Don't go back near the car.'"

"Did he tell you what would happen to you if you went back to the car?"

"Yes, sir."

"What was that?"

"He told me there was plenty of room out here for me, too. He said, 'There's plenty of room out here for you, also, so don't go near the car.' I told him I was going to get a couple of beers out of the car and then he just said, 'Don't bother us. Just leave us alone.' I said, 'All right.' He followed me back to the car. As I was getting in the car, I reached up and got the gun from under the dashboard and put it in my pocket. And he got in on the driver's side of the car."

"Did you tell Miss Tidwell anything when you got in the car?"

"Yes."

"What did you tell her?"

Jimmy's eyes closed for a moment, as if he were being transported back in time, and then he said earnestly, "I told her, 'Don't panic and everything will be all right. I'm not going to let him hurt you.' If she had jumped out of the car then and run, he probably would have killed her, or I imagine he would have. It was my opinion."

"Okay. After you told her that, then what did you do?"

"Well, I was still sitting in the car, and I got a couple of beers. And he got in the car and he kept looking at me, gave me dirty looks and nodded his head. So I got out of the car and I walked back to the place where we was at, maybe from here to the door, and the window was down. And I didn't know what to do. I knew if I got up close to the car, he was going to either shoot me or hurt her or something. He was drunk, he was pretty well mad. I was sitting on this log, standing by the log or something. It was dark. And I heard her scream. And I heard a lot of banging and bumping around, and I heard her scream for help."

"Was it a loud scream?"

He nodded vigorously. "Yeah. I heard it from where I was at, and it was loud enough for me to hear."

"Did she scream more than once?"

"Yes."

"Was it a constant repetition of scream?"

Jimmy grimaced. "No. First she told the guy, I heard her, 'Get away from me.' And then I heard her screaming and kicking and making noise. And then I heard her scream for help, so I ran over to the car."

"Which side of the car did you run to?"

"The passenger side. The window was down. And he had her down on the seat with his arms by her arms. And she was fighting and kicking and hollering. I told him, yelled at him, 'Leave her alone.' And I don't know if he didn't hear me, or—but he didn't, not the first time. I pulled the gun out and pointed at him and said, 'Get up and leave her alone.'"

"Was the door opened or closed at this time?"

"It was partly open. She got the door opened some-how a little bit. But she was laying with her head toward me, and he was also. . . ."

"And he was coming in through the driver's side?"

"Yes. He was in the car when I got out of the car."

"Okay. What happened then?"

"He glanced up and saw the gun, and he stopped."

"Was he . . ."

"Or he pushed her away."

"Was the dome light on at this point because the door was open?"

"I don't know. I don't think so."

"Okay, but he did recognize you had a gun?"

"Oh yes."

"Okay."

"I told him, 'Get out of the car and leave her alone.' So

he got out of the car. Then I realized that wasn't too good of an idea. I should have gotten her out first and let her run. He was already out of the car, and when he got out that side, she jumped out the side I was on and she ran around the back of the car. And I was standing on the opposite side of the car that he was on, and I still had a gun on him. And I told him to keep his hands so I could see his hands, because I knew he had the gun.

"I walked around to where he was at, and I got there just about the same time that lady got there, Miss Tidwell. And she was scared, and I was scared. And she was screaming and hollering. And he was hollering, cussing at me. I can't remember—I remember part of it, but everything was going on all at one time there."

The words were a torrent now.

"I remember she was standing there screaming and screaming and screaming. I didn't know if he had stabbed her, cut her, or beat her, or hit her, or what. She was sure hollering. He was cussing at me, kept pointing his finger at me. I had him stand directly in front of one of the headlights. And I told him to sit down, kept on telling him to sit down. She was screaming and hollering. And he was hollering at me. And she was screaming. I couldn't see too much because the lights were in my eyes. But I could see him from where he was at; it wasn't too far. But I couldn't see her. She was further over. But she was hollering. I didn't know if she was hurt.

"I backed up about four feet, three or four feet, to get out of the headlights of the car, and I could see her from the side. And I didn't want to turn my head to take my eyes off him, but I did. And when I turned my head to ask if she was all right, she said no. And she got in the car — it wasn't a four-door; it was two-door—and she was in the back seat of the car real fast, and backing out with, came back out with her suitcases. And I asked her again, 'Are you all right?' And I seen him move. And as I turned around, he was bringing a gun out. And I fired a shot. Well, first before I fired a shot, I asked her if she was all right."

Assistant District Attorney Richard Samuels, Dentoni's assistant, stood up. "Your Honor, I'm going to object to the narrative form. He's not answering any questions."

Judge Roberts said, "Objection overruled. Go ahead."

"Oh, she got out of the car, and he was still standing there. I asked her if she was all right. And she said, 'No. I'm leaving.' And she took off running that direction, through the trees with her suitcases, down this little road. And as I turned around, I seen him bringing the gun up, I heard the shot and I fired. And it hit him right there. It was—he was, oh, ten feet from me, maybe. And he went down on one knee.

"And when he grabbed the gun, the gun fell over beside him here, and he was holding his chest and just looking at me. So he looked down at the gun. And I told him to back up, don't try to touch it. And I started walking around behind him just so if he did grab the gun, he wouldn't be able to shoot me. And he grabbed for the gun, and I fired again. And that time I fired, I thought I hit him in the shoulder, but evidently I didn't, and he fell sideways on his back."

Garbutt began to interrupt to ask a question. The judge took advantage of the opening and recessed for lunch.

After lunch, Garbutt continued the questioning.

"Mr. Taylor, I believe the last thing you indicated was that you shot a second time and you thought you hit him in the shoulder, but then you found out that you had hit him in the head. I'd like to digress a little bit. There was this testimony about his shirt being taken off. How did that whole scene evolve?"

"Well, I didn't know where the gun was at, and I told him to take his shirt off to see if it was stuck in his belt or whatever."

"After you fired the second time, what did you—did you take any action regarding Miss Tidwell?"

"No."

"She testified that you were calling after her. Do you remember any of that?"

"No. I asked her if she was all right before she left."

"What did you do at that point?"

"I panicked. I went over to him and first the gun was still there. And I still had the gun pointed at him. And he was laying next to the car, so I went over and picked the gun up, put the gun in my pocket, and went over to where he was at to see if I could find a pulse or something. I decided I would move him so I wouldn't run over him with the car. And I moved him to where he's laying up there.

"And I walked around for a few minutes, didn't know what to do. I looked down and saw the blood on my hands, and I just took off. I got sick, shaky, I panicked."

Jimmy told about how Clark always put his watch on the turn signal handle and that Jimmy had taken neither watch nor wallet. He had taken the guns and later thrown them away. He left the scene, ran out of gas, was assisted by a patrolman, and returned to San Francisco.

Garbutt stopped him from going on. "That will be all for now, Mr. Taylor."

Richard Samuels conducted the cross-examination. He attempted to trap Jimmy in inconsistencies about that night and the crime, going over much of Jimmy's testimony.

Samuels challenged, "So at the time that the victim was getting back into the car, you were the only one that had easy access to a loaded, unholstered weapon, is that right?"

"No," Jimmy said defensively.

To unsettle him, the questions were delivered rapid-fire, but Jimmy stuck to the story he had told on the stand that day and to his lawyers only a short time before.

"You had just taken it out from under the dash, hadn't you?"

"Yes, sir."

"And you knew full well what he intended to do with Miss Tidwell, isn't that right?"

"Yes."

"And isn't it also true that, at that time, you told Miss Tidwell not to worry, that you would kill him if you had to?"

"No, sir."

"So her testimony is not right?"

"That's right."

"You made no effort to warn Miss Tidwell of what was about to happen to her, did you?"

"I didn't have a chance."

"Well, you had a chance to tell her that you had a gun, didn't you?"

"No. I told her—no, I told her, 'Don't panic,' and that's all I had a chance to say before he got in the car, and get two beers. And then he just started looking at me funny, staring at me. So I got out of the car."

After they had moved ahead to when Jimmy ran over to the car, Samuels said, "You ordered him out of the car?"

"Yes."

"And he complied?"

"Yes."

"And you ordered him out in front of the car, right?"

"After. Yes, sir."

"And he also complied with that, didn't he?"

"Yes, sir."

"And you ordered him to remove his shirt?"

"Yes, sir."

"And he complied with that, didn't he?"

"Yes, sir."

"So it would be fair to say up to that point you are in control of the situation, wouldn't it?"

"Semi. Up to. Yes, sir."

"Well, let me put it this way, Mr. Taylor. You're the only man at the scene with a gun drawn and pointing at the other man. Isn't that right?"

"Yes, sir."

"And up to that point he had complied with each and every one of your orders. Isn't that right?"

"Yes, sir."

"And while you were in this position of advantage, never once did you attempt to disarm him, did you?"

"Yes, sir."

"And, for some reason, he chose not to comply with the gun trained on him?"

"No. He was cussing me, yelling at me. She was screaming. It was one big bunch of noise."

Discussing Jimmy's actions after Glenn had been shot the first time, Samuels asked, "At that point, you made no effort to kick the gun away from him; did you?"

"No."

"You didn't make an effort to rush him and push him over without shooting him again, did you?"

"No. I didn't want to go near him."

As for the second shot, Samuels inquired, "And you thought you were shooting at his shoulder?"

"No. I didn't aim at anything. I just pulled the gun up and fired. I thought that would probably be the area that it hit. I didn't know it hit him in the head."

Jimmy admitted under further questioning that he had made no effort to find Terrie after the shooting.

Samuels continued, "You also mentioned something while you were speaking with Mr. Garbutt about how you didn't know whether she had been shot or cut. Had you seen a knife on the victim?"

"No, sir. Just the way she was screaming, I didn't know what happened."

Jimmy admitted that he had left the scene and that he had never reported the shooting.

Samuels switched the focus of questioning.

"Earlier today you testified that you have thought about this incident every day of your life since it happened. Is that right?"

"Just about. Yes, sir."

Under further questioning, Jimmy admitted that he had not thought of it every day of his life, but quite often. Samuels thought that if this was so, then Jimmy should have known what Peter Jones was referring to when the detective asked Jimmy if he had ever been in Oregon, and told Jimmy that he was arrested for murder. After a few more questions, Samuels finally said, "I have nothing further."

Garbutt walked slowly toward the witness stand and inquired of Jimmy, "Were you afraid at the time of the shooting?"

"Yes."

"Again, were you afraid?"

"Yes."

"Were you afraid for your own life?"

"Yes."

"Were you afraid for Miss Tidwell's life?"

"Yes, sir."

"I have no other questions," Garbutt said, his eyes fixed on the jury.

Court was adjourned until Monday afternoon at 1:30. Jimmy was taken back to his quad. There he would spend the longest weekend of his life.

So would Jeannie. She felt trapped in Guthrie with the children, far away from the man she loved, the father who might never live with his family again. The man she thought she knew so well was on trial for murder. Briefly, she thought back to their earlier days together. His moodiness. His constant flights from place to place. Now she understood why, but it still made no sense. Jimmy could never have killed anyone in cold blood. There had to be an explanation. She loved and believed in him no matter what. She held on to that now. It was all she had. At the end of each day of the trial, Jimmy had called their friend Les collect so that an account of what happened could be passed to her. Even so, Jeannie felt helpless. All she could do was wait. And wait some more.

23

THE VERDICT

Pacing back and forth in his quad, Jimmy agonized over the trial. Had the jury believed him? Had he laid bare his soul for nothing? He couldn't know what the outcome would be. He only knew that the hour of decision was drawing near.

He wanted so much to talk with Jeannie but it still wasn't possible. And so, on Sunday, March 5 he wrote his feelings in a letter. He said, "I don't know if the jury will give its verdict tomorrow or the day after, but by the time this letter gets to you it will be over and I will know what is going to happen. When I think about it, I really get nervous.

"Boy, this place is starting to get to me pretty badly. We all walk around in here like animals in cages. I have to be careful what I say or do so as not to start a fight. I spend more and more time inside of my cell by myself, reading my Bible or thinking of you and the children. I need your mail! It helps me through the hard times. I have read your letters over and over.

"I have now been locked up for over one-hundred-and-fifty days and I feel every day of it. Although I hope and pray I will be free, I will be so glad when they do whatever they are going to do.

"They will be coming to get me soon to take me to court. This is the last letter you will get from me before the verdict. The next time you hear from me I will know what's going to happen to me."

When court resumed on Monday afternoon, those who took the witness stand showed unusual courage. They were a friend and relatives of Clark, including his ex-wife, who had been found by Paul Arritola and had agreed to testify for Jimmy.

First to take the stand was Glenn's attractive blond sister, Marion Parker. Gitnes handled the direct examination. After establishing her relationship to Clark, he asked, "Was he older than you or younger than you?"

"Younger. Four years."

"Did you have other brothers?"

"Yes. I had two older brothers and two younger brothers."

"Mr. Clark—Glenn Clark—did he have a special place with you? Was he one of your . . . ?"

Her voice was far away, sad. "He was kind of a favorite brother, yes."

"You did a lot of things together?"

"Yes."

"When you knew your brother, the last couple of years before he died, had he become a changed person?"

"Yes."

"How would, how had he changed?"

"Oh, not towards me, but his talking and his attitude were altogether different."

"Based upon your contacts with him and your knowledge of your brother, would you be able to form an opinion as to his disposition or character towards violence?"

"Yes. He was. . . . He—I don't know how to say it. He could have been violent, yes."

Looking away for a moment, tears sprang to Jimmy's

eyes. He could not help but feel compassion for this woman who, like him, had to bare her family's secrets to strangers. He moved his head to see her again.

"Would intoxication exacerbate that situation?"

"Yes," she said softly but firmly.

"Regarding weapons, did your brother like weapons?"

"Yes."

"Did he carry a weapon in his car?"

"Yes." Her voice quivered.

In his cross-examination, Daniel Dentoni asked, "Was it also true that your brother could be a kind, compassionate person?"

"Yes."

Marion was followed by her brother Avery. His testimony was very brief. There was no cross-examination.

Next to be called was Ted Ryder, the friend and neighbor who had assisted the police twenty-one years before. After it was established that he and Glenn True Clark had socialized several times and that Ted had seen Glenn carry a handgun into a bar and believed that he always carried one in his car, Gitnes asked, "Based upon your relationship with him, are you able to form an opinion as to his disposition or character towards violence?"

"When he was intoxicated, he would get very violent."

"Did you ever see him carry a wallet?"

"Never did."

"Why would that strike you as being significant?"

"He never paid for anything. When he was out with a man, he expected you to pay all the deals. And when he did have money, he'd take it out of his pocket. His credit cards and stuff like that he carried in his pocket."

On cross, Dentoni asked, "Was it your testimony just now that he carried credit cards in his pocket?"

"He always did, and any money he had."

"He always had money and credit cards in his pocket?"

"Well, but he never paid for anything."

When Glenn's ex-wife testified, she said that they had been separated since May 1966.

Gitnes asked, "Prior to the separation, had you had a difficult relationship with him?"

"Yes. Prior to the separation, yes."

"Based upon that difficulty, are you in a position to form an opinion as to his disposition or character towards violence?"

"He was becoming very violent."

"Would intoxication enhance that violence?"

"Yes. It did."

"During the period of separation, did you have an amicable time during that period of time with him?"

"During the period of separation, I did not see him."

"Did you avoid him?"

"Yes. I did."

There was no cross-examination. The defense rested its case.

Samuels presented closing argument for the State. He told the jury, "Because the State has the burden of proving this case beyond a reasonable doubt, I get to speak with you twice. I'll argue my case now.

"The defendant's attorneys will have their chance to argue their case to you. And then I'll have a chance to respond to the issues that are raised during their closing."

He began by saying, "Let's look at the evidence that you heard during the trial. We started off with the testimony of Terrie Trina Tidwell. She's one of two people still living today that were up there off Shell Peak Road on that logging spur on August twenty-ninth, nineteen sixty-seven. And of the two people that survived, she's the only person that's truly unbiased. Truly the only disinterested person that's testified in this case."

Samuels took the jury once more over events after Terrie had been picked up to when they were in the clearing on Dead Indian Mountain. He said, "I suggest to you that from the time that John left the front of the car until he got in and told Miss Tidwell that he'd shoot Jay if he had to, he had deliberated and premeditated and decided he was going to kill Jay.

"As we know, she said he left the car, Jay made a grab at her, and she screamed. She screamed for help. And John, the man we later found out is the defendant, came running out of the darkness with a gun drawn and stuck it in Jay's face. Told him to leave Miss Tidwell alone and Jay complied."

Samuels used the same argument, trying to show that Jay took his shirt off and got on his knees, as ordered by John. He told the jury that Jay was pleading for his life. "Terrie knows that John shot Jay in cold blood while he was pleading for his life. The car left, and they didn't see one another in twenty-one years."

According to Samuels, the defendant ditched the car in an area where he knew it would be stripped, thus covering his tracks. Meanwhile, Miss Tidwell was cooperating with police officers. He said, "She was truly detached and uninterested, just here to tell the truth. They found a knee print near a footprint, essentially where she said it would be. One other thing they found. They found a body nine feet from the spur road lying on its back devoid of any identification and missing its watch.

"I ask you to remember Dr. Morgan's testimony. The victim suffered two wounds, one just below the clavicle or collar bone. And one in the back of the head. I suggest to you that the placement of that shot alone shows a clear intent to kill. You don't shoot somebody in the middle of the back of the head by accident."

Samuels kept returning to the shot to the back of the head and also laid out other evidence. "Look at the defendant's rapid departure from the scene and his taking the car to San Francisco and dumping it in an effort to cover his tracks."

Soon after this, he concluded, "When you so view the evidence, it becomes clear that this defendant is guilty of murder in the first degree."

After a recess, Myron Gitnes walked slowly to the front of the courtroom and began the closing argument for the defense.

He said, "Here we are twenty-two years after a violent time in two people's lives. We're trying to decide what happened."

Gitnes believed there were two important pieces of evidence. One was Terrie's statement from 1967 and the other was Jimmy Taylor's testimony to the jury.

Gitnes said, "We have a case here—and I think I explained this to you in the opening—in which you must decide murder versus self-defense. The fingerprint expert—and he was an expert, no question about that—doesn't help you to decide this case at all. The police officers who drew this diagram, took the measurements, and did the hard work really don't help you that much to decide this case.

"The real question is, are we talking about murder or self-defense? Murder is the deliberate killing of another person. Self-defense has a definition in law, too. That is, a person is justified in using force against another person whom he reasonably believes is going to use imminent force against him."

Then Gitnes asked, "How has the State proved premeditated murder to you? Well, the only evidence I can see in this whole case is the testimony of Terrie Tidwell. There is no physical evidence at all that proves premeditated murder. The physical evidence here just shows you that Mr. Clark was shot under some circumstances.

"I also point out that Terrie Tidwell was not even physically present when these two shots were fired."

Gitnes reminded the jury of Dr. Morgan's testimony. The path of the bullet to the chest was horizontal. This meant the two men were standing. They found bare footprints. Only one knee print. The position of the body where it fell was not consistent with where Terrie Tidwell had said it should be. There were no powder burns.

Gitnes went over the prosecution's case point by point.

He didn't say Terrie was lying, but he opined, "What I am going to suggest to you is that she embellished her story. What are her in-court embellishments? Well, I think there are a few. Number one, 'Mr. Taylor called after me.'

Number two, 'I watched the whole incident from behind a tree.' You remember her telling us that. This is where this helps us out a lot. In nineteen sixty-seven she told the police, 'The last thing I heard, the last thing I heard was two gun shots.'

"She didn't stop and hide behind a tree and watch this scene like she told us in court. At one point she says, 'I was crying and screaming as I walked.'

"The crux of the matter is that Terrie Tidwell's nineteen-sixty-seven statement and Jimmy Taylor's in-court statement a couple of days ago are almost identical. And they are almost identical in all the crucial ways."

Gitnes went on, his voice gathering force. "If you believe Terrie Tidwell's own testimony, you have to think that Mr. Taylor got so offended by someone trying to rape a stranger that he was the executioner himself."

Not long after this, he concluded, "Ladies and gentlemen, we don't have to, but I think we did prove to you that this was an act of self-defense."

Samuels fired the last shot for the prosecution. He portrayed Terrie Tidwell as an unbiased third party. According to him, she was the one who stuck around and told the police what she had seen. She helped the police with the composite drawing. He added that the evidence all pointed to first degree murder.

Later, he said, "Now in terms of deliberation, the judge will instruct you, and I'd ask you once again to listen very care fully to his instruction because he will tell you just how quickly deliberation and premeditation can occur. And I suggest to you that it happened in that brief span of moments from the time the defendant left the front area of that car and walked back and sat down and talked to Terrie."

Samuels went on, "Now to the testimony about the wallet. You heard Mr. Ryder testify that Glenn didn't like to pay for drinks. And that he never saw him with a wallet.

That doesn't mean he didn't have one. And the issue here is not really whether he had a wallet, but rather the issue is the ID that is usually contained in such a wallet. What we do have is a statement from Mr. Ryder that the victim always carried money and credit cards in his pocket. Credit cards identify you. The body didn't have any identification on it.

"Defense Exhibit One Hundred Eight shows the right rear pocket, and it appears that the pocket has been turned inside out. This is completely consistent with someone going through that pocket attempting to remove anything that would identify the victim in this case and covering his tracks."

Samuels recalled Terrie's disappearance and the fact that Jimmy pulled out pretty fast after the killing. And then he switched to the time of the arrest in Oklahoma.

Speaking of Jimmy, Samuels said, "He wasn't indignant, as he testified. He was rather soft-spoken." Gitnes glanced at Jimmy. It was bad news when being a decent guy was equated with being guilty of murder. "Not very forceful in his testimony. Put yourself in that position. If you're here to defend yourself and claiming self-defense, you'd be indignant if you were really and truly acting in self-defense.

"Mr. Taylor would also like you to believe that he was acting in defense of Miss Tidwell, but, if he was, how come he didn't go look for her? How come he hopped in the car and took off? Because he wasn't concerned about her. He shot Glenn Clark, and he just wanted to get out of there. He murdered him. You don't shoot someone in the back of the head if you're acting in self-defense."

Samuels ended, "Look at it altogether, and you should find the defendant guilty of murder in the first degree."

There was no verdict that day. Although the final arguments were concluded at 3:47 P.M., Judge Roberts recessed until 9:00 the following morning.

Jimmy's defense team had had their last chance with the jury. Much was made throughout the testimony about Glenn Clark not carrying a wallet, even suggesting that the man never carried one. Ted Ryder testified in this trial that he did not. Memory over time sometimes plays tricks on us all. The defense would have liked to have said that a back pocket turned inside out could also have been caused by removing a gun in a hurry, but it was too late.

It was Ryder who, in 1967, had told Pauling that Clark did carry a wallet, one with smooth leather in a dark brown color that looked old. At that time Clark's niece described the wallet Glenn carried as being soft brown leather, made by his brother who was in prison, and with "Glenn" engraved on its face. Clark's daughters recalled that he carried a brown leather wallet. Avery told officers that when his brother was at his house not long before his death, while standing in the driveway, he pulled his wallet out of his pocket and later that's where a piece of credit card with the name John was found. Also, it was a fact that Clark bought items on credit cards on his last trip, and these credit cards were not on his person when searched by the lawmen. The wallet was still inside the car.

If the past weekend had been Jimmy's longest ever, this night felt even longer. He didn't know what the outcome would be.

Shortly after nine on Tuesday, Judge Roberts gave the jury its final instructions. He reminded them that even though an indictment has been filed, an indictment is not evidence. Concerning reasonable doubt, he said, "It's not a mere possible doubt because everything relating to human affairs depending on moral evidence is only some possible or some imaginary doubt. It is that state of the case which after the entire comparison and consideration of all the evidence leaves in the mind of the jury that condition that they could not say they feel an abiding conviction to a moral certainty of the truth of the charge."

He defined first degree murder as, "All murder which is committed by any kind of willful, deliberate, premeditated killing with malice. The word deliberate means formed or arrived at or determined upon as a result of careful thought and weighing of considerations for and against the purpose, the proposed cause of action.

"The word premeditated means considered beforehand. If you find that the killing was preceded and accompanied by a clear deliberate intent by the part of the defendant to kill, which was the result of deliberate and premeditation, so that it must have been formed upon preexisting reflex and not upon a sudden heat of passion or other condition, precluding the idea of deliberation, it is murder in the first degree.

"The law does not undertake to measure the units of time, the length of period during which the thought must be pondered before it can ripen into an intent to kill, which is truly deliberate and premeditated. The time will vary with certain individuals and under varying circumstances."

He defined further the guidelines for determining first degree murder and told the jury that if they cannot agree upon a verdict of first degree, they then should consider murder in the second degree. After defining this, he talked about self-defense.

"Now the defense of self-defense or defense of another person has been raised. A person is justified in using physical force upon another person to defend himself or a third party from what he reasonably believes to be the use of imminent or the imminent use of unlawful physical force." He further defined physical evidence and expert testimony.

Judge Roberts went on, "On the charge of murder in the first degree, each and every juror must agree on that verdict to return a verdict of guilty. Now that would be a unanimous verdict of murder in the first degree.

"Ten or more must agree to return a verdict of not guilty of the crime of murder in the first degree.

"Ten or more jurors must agree to return a verdict of

murder in the second degree or not guilty of murder in the second degree."

After completing his instructions, the bailiff was sworn.

At 9:18 that morning, the jury retired for deliberations. At 9:19 they asked for Defense Exhibit 105, Terrie's statement from 1967. It was sent to the jury room. At 9:21 the court stood in recess.

Jimmy was taken to the holding cell. Soon he was joined by Gitnes and Garbutt.

"Jimmy, it could go either way," Myron said. "I don't know. All we can do now is wait and see."

No matter what happened now, Jimmy was glad to have these lawyers on his side.

"Yeah, I know," he said. He had been studying the faces of the jurors for days, but he had no clue as to how they felt. He knew that Samuels had had the final word. He knew, too, that Gitnes, Garbutt, and Arritola had done all they could.

The feeling kept gnawing at Jimmy that the State of Oregon had not gone to all this trouble and expense just to turn him loose. Murder one: twenty-five years minimum. Murder two: ten. Either term would ruin his life.

The guards brought lunch but he couldn't eat. It seemed as though the jury had been out a long time. "Is that a good or bad sign?" he asked Gitnes.

"It's hard to say, Jimmy."

It was almost three in the afternoon when Jimmy was led back into the courtroom because the jury had returned. Jimmy stood. He was trembling so much that his knees would hardly hold him.

Judge Roberts said, "The presiding juror please give the verdict to the bailiff."

The bailiff handed the paper to the judge, who looked it over and then in his sonorous voice began:

"The verdict reads as follows. 'We, the jury, being duly impaneled and sworn in the above-entitled court and cause, ten or more of our number concurring, find the defendant not guilty of murder in the first degree."

Jimmy felt a wave of relief and then one of fear. It was still too early to celebrate. There was another verdict to be read.

Judge Roberts continued. "And we the jury, being duly impaneled and sworn in the above-entitled court and cause, ten or more of our number concurring, find the defendant not guilty of murder in the second degree."

Jimmy took a deep breath.

It was all he could do not to yell out. They had believed him. He was to be a free man!

After thanking the jury, Judge Roberts said, "The defendant will be ordered released from custody immediately."

24

HOME AGAIN

There was bedlam. Other than the prosecution, everyone seemed happy. Jimmy and his lawyers hugged, and tears fell from Jimmy's eyes. People came from the gallery to congratulate him and said that the right decision had been handed down.

Moments later, the judge retreated to his chambers, and the sounds of cheers and congratulations died down. The spectators began shuffling out of the courtroom. Jimmy was ready to walk out with his attorneys when the bailiff came up to him and said, "Jimmy, I got to hand-cuff you again."

"What? I'm a free man. You heard the judge."

"Jimmy, I gotta take you back inside. It'd be my job if I brought you in without the cuffs. There's this procedure we gotta go through to get you checked out. Do this for me, will you?"

Jimmy bristled. "Man, I've been locked up for the last time. You aren't about to put handcuffs on me again."

They were at a stalemate. Jimmy knew the bailiff had

been decent to him, but he wasn't about to be treated like a criminal again. Gitnes intervened.

"Jimmy, let's do it their way. Another hour or two isn't going to make that much difference."

After what these guys had done for him, Jimmy couldn't go against his lawyers. Although it hurt to do so, he allowed himself to be handcuffed, led into the elevator and down into the basement. The bailiff didn't even consider leg shackles. They crossed through a tunnel until they reached the jail where they took the elevator up to the maximum security floor. Jimmy even had to dress himself in jail clothes before he could go into the quad.

His three cell mates were there waiting.

"How much time'd you get?" one called "Beast" asked.

"None. I'm a free man."

"Yeah, it looks like it. That why you're back up here with us?"

"I'm telling you, man. They found me innocent."

"With them lawyers?"

"Hell yes, man. They're the best."

Another jailhouse theory blown all to hell.

Jimmy entered his cell and gathered his meager belongings. Meager, yes, and yet he found them to be priceless. Letters from Jeannie had carried him through, as had the letters from his mother and sisters. Also from his brother and sisters-in-law. Jeannie's sisters Carol and Joanie had both been a big help. So had a host of friends. Many had written. Some had told of their prayers on his behalf. He clutched the mail to him. He would never forget.

He debated whether or not to keep the envelope filled with police reports and newspaper clippings, some dating back to 1967. Eventually, he decided to take it all home. Perhaps reading them would help Jeannie understand. He would return the Bible to the library and pick up his own on the way out.

When he came out of his cell, the other prisoners finally believed. "I'll be damned," Beast said. "You beat the system, didn't you?"

"I sure as hell did."

"You're one lucky son of a bitch."

Jimmy wasn't sure whether his good fortune was due to luck, his innocence, or his attorneys. However, it had been him who had decided to keep these attorneys in spite of the advice from other prisoners. And he had leaned on Jeannie's belief and on God.

The others went wild, hugging and congratulating Jimmy. He felt an empathy for these men who faced dismal futures. He accepted their good wishes, but, in spite of the euphoria he felt, the hour-and-a-half wait was more like an eternity. At last the guards came for him.

Jimmy changed clothing again and signed for the possessions he'd brought with him from Oklahoma those many months ago. On the way out he was cheered by inmates and given well wishes by some of the guards. By the time he reached the yard between the jail and the courthouse, his head was spinning. Free! Only hours before he had been fearing spending the rest of his life in prison. This was the most wonderful feeling he could remember ever having. If only he had some way of telling Jeannie.

Although their phone had been disconnected months earlier for nonpayment, Jeannie heard the news of Jimmy's acquittal even before he left the courthouse. While Jimmy was being mustered out, Les called the court from Matt's house, as he had been doing daily since the trial began. He had felt somehow that this was to be the day of decision. Either Jimmy would be free to return home or else he would be put away, probably for a long time. If the news was good, he would hurry to tell Jeannie and the kids. If not, well, he would have to tell them anyway.

On the long-distance telephone Les heard an unknown voice respond to his question by saying, "Mr. Taylor has been acquitted on all charges."

Along with Matt, he jumped into his pickup and tore out to Jeannie's house.

* * *

For someone who has led a private, somewhat secluded, life, harboring a secret for those many years, the scene unfolding outside the courthouse when Jimmy eventually emerged was more than he could comprehend. It was his moment, his vindication. The happiness he displayed he felt deep inside.

Breathing free air! The newspapers snapped his photograph with arms outstretched and his joyful face tilted to the heavens. More flashbulbs popped. Microphones were pressed in his face. Video cameras rolled.

He hugged Gitnes and then Garbutt. Arritola clapped him on the back. These three men whom he had mistrusted only weeks earlier had done the impossible. Now, instead of facing the prospect of spending the rest of his life in prison and losing not only Jeannie but his children as well, Jimmy would soon be able to go home.

In the crowd were three women Jimmy had been watching intently for the past week. He recognized them at once. All three were jurors. *What are they doing here?* he wondered. He peered more closely. At least they didn't look hostile. In fact, they were smiling.

One lady stepped forward and gave him a hug. "Thank you," she said, "for saving that girl's life that night on that mountain."

"Ma'am, I . . ."

When she stepped back another woman took her place. "That little fool, Terrie, doesn't know it," she said, "but she wouldn't be alive if it wasn't for you. It's her who should be out here thanking you."

Terrie didn't thank him. Jimmy never saw her again.

The third juror was a little more timid. No hugs this time. She simply took Jimmy's hand in hers and said, "Thank you."

"Thank you for setting me free," Jimmy said. "Thank you very much."

He thought it quite remarkable that these three women

had not only exonerated him but had waited hours with the crowd in order to express their appreciation.

Over the years the state of Oregon had spent tens of thousands of dollars investigating, hunting, and eventually arresting Jimmy Dale Taylor. They had flown him to Oregon to stand trial and incurred more costs for his imprisonment and prosecution. However, once the not guilty verdict was handed down by the jury and he had been properly checked out of the jail, they were through with Jimmy forever. He would have to find his own way home. The state was not spending one more penny.

Jimmy didn't mind. He would have hitchhiked if necessary.

He and his three defenders rode together to the Red Lion Inn.

When they were shown to a table and seated among the other diners, Gitnes said, "I know you don't drink anymore. However, we ordered a bottle of Scotch so that we can all toast your freedom. If you'd rather not, we understand."

Jimmy, who had stopped drinking when he'd joined the church, felt as though it would be rude not to join in. He drank his share and more. When the diners heard who he was, some wanted his autograph.

Afterwards, his defense team drove to the mountain hideaway where they had been staying since the beginning of the trial and loaded their suitcases. On the seventy-seven-mile ride to Klamath Falls Jimmy was laughing, crying, and often shouting. The attorneys supposed the man deserved the opportunity to blow off a little steam. He had reason to rejoice. When they passed a certain intersection, one of them said, "Up that mountain, that's where it all happened. That's where Clark died." Though he would never forget, Jimmy looked away as if he hadn't heard.

Jeannie knew that something had happened concerning Jim when two wild men tore into her backyard in the company truck, brakes squealing. They jumped out and raced to the back door. Les won the right to tell. With tears streaming down his face, he said, "He's free! Jim's coming home, Jeannie. They found him not guilty!"

Jeannie sank down into a chair. She said a silent thank you to God. She had been praying so hard these many months. The children, too, came running in. They all hugged each other.

"When will he be home?" Jeannie asked.

"We don't know," Matt said. "Les just talked to somebody at the courthouse. Probably within a day or two though."

They stopped in Klamath Falls and went upstairs to the offices of Gitnes and Garbutt, as well as that of Paul Arritola. Jimmy was still floating. He could not believe that he was actually free and soon would be on his way home. That his nightmare was finally over.

Early the next morning, Jimmy was on a plane, putting space between himself and Dead Indian Mountain. As the miles increased, he began to relax a little. To allow himself to believe the unbelievable. He was really going back.

Les was waiting at the airport in Oklahoma. The men who felt like two brothers embraced and were soon speeding up I-35 towards Guthrie, Jeannie, and the children.

When Les parked his truck in back of the Taylor home, Jimmy sprung open the door and jumped to the ground. The children ran out. A banner prepared by the three of them was draped across the back door. It read, "Welcome Home, Dad!"

As they were all hugging, out of the house came Jeannie. Jimmy pulled away from his children and ran to his wife. They clung to one another with desperation and elation. Les drove away. This moment belonged to the Taylor family.

It was a time to celebrate.

EPILOGUE

"Jim, tell me what happened that night. What was this all about?"

Jeannie didn't ask right away. Weeks had passed since Jim had returned home before she felt as though it was the right time. They had taken up their lives where they'd left off on that dreaded day in September, almost as though nothing out of the ordinary had ever happened. Only memories remained, reminding them of how near they had been to being apart forever.

The morning was early. The children were still in bed. The two adults sat on the living room sofa watching the television news, drinking coffee, and sharing a cigarette.

"You know, I quit smoking for a while," Jimmy said.

"We both should quit," Jeannie said. "Are you trying to avoid my question, Jim?"

"No, not really. Just a minute."

Leaving Jeannie for a moment, Jimmy went into the bedroom and pulled a box out from under the bed. Inside were copies of reports by the police detectives, interviews with those who had been involved those many years ago, including Terrie and the loggers, and reports from the FBI. Then there were the reports from 1988 and 1989 telling of the trail that had led straight to the door of Jimmy Dale Taylor in Guthrie, Oklahoma.

It was time that Jeannie knew the whole story. He carried the box into the living room and placed it on the coffee table. "Read all this first," he said. "We'll talk about it later."

Jim went off to work, and soon after that the children got up and went to school. Jeannie read. Housework was neglected, uncharacteristic of Jeannie. When Jim came home that night, neither of them spoke of it. Days passed and Jeannie kept reading, attempting to absorb what she had learned. She read some passages over and over in an attempt to understand. Terrie's statement given to Armand and Pauling in 1967 Jeannie read time after time. *How,* she wondered, *could Terrie have testified against Jim? Jim had saved the girl's life.*

The following week, Jeannie joined Jim on their tiny front porch. The afternoon was late with the sun a red ball of fire resting on distant trees. They could hear carnival noises coming from the uptown area, only a few blocks distance. The children were all up there, joining in the festivities. Guthrie was celebrating the one hundredth anniversary of its land run, making an attempt to relive its past.

The Taylors were attempting a new beginning in an old environment. Yet it was not all old. The garden had been plowed and enough seeds planted that new life was taking shape. Grass was turning green as were the trees on Cottonwood Creek. Around them was the promise of new life, the rebirth of an eternal cycle.

"Did you read it all?" Jimmy asked.

"Yes. I read it all," Jeannie said softly. "You really did kill a man, didn't you, Jim?"

"It was either me or him."

"Why didn't you tell me before all this happened? When they came for you, I was completely in the dark. That man kept saying to me, 'You have to know about this,' but I didn't. Why didn't you tell me twenty years ago?"

"I tried to."

Jimmy lit a cigarette and passed it to Jeannie. "I tried lots of times. Back when we were first together, I was afraid you would leave me if you knew. After that, I didn't think

I'd ever be caught. Too much time had passed. I had no idea they'd still be looking for me after twenty-one years."

"Why did that girl testify against you?"

He sighed. His voice was serious, genuine. "I don't know. I think she was scared when she first told her story to the police. Maybe she was afraid they suspected her, I don't know. Or maybe they thought that she and I had planned to kill Clark, and they offered her a way out if she would turn on me. After she'd settled on a story, she couldn't just do an abrupt about-face. But I can only make guesses; we'll never know for certain why."

Jeannie looked directly into his eyes. "Is there anything else about you I don't know, Jim?"

Jimmy took Jeannie's hand in his. Such a short time back, he hadn't thought that he would ever be able to do this again. Thanks be to God, he thought.

"No, Babe. Nothing else, I promise you."

They sat in silence, touching as they had that night so long ago at the Logan County Jail, listening to the joyful sounds coming from uptown and watching the red-orange sun as it settled behind the tall, light-edged trees. At last they were at peace.

UPDATE

FREE TO LIVE

For Jimmy and Jeannie Taylor, life after their terrifying ordeal left them temporarily unsettled, but this condition was soon replaced by calmness. Their horrific nightmares seemed to be little more than a brief interruption. They would have to build anew, but the dark experiences were pushed into deep recesses of the mind, and it was as though little out of the ordinary had ever happened.

Although many years have passed since the jury found Jimmy not guilty, they continue to reside in Guthrie, Oklahoma, living in the same house where they were living when Jimmy returned from Oregon. The children are all grown and have moved away from home. The two girls have families of their own, but close ties keep them all near their parents and to one another, as well as to their brother. Lynn has two children, while Julie, the little tyke who beat on the lawman with her tiny fists when they came to arrest her daddy, has four. Coming home often, they bring their children for visits. This suits Grandma and Grandpa just fine.

Not long after this book was originally published by New Horizon Press, Rick Kramer, of *Inside Edition*, contracted with a cameraman from Oklahoma City. They came to Guthrie to interview and film both of the authors, primarily Jimmy, along with his family. Soon after completion, the work was edited and became a lead story on one of their broadcasts. For the young hitchhiker whose life was forever changed, they used the name "Terrie Trina Tidwell," even as we had in the book. At her request, they kept her identity and geographic location secret. As one watches the interview with the lady who experienced such a traumatic ordeal, it becomes obvious that Terrie has developed into an attractive and well-adjusted woman. Until she spoke to the producers of *Inside Edition* and read the book, she had no idea of what had really happened on Dead Indian Mountain that dreadful night.

Speaking of her ordeal, Terrie said, "It was probably the most traumatic time of my life. I was on my way to Pasadena. Glenn stopped and said, 'We're going that way and would be glad to give you a ride.' As we headed up the mountain, I could see that we were getting off the main road. That is when I began to be alarmed."

Although court-appointed attorneys often receive a bad rap, and sometimes rightfully so, Jimmy has nothing but the highest praise for those who represented him. After all, the results speak for themselves. Myron Gitnes and Richard Garbutt, along with the private investigator Paul Arritola, worked hard for their client, even though Jimmy was reluctant to cooperate. Each week, they would make the long drive from Klamath Falls to Medford, Oregon, and each week they would return home frustrated at the lack of cooperation. Jimmy listened to his fellow inmates who insisted that these guys couldn't be any good or they wouldn't be court-appointed. Eventually Jimmy's cooperation allowed them to present a defense when his trial began.

While being interviewed for *Inside Edition,* Richard Garbutt said about Glenn True Clark, "He was a loser, a small-time hood. He had a big ego and was trying to impress women all the time."

Speaking of Terrie's testimony at the trial, Myron Gitness, said, "Basically, what she volunteered was 'I told you what I think happened, but I'm not sure.'"

Terrie said, "I was scared. I was shaking. I was crying.

I knew that I had made a bad decision. I know that I had had too much to drink. Everything was closing in on me. I saw Glenn on his knees with his hands up. I heard the gun go off as Jimmy shot Glenn."

The narrator on *Inside Edition* broke in and said, "She never knew that Glenn had a gun or that he had threatened to rape and murder her. That was the last time she and Jimmy saw one another for twenty-one years."

Even so, the only way the two of them have been able to see or speak to one another, as of this date, has been through the efforts of *Inside Edition*.

When the program interviewed Joe Reale, Jimmy's boss at Farm and Home Termite and Pest Control, Joe—being very complimentary—said, "I've been in business for forty years. I've never seen anyone like Jimmy."

The producers also arranged a telephone hookup between Jimmy and Terrie. From her location, they dialed Jimmy's number. After she had identified herself, Jimmy replied, "How are you doing?"

She answered, "I've had a good life, thanks to you. I never did say thank you."

After the phone call, Terrie said to the vast audience of the program, "It very well could be that the Lord sent Jimmy to save my life. I truly do believe that God put Jimmy in my path and he saved my life."

The moderator told the viewers, "Jimmy said he would like to meet Terrie in person, so he has asked her and her family to visit him in Oklahoma."

As of this writing, the reunion in person has not taken place.

Next came a movie based on Jimmy's adventure, produced by von Zerneck/Sertner Films after executive producer Anat Baron became interested enough to run with the story. The movie starred Michele Lee and Peter Coyote and was first shown on CBS. Since its initial showing, it has been on the Lifetime Channel, as well as the Lifetime Movie Channel, numerous times. The movie came out under the title *A Murder On Shadow Mountain*. The plot was changed somewhat in that Michele Lee, portraying Jeannie, flew to Oregon and, once there, proved that Peter Coyote, portraying Jimmy, acted in self-defense. In real life, Jeannie did not have the monetary means to travel to Oregon, even to be with Jimmy, as he went through the hell of a trial. Even so, the movie was well done and is a very interesting story.

More than twenty-one years have passed since the Taylor family moved into their modest home in Guthrie, Oklahoma, and more than seventeen years have passed since Jimmy returned from his ordeal in Oregon. Jimmy is now sixty years of age, and Jeannie is eight years younger. Neither of them thought they would still be living in this house at this stage of their lives. After the book was originally published and the movie made, they seriously considered buying a larger house and moving, but when the time came, they couldn't force themselves to do so. Not only had this house provided them with a safe haven when they had finally settled in one place after years of a no-madic life, but it had been a place for them to reunite after the "not guilty" verdict.

Jeannie said, "This house has a hold on us. Because of a lot of memories, I guess. Soon after Jimmy returned from Oregon, everything just fell back in place. We went back to our normal routine. Jimmy went back to work to make money to support us, and I went back to taking care of the kids and the house."

Jimmy worked for Farm & Home Termite & Pest Control until Joe Reale sold the company to a large corporation in 2000. Without steady work for a while, Jimmy did what he could to support his family. He did do odd jobs, such as painting or yard work—anything to put food on the table and pay the monthly bills. Then, in 2001, he found steady work with a livestock feed company.

A trusted employee, Jimmy often works away from the main business, overseeing the unloading of feed on the rail siding. There, cattle food is transferred into the beds of tractor trailers that haul their load, often to distant destinations, where it is needed to feed cattle. His workplace is cold in the winter and hot in the summer, but Jimmy finds the work interesting and likes his job. More often than not, he works six days a week and often seven. He doesn't mind the busy schedule—other than it makes it impossible for him and his wife to be active in church.

Jeannie has had health problems that have tended to slow her somewhat. Several years ago, she had neck surgery and still has pain in this area. Even so, on days that Jimmy is working, she arises at five-thirty in the morning, along with her husband. She fixes his breakfast and lunch, and they enjoy a cup or two of coffee together before Jimmy heads off.

Jimmy's only health problem these days is trouble with his left eye. Jeannie says it twitches and Jimmy says that he can hardly see out of it. Soon he will have to have his vision checked out.

Being Christians, they both pray daily and give God the credit for the love they feel for one another and for the life they now have together. Although there was a time when they didn't think it would ever happen, they are free to live!